| DATE DUE | | |
|---|---|---|
| JUL 17 1995 S | | |
| DEC 15 1999 | | |
| | | |
| | | |
| | | |
| | | |
| | | |
| | | |
| | | |
| | | |
| | | |
| | | |

# Banking and finance in Japan

# Banking and finance in Japan
## An introduction to the Tokyo market

Kazuo Tatewaki

London and New York

First published 1991
by Routledge
11 New Fetter Lane, London EC4P 4EE
29 West 35th Street, New York, NY 10001

© 1991 Kazuo Tatewaki

Typeset in Times by LaserScript Limited, Mitcham, Surrey
Printed and bound in Great Britain by
Biddles Ltd, Guildford and King's Lynn

*British Library Cataloguing in Publication Data*
Tatewaki, Kazuo, *1935–*
Banking and finance in Japan: an introduction to the
Tokyo market.
1. Japan. Finance
I. Title
332.0952

ISBN 0-415-00992-8

*Library of Congress Cataloging in Publication Data*
has been applied for

For Vernon A. Mund

# Contents

*Contents*

**Part II Financial markets**

**Part III Financial institutions**

viii

# Tables and figures

## Tables

## Figures

# Preface

At present, financial deregulation, innovation, and globalization are in progress on a world-wide scale. Financial markets are integrated into a huge, single global market, in which New York and London play a major role. Tokyo seems destined to play a growing role in the immediate future due to its capital resources and its geographical location connecting New York and London.

People want to know about the Tokyo market, especially up-to-date information, because the market is changing so rapidly. Much information is available via newspapers, magazines, and books, but most is in Japanese. Information in English is limited. This book offers general and up-to-date information on the Tokyo market to English-speakers. Hence, it is not my intention to present academic research. That's why notes signifying sources are omitted other than for tables and figures. However, a bibliography is available at the end of this book.

I am indebted to Dr Yoshio Suzuki, Vice-Chairman of the Board of Councillors, Nomura Research Institute, and Mr Peter Sowden of Routledge, who gave me the opportunity to write this book. Dr Suzuki was formerly Managing Director of the Bank of Japan and editor of *The Japanese Financial System* from which I have learned a great deal. The book's description of the basic functions of the financial institutions, financial markets, and monetary policy is very informative, although difficult to keep entirely up to date due to the rapid change in Japan's financial markets.

I should also thank Dr Adrian E. Tschoegl, Economist of SBCI Securities (Asia) Ltd, Tokyo Branch, for his valuable comments, corrections, and suggestions. Dr Tschoegl was formerly Assistant Professor of International Business at the School of Business Administration, the University of Michigan. Needless to say, the author is responsible for any possible errors or omissions.

I hope this book may help those people interested in Japan to understand financial markets and other related matters in contemporary Japan.

Kazuo Tatewaki
Shizuoka, Japan

---

**Remarks**

Readers are recommended to pay attention to certain words which have specific meanings in this book, as follows,

| | |
|---|---|
| billion (bn) | : million (m) x million (m) |
| dollar ($) | : US dollar, unless specified |
| fiscal year (FY) | : from 1 April of the current year to 31 March of the following year |
| yen (¥) | : Japanese yen |

It is also noted that the private sector's financial figures, such as assets, liabilities, and profits, are principally based on unconsolidated statements of conditions and incomes.

# Publisher's acknowledgement

In certain sections of this volume, some of the material has been closely based on the text of *The Japanese Financial System*, a book edited by Yoshio Suzuki for the Bank of Japan and published by Oxford University Press in 1987. The Publishers would therefore like to thank Oxford University Press for permission to use the copyright material in this present volume.

# Introduction

## Japan's role in the world economy

Japan's role in the world economy has been significant since the beginning of the 1980s, and its financial and banking systems have experienced a revolution.

The Japanese economy underwent drastic changes in the early 1970s, stemming from the Nixon shock,† the oil crisis, and the move to a floating exchange rate system. As a consequence, the Japanese economy slowed after a fast growth period. During the fast growth period (1955–70) the Japanese economy achieved more than 10 per cent average annual growth in real terms. Reflecting the energy crisis, the Japanese economy recorded a decline (–0.4 per cent) in 1974 for the first time during the post-war period.

Since then, however, the Japanese economy has continued a steady growth of about 4.5 per cent per annum, higher than any other major country in the world. As a result, Japan's role has increased in the world economy while that of the United States has declined relatively in several dimensions, such as GNP, balance of payments surplus, net external assets, trading volume of the stock exchanges and the level of interest rates.

After 1968, Japan's GNP was second in the free world after that of the United States. However, Japan's per capita GNP ($19,553) exceeded the United States ($18,569) in 1987. The spread *vis-à-vis* the United States had increased from $984 in 1987 to $3,598 in 1988, due partly to a sharp appreciation of the yen against the US dollar, especially after the Plaza agreement in September 1985. In early September 1985, the Japanese yen stood at ¥240/US$1. The rate appreciated to ¥120/US$1 in early 1988. It is hard to remember that the Japanese yen was ¥360/US$1 before the Nixon shock.

†The Nixon shock refers to the serious impact made on the world economy by President Nixon's statement on 15 August 1971. The statement announced important policy changes including an immediate suspension in conversion of dollars to gold, and a proposal to restructure the exchange rates of major countries.

1

In spite of such a sharp appreciation of the yen, Japan's current account surplus has continued to grow since 1981, while the United States has experienced current account deficits since 1982. In addition, from 1986 on, Japan sold a large volume of US dollars in the foreign exchange market to cause the US dollar rate to depreciate. Nevertheless, Japan's external reserves continued to increase and surpassed those of the United States by 1987 and West Germany by 1988. In April 1989, the external reserves of Japan, the United States, and West Germany were $100,361 million, $50,303 million, and $60,642 million, respectively.

Japan's nominal net external assets were the largest in the world in 1985, while the United States had a nominal net external debt in the same year. Since then there has been no reversal of this position. At the end of 1988, Japan's nominal net external assets were $291,746 million while United States nominal net external debt was $532,500 million.

Until recently, the New York Stock Exchange (NYSE) was the largest stock exchange in the world in every respect. However, since 1987, the NYSE has been exceeded by the Tokyo Stock Exchange (TSE) in terms of the total market value of listed stocks. The TSE also exceeded the NYSE in terms of total trading value in 1988. Total market value of listed stocks at the end of 1988 and total trading value during 1988 at both exchanges were as follows (in millions of dollars):

|  | New York | Tokyo |
|---|---|---|
| Total market value of listed stocks | 2,457,461 | 3,789,035 |
| Total trading value of stocks | 1,356,050 | 2,234,233 |

Before 1977, the discount rate of the Federal Reserve Bank of New York (FRBNY) was below the discount rate of the Bank of Japan (BOJ), except for a few months in 1972 and 1973. In April 1977, the BOJ reduced its discount rate from 6 per cent to 5 per cent, while the discount rate of the FRBNY was 5.25 per cent. Since then, the BOJ's discount rate has continued to decline, reaching its lowest level of 2.5 per cent in February 1987 (it was raised to 3.25 per cent in May 1989). On the other hand, the FRBNY's discount rate has been 7.0 per cent since February 1989 (see figure I.1).

## Restructuring and deregulation of the financial system

There are three key types of regulation in the financial field: regulation of interest rates, regulation of international or foreign exchange transactions, and regulation of the scope of business. The last type includes the separation of short-term from long-term financing, the segregation of commercial banking and trust banking, and the separation of the

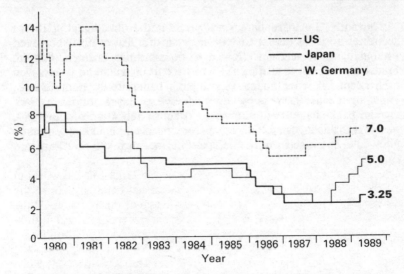

*Figure I.1* Central Bank discount rates in Japan, US, and West Germany
*Source:* BOJ, *Economic Statistics Monthly*.

banking and securities businesses.

International transactions were entirely deregulated when the revised Foreign Exchange and Foreign Trade Control Law took effect in December 1980. Interest rates were gradually deregulated but this process is now approaching an end. The minimum amount of non-transferable large-sum time deposits was reduced from ¥30 million to ¥20 million between April and September 1989 and was further reduced to ¥10 million in October 1989. In addition, the 'super MMC' was introduced in June 1989, with minimum amounts of ¥3 million for small savers. The minimum amount is scheduled to be ¥1 million in April 1990 and ¥100,000 by 1992.

The regulation of the scope of business or segmentation of financial institutions is now the most contentious issue. In December 1987, the Research Committee on Financial System, an advisory body to the Minister of Finance, proposed that financial segmentation be reviewed to promote the rational allocation of resources and competition among financial institutions. In fact, in March 1985, the Ministry of Finance (MOF) approved commercial banks issuing convertible bonds to procure long-term funds in overseas markets. This was expanded to the domestic market in April 1987. In addition, the MOF permitted mutual banks to convert themselves into commercial banks in early 1989. The separation of banking and securities business is currently under discussion with a view to further reduction in barriers.

Currently, Japanese banks are prohibited from engaging in the securities business except for public securities. Since 1985, however, foreign banks have been allowed to do securities business through branches of securities affiliates of which the foreign banks own less than 50 per cent. Likewise Japanese commercial banks are discouraged from engaging in trust business by administrative guidance but, since 1985, foreign banks have been allowed to establish subsidiaries doing trust business in Japan. Therefore, Japanese commercial banks may also be allowed to enter the securities and trust businesses in the near future.

# Part I

# Financial structure and deregulation

# Chapter one

# Historical background

## Formation of Japan's modern banking system, 1868–99

Japan's banking system was formed under the strong influence of the United States and Europe rather than on the basis of any tradition from feudal days. The new government of 1868 born out of the Meiji Restoration tried to establish its banking system by imitating the systems of western countries.

The government felt that a modern financial system was a prerequisite to Japan's development and transformation from a feudal state into a modern capitalist economy. The government introduced Japan's new decimal currency, the yen, in 1871. In the following year, the government enacted the National Bank Act which was a copy of the National Currency Act of 1864 in the United States. Private entrepreneurs created the First National Bank (*Dai-ichi Kokuritsu Ginko*) in 1873, and several other banks followed shortly thereafter. In 1882, the Bank of Japan (BOJ) was founded as Japan's central bank, modelled on the Banque Nationale de Belgique, which was at that time considered the modern version of the Bank of England. Under the Banking Act (Law No. 72 of 1890), the national banks lost their note-issuing function and were transformed into British-style commercial banks.

The government took another step towards founding savings banks by inaugurating the postal savings system in 1874. Private savings banks followed after. By 1880, Japan's financial system came to be organized on European lines with the BOJ at the apex of a financial structure based on the commercial banks and the savings banks. It was, however, difficult for voluntary savings alone to satisfy the enormous demand for capital generated by the desire to develop the economy in a short period of time. Hence the government had to assume the important role of promoting industrial growth. The result was the establishment of a number of government-supported 'specialized banks': Yokohama Specie Bank (1880), Nippon Kangyo Bank (1897), Hokkaido Takushoku Bank

(1900), the Bank of Taiwan (1900), the Industrial Bank of Japan (1902), and others.

Commercial banks also found it difficult to follow British practice too faithfully, being compelled to work as investment banks supplying long-term funds to industry. Thus long-term time deposits dominated deposits; in lending, loans were overwhelmingly more important than the discounting of bills. Reflecting the steady growth of the commercial banks, clearing houses were established in Osaka in 1879 and in Tokyo in 1887.

## Development of the banking system before the Second World War, 1900–44

The number of commercial banks increased rapidly, reaching a peak of 1,867 banks in 1901. The collapse of small and unsound banks accounted for most of the subsequent decline; merger was a minor phenomenon and did not contribute significantly to the initial growth of Japan's big banks. Merger only became important during and after the depression years following the First World War, and particularly after the financial crisis of 1927. The minimum bank capital requirement of the Banking Law (Law No. 21 of 1927), which took effect in 1928, accelerated the process. The law disqualified more than half of 1,400 then existing banks.

Many banks preferred merger to liquidation, but there were few cases in which big banks participated in such mergers or amalgamations. The usual pattern was one of horizontal merger between regional, small- or middle-scale banks. The cause was the marked difference in the basic character of big urban banks from small rural banks. Even so, local merger improved the quality of banks in rural areas.

In 1942, with the expiry of its founding charter, the BOJ was reorganized along the same lines as the Reichsbank in Germany. Since reorganization took place during the Second World War, the new BOJ was destined to control currency, credit, and finance pursuant to government policy so that the general economic resources of the nation could be utilized adequately.

By 1936, the number of commercial banks had been reduced to 418. Bank mergers during the Second World War reduced the numbers further. By the end of the war, only sixty-four banks remained. The survivors consisted of eight major banks in metropolitan areas and generally one regional bank in each prefecture. The number of savings banks also declined. A legal amendment in 1943 allowing commercial banks to engage in savings banking concurrently proved devastating. As a result of such changes, only four savings banks remained by the end of the war in 1945.

Trust companies were founded one after another at the turn of the century. However, their character was not always distinct in the earlier periods as some of them deviated from genuine trust business. It was only after the promulgation of the Trust Law and the Trust Business Law (Law Nos 62 and 65 of 1922) that genuine trust companies came into existence and started to grow rapidly. The limited private assets and traditional family organization in Japan, however, handicapped their development. The bulk of trust funds were placed in an account called 'money in trust' which was virtually identical to bank deposits.

The Nippon Kangyo Bank and the agricultural and industrial banks (noko ginko) were set up to provide agricultural finance. Eventually, the Nippon Kangyo Bank absorbed the others through mergers. In addition, the financial activities of agricultural co-operatives gradually gained importance, being legally endorsed by the Industrial Co- operative Law (Law No. 34 of 1900) in 1900. In 1923, the Central Bank for Industrial Co-operatives (the predecessor of Norinchukin Bank) was established as the central body of the industrial co-operatives.

In the area of the financing of small businesses and petty loans to the public, Japan had for a long time had organizations for mutual financing called *mujin* or *tanomoshiko*. In 1915 the *tanomoshiko* were incorporated into the *mujin* companies. In addition, co-operative financing was no longer confined to agriculture alone, as urban credit co-operatives came to be established after 1917. In 1936, the Central Bank for Commercial and Industrial Co-operatives (Shokochukin Bank) was formed as an institution to finance the co-operatives of small enterprises.

The securities markets contributed little to development for many years since actual transactions were highly speculative. One major obstacle to the development of the securities markets was the fact that enterprises tended to belong to a group of companies or *zaibatsu*. The *zaibatsu* dominated the nation's economy and could rely on capital supply from within the group. Despite such hindrances, development of heavy industries and the growth of large enterprises during the First World War led to a slow expansion of securities markets.

## Restructuring of the banking system after the Second World War, 1945–54

### Drastic changes in the banking system

After the Second World War the Supreme Commander of the Allied Powers' (SCAP) directives and instructions brought drastic changes to most Japanese institutional arrangements. Shortly after the end of the war, all the wartime financial institutions and colonial banks such as the

Bank of Taiwan were closed. In 1950 all the specialized banks were converted into commercial banks. However, no revision was made to the Banking Law (Law No. 21 of 1927) and no drastic reforms touched banking itself. The role of commercial banks increased rather than declined because their credit creation was vital to business enterprises.

Probably the most important post-war reform affecting commercial banks was the revised Securities and Exchange Law (Law No. 25 of 1948). The law was modelled after the Glass-Steagall Act in the United States and prohibited commercial banks from underwriting securities except for public bonds. Thus underwriting business, which commercial banks had dominated before the war, was taken over by securities firms, boosting their importance in subsequent years.

In 1949, the BOJ was reorganized and the Policy Board was established, modelled on the Board of Governors of the Federal Reserve System in the United States. The Policy Board, comprising representatives of various sectors of the nation's economy, took over the responsibility for major decisions on monetary policy, including changes in discount rates. The reorganization strengthened the BOJ's powers.

The accelerated inflation after the war had a great impact on banking. Spiralling inflation strangled financial institutions engaged mainly in mobilizing long-term savings. The four remaining savings banks were converted to or merged with commercial banks. Trust companies were transformed into commercial banks concurrently engaging in trust business and renamed 'trust banks'. The specialized banks established before the war were unable to maintain their status. Their conversion to commercial banks, therefore, was inevitable even without the 1950 reform.

The post-war inflation turned various other financial institutions as well into *de facto* banks relying on deposits. A reform of the financial institutions for small businesses followed in 1951. Small businesses were faced with depression and financial crisis resulting from the severe anti-inflationary measures of 1949–50. The 1951 reform made *mujin* companies convert into mutual banks (*sogo ginko*) and urban credit co-operatives into credit associations (*shinyo kinko*). These new institutions were allowed to offer current accounts and subsequently grew tremendously. Their total deposits grew faster than those of commercial banks.

The stabilization of the economy in 1949–50 enabled the trust banks, the insurance companies, and other organizations for long-term finance to recover. Two new financial instruments were introduced by the government to spur the growth of trust banks. These were the securities investment trust (1951) and the loan trust (1952). Loan trusts facilitated lending to important industries. When these new instruments proved to be a great success, the government decided as a matter of policy to guide trust banks towards greater emphasis on trust business and towards a reduced emphasis on banking activities.

The Long-term Credit Bank Law (Law No. 187 of 1952) was promulgated in 1952. The legislation was a response to the lack of an active market for long-term capital after the war. The long-term credit banks (LTCBs) were authorized to raise funds for long-term lending by issuing bonds. The Industrial Bank of Japan, a specialized bank in the pre-war days, was converted into a LTCB. The Long-term Credit Bank of Japan and the Nippon Fudosan Bank (currently the Nippon Credit Bank) were also founded under the law.

The Foreign Exchange Bank Law (Law No. 67 of 1954) established the Bank of Tokyo, successor to the Yokohama Specie Bank, as the specialized foreign exchange bank. However, the bank lost many of the privileges which its predecessor had enjoyed. In fact, today most major banks engage in foreign exchange business on an almost equal footing.

*Government financial institutions*

The Reconstruction Finance Bank (established 1947) engaged in construction finance after the Second World War by relying heavily on borrowings from the BOJ and contributed significantly to the post-war accelerating inflation. The institution ceased its operations in 1949. A number of the government financial institutions were established in subsequent years to ensure the supply of funds to sectors of the economy which private financial institutions were unable to serve adequately: the People's Finance Corporation (established 1949), the Export-Import Bank of Japan (1950), the Japan Development Bank (1951), the Agriculture, Forestry and Fisheries Finance Corporation (1952), the Small Business Finance Corporation (1953), the Hokkaido-Tohoku Development Corporation (1956), the Okinawa Development Finance Corporation (1972), etc. These institutions depend on capital subscriptions and borrowings from the government for their funds. In principle they do not compete with private financial institutions but supplement them.

Following a decade of recovery, Japan's economy enjoyed a fast growth period from 1955 to 1970 in which the average real economic growth rate exceeded 10 per cent per annum. This period saw no major legislation affecting the private banking system. It should be noted, however, that the Deposit Reserve Requirement System and the Deposit Insurance Corporation were established in 1957 and 1971, respectively.

The Research Committee on Financial System made an extensive study on modernizing the central banking system in the late 1950s, but its efforts did not result in any reform. The Ministry of Finance (MOF) wished to retain its power and blocked reform.

Serious recession in the securities industry occurred in 1965. Yamaichi, then the number two securities firm, faced bankruptcy and called on the BOJ for help as the lender of the last resort. In the following year, the government began to issue government bonds. This led, in time, to financial deregulation through the rapid growth of the secon- dary market for government bonds.

External events in the early 1970s proved to be much more important factors in the development of the financial system than those described above. In 1971, President Nixon declared that the United States was no longer willing to change US dollars into gold and imposed a 10 per cent surcharge on imports to the United States. After the short-lived Smithsonian Agreement, the currencies of the major countries including the Japanese yen moved to a floating exchange rate system in 1973 (see table 1.1). In the fall of 1973, the OPEC countries decided to raise oil prices substantially and to reduce oil production. All these events had a serious impact on Japan's economy and financial system.

*Table 1.1*  Yen/dollar rate since 1949 (interbank rate in Tokyo)

| Year | High (¥) | Low (¥) | Average (¥) |
|------|----------|---------|-------------|
| 1949–70 | (IMF parity) | | 360.00 |
| Dec. 1971 | (Smithsonian rate) | | 308.00 |
| 1971 | 314.20 | 358.50 | 349.33 |
| 1972 | 301.10 | 314.84 | 303.17 |
| 1973 | 253.20 | 302.75 | 271.70 |
| 1974 | 272.00 | 304.40 | 292.08 |
| 1975 | 284.90 | 307.00 | 296.79 |
| 1976 | 286.00 | 306.25 | 296.55 |
| 1977 | 238.00 | 293.05 | 268.51 |
| 1978 | 175.50 | 242.50 | 210.44 |
| 1979 | 194.60 | 251.80 | 219.14 |
| 1980 | 202.95 | 264.00 | 226.74 |
| 1981 | 198.70 | 247.40 | 220.54 |
| 1982 | 217.70 | 278.50 | 249.08 |
| 1983 | 227.20 | 247.80 | 237.51 |
| 1984 | 220.00 | 251.70 | 237.52 |
| 1985 | 199.80 | 263.65 | 238.54 |
| 1986 | 152.55 | 203.30 | 168.52 |
| 1987 | 121.85 | 159.20 | 144.64 |
| 1988 | 120.45 | 136.80 | 128.15 |
| 1989 | 123.80 | 151.35 | 137.98 |

*Sources: BOJ, Economic Statistics Annual, 1988; Economic Statistics Monthly, January 1990.*

Chapter two

# Financial structure and the flow of funds

## Financial structure in the fast growth period, 1955–70

*Japan's financial structure*

The financial structure of the post-war period was one confined by regulations, particularly from the viewpoint of the 1980s with its slow growth rates, floating exchange rates, on-line computers, and rapid telecommunications systems. Regulations in the fast growth period was focused on interest rates, particularly those of depository institutions and the private sector, and provided incentives for the private sector to circumvent the regulations. Regulatory authorities realized that regulations did not answer the financial needs of the economy and was a barrier to efficiency and fairness. Consequently, regulations were relaxed and gradually abolished.

The financial system in the post-war period was characterized by the conditions that Japan's economy had to face. In the immediate post-war years, sacrifices of capital and raw materials constrained economic growth, although there was an ample supply of labour. As a result, the path to economic recovery and development for Japan lay in giving first priority to investment and exports which allowed the import of raw materials. Given this background, it was quite appropriate for the economic policy of the post-war period to give priority to investment and exports.

Various types of policy were implemented to achieve these targets. For example, important roles in encouraging investment and exports were played by protectionist industrial policies and by preferential taxes that promoted savings and investment. At the same time, policies on financial structure also played an important role. Thus funds were allocated to the investment and export sectors by means of various types of regulations, particularly interest rate regulations. Other policies insulated domestic markets from foreign influences.

It was often argued that investment and exports could be encouraged by reducing financing costs, particularly by keeping the level of interest rates as low as possible by means of interest rate regulation. However, there is a point of view which questions whether so-called intentional low interest rate policy was, in fact, able to reduce financing costs to corporate businesses and thus encourage investment and exports. Except for the long-term prime rate, the interest rate on loans fluctuated freely to some extent, and there is some doubt whether the effective rate of interest on loans including compensating balances was low enough to actually encourage investment and exports.

However, in the case of loans from the government financial institutions, there were no compensating balances and hence the agreed loan rate was identical to the effective loan rate. Therefore, government financial institutions supplied long-term funds at lending rates considerably below those of private financial institutions. Thus these institutions played a role in encouraging investment and exports. In addition, the BOJ's preferential export financing scheme reduced the financing costs of exports.

The most important point for the financial system was that interest rate regulations, and particularly regulations on deposit interest rates, prevented cut-throat competition. The lack of competition stabilized the business environment for the financial institutions that carried the burden of 'indirect finance'. Indirect finance is a form of finance that final borrowers may obtain funds from financial institutions, while direct finance is a form of funding that final borrowers sell new securities to investors other than the financial institutions.

Regulations that separated long-term and short-term financing business further restricted competition among financial institutions. As a result of this stable business environment, financial institutions were able to respond to the vigorous demand for funds by the corporate sector.

Fast economic growth meant that the expected rate of return to corporate businesses was high enough to compensate for effective loan rates and firms were willing to embark on investments as long as sufficient liquidity was available. Interest rate regulations promoted growth in the sense that they allowed indirect finance to flourish. In addition, the isolation of domestic financial markets from overseas markets prevented foreign influences from undermining the various financial regulations.

Thus, the economic framework of the fast growth period was one in which economic growth was mainly based on investment and exports and relied on a regulated financial system. This system had three features: predominance of indirect finance, over-borrowing and over-lending, and maldistribution of funds.

## Major features of the financial structure

The predominance of indirect finance through financial institutions was best illustrated by its overwhelming share in the supply of funds, which almost always exceeded 90 per cent throughout the fast growth period and the early 1970s. Contemporary reasons for the predominance of indirect finance during the fast growth period include the low level of public bonds flotation, and the use of regulations on interest rates and foreign exchange transactions.

Over-borrowing and over-lending are two sides of the same coin. Over-borrowing by the corporate sector means a situation in which the corporate sector's funding relies heavily on borrowing from financial institutions. Such over-borrowing was particularly notable during the fast growth period. Along with growth based on investment and exports, the investment-to-GNP ratio was extremely high, and thus a mechanism was at work which greatly expanded the funding requirements of the corporate sector.

With insufficient accumulation of liquidity of its own, corporate businesses had no choice but to rely on outside funding, and were actually forced to rely on borrowing from financial institutions, given the priority accorded to indirect finance. Moreover, over-borrowing could not be avoided through capital inflows from abroad. Regulations separating the domestic and overseas financial markets meant that corporations were restricted in their ability to float foreign currency bonds and to use foreign currency loans (impact loans). In addition, the purchase of shares by non-residents was prohibited.

On the other hand, over-lending by the banking sector denoted a condition in the private banking sector in which the banks' credit extension, either by lending and/or by purchase of securities, exceeded the deposits they acquired and their own capital. The gap was filled primarily by relying on borrowing from the BOJ. Over-lending emerged for the first time around 1900 but was reduced by the growth of government expenditures. It emerged again during the Second World War and intensified during the post-war period, particularly in the fast growth period.

Over-lending during the fast growth period was attributable mainly to the concentration of demand for funds on city banks as the most important sources of funds for the corporate businesses. The city banks found it profitable to rely on low interest loans from the BOJ and were able to continue their own excess credit extension in the stable business environment under regulated interest rates.

The BOJ solved the problems of insufficient funds in the banking sector by direct lending, since neither long-term nor short-term markets were developed. Thus, the BOJ was unable to conduct open-market operations. Moreover, given the framework of the intentional low interest rate policy, there was continuous, latent excess demand for BOJ lending and no way to satisfy this demand other than by credit rationing. It was quite convenient to transmit guidance for the day-to-day funding of banks through direct lending.

Maldistribution of funds was the third feature of the financial system during the fast growth period. The city banks were chronically in need of funds while regional banks, mutual banks, credit associations and other financial institutions usually had surplus funds. From this imbalance, an interbank market was developed. The city banks were chronic borrowers and the regional banks and other institutions were chronic lenders in a one-way flow of funds.

Maldistribution of funds emerged during the Second World War and intensified during the fast growth period. There were principally two reasons why the city banks became chronically dependent on borrowing from the BOJ and the money markets. First, loan demand was concentrated on the city banks since their customers were closely related to investment and export activities. Second, the city banks were not permitted to issue bonds or certificates of deposits (CDs).

These three features of the financial structure during the fast growth period were interrelated. For example, over-borrowing by the corporate sector reflected the predominance of indirect finance. Also over-lending occurred because the BOJ was more or less forced into granting credit due to the underdevelopment of long-term and short-term financial markets, which resulted from the predominance of indirect finance. In addition, over-lending could be maintained only because the BOJ engaged in direct lending primarily to the city banks, and thus underpinned both the maldistribution of funds and over-borrowing by the corporate sector.

## Financial structure in the 1970s and 1980s

### *Drastic change in the early 1970s*

During the fast growth period, the structure of the financial system did not cause any major problems. But three major incidents changed this. They were the Nixon shock in 1971, a shift to a floating exchange rate system from a fixed rate system, and the first oil crisis in 1973. The Japanese economy was no longer an environment in which investment and export-led fast growth could be supported as an economic target. A slow-down of economic growth and internationalization of markets were required.

The major changes in the economic structure between the fast growth period and the second half of the 1970s had a major impact on the financial structure. The resulting changes in the financial structure meant the emergence of contradictions between the financial framework that had worked satisfactorily during the fast growth period and the financial needs of a new era. As a result, it was necessary to review the regulations governing the financial system.

The most remarkable change under the slow growth economy was the change in the flow of funds. This will be discussed later. The expansion of the public sector deficit brought large-scale flotations of government and municipal bonds to finance these deficits. The bond-financing ratio or ratio of bond flotation to the government's general account peaked at 34.7 per cent in fiscal 1979. Thereafter attempts at retrenchment were made to reduce the flotation of government bonds. As a result, the bond-financing ratio declined substantially in the 1980s, although government bonds outstanding were still growing (see table 2.1).

The large-scale flotation of government bonds provided the impetus for the development of direct finance through the securities market. The development of the secondary market where existing securities held by investors are traded, was the most important factor ensuring that bond issues were absorbed smoothly. There were also some modifications in the primary market through such methods as diversifying the types and methods of flotation, through, for example, the tender issue of medium-term coupon bonds.

The relatively underdeveloped state of open financial markets in Japan prior to 1975 was attributable to several factors. First, trading on open markets needs assets to be traded, and the short-term government bills, the most appropriate assets for such purposes, were in limited supply. In addition, banks and other financial institutions which had underwritten the largest portion of issuing bonds were required to hold these bonds for a certain period of time. Second, even direct finance was quite restricted. Under the intentional low interest rate policy, corporate businesses able to float bonds were those with close ties with financial institutions because such bonds were bought by these institutions. Third, interest rate regulations kept the subscribers' yields of bonds at low levels, which meant that bond sales before maturity incurred losses. This factor also restrained development of the secondary market.

However, consecutive issues of large-scale government bonds had a major impact on all three factors. Along with the expansion of the secondary market for government bonds, there was a substantial increase in short-term market transactions such as *gensaki* (equivalent to RP [repurchase agreement]). Because the interest rates in these open markets were freely deter- mined by market forces, the open markets had a major impact on the financial structure.

One of the most important effects of slower growth on the financial

*Table 2.1* Government revenues, expenditures, and bonds outstanding (¥bn)

| Fiscal year | Total revenues* | Taxes and stamps | Bond issues | Bond issue to total exp. ratio % | Total expenditures* | Social security | Debt services | Government bonds outstanding |
|---|---|---|---|---|---|---|---|---|
| 1965 | 3.8 | 3.0 | 0.2 | 5.3 | 3.7 | 0.6 | – | 0.7 |
| 1970 | 8.5 | 7.3 | 0.3 | 4.2 | 8.2 | 1.3 | 0.3 | 3.6 |
| 1975 | 21.5 | 13.8 | 5.3 | 25.3 | 20.9 | 4.6 | 1.1 | 15.8 |
| 1979 | 39.8 | 23.7 | 13.5 | 34.7 | 38.8 | 8.4 | 4.4 | 57.3 |
| 1980 | 44.0 | 26.9 | 14.2 | 32.6 | 43.4 | 9.2 | 5.5 | 71.9 |
| 1981 | 47.4 | 29.9 | 13.0 | 27.5 | 46.9 | 10.0 | 6.7 | 83.6 |
| 1982 | 48.0 | 30.5 | 14.0 | 29.7 | 47.2 | 10.4 | 6.9 | 97.9 |
| 1983 | 51.7 | 32.4 | 13.5 | 26.6 | 50.6 | 10.5 | 8.2 | 111.5 |
| 1984 | 52.2 | 34.9 | 12.7 | 24.8 | 51.5 | 11.0 | 9.2 | 123.8 |
| 1985 | 54.0 | 38.2 | 12.3 | 23.2 | 53.0 | 11.1 | 10.2 | 136.6 |
| 1986 | 53.8 | 39.4 | 11.5 | 21.4 | 53.8 | 11.3 | 10.7 | 147.3 |
| 1987 | 61.4 | 46.8 | 9.4 | 15.3 | 57.7 | 11.1 | 11.3 | 151.8 |
| 1988** | 56.7 | 45.1 | 8.8 | 15.6 | 56.7 | 11.4 | 11.5 | 159.1 |
| 1989** | 60.4 | 51.0 | 7.1 | 11.8 | 50.4 | 10.9 | 11.7 | 162.0 (p) |

*Notes:* *General account only.
**These are initial budgets, but the supplemental budget for 1988 stood at ¥5.1 billion.
(p) = projection.
*Source:* BOJ, *Economic Statistics Annual and Economic Statistics Monthly.*

structure was growing demand for high yield assets by the private non-financial sector, particularly by households. From the 1950s till the mid-1970s, with only minor exceptions, accumulation of financial assets by the private non-financial sector rose at a rate exceeding the growth rate of nominal GNP, on the back of two digit wage hikes. However, after 1975, wage hikes slowed down to single digit levels. Meanwhile, considerable financial assets had already been accumulated. It was quite natural for households to become more sensitive to interest rates and, in particular, to real interest rates.

Major trends may be described numerically by examination of the personal sector (households and non-corporate businesses), which held the largest portion of total financial assets. Table 2.2 shows that the gross financial assets held by the personal sector rose more rapidly than personal disposable income after 1965. By 1985, gross assets of the personal sector were ¥372 billion, over eighteen times the level at the end of 1965. Taking a look at the components of these assets, it is evident that cash and securities grew more slowly than the average, and that time deposits, trusts, and insurance grew more rapidly. These trends demonstrate increased preference for high yields on the part of households.

*Table 2.2* Financial assets of the personal sector (¥bn)

|  | 1965(A) | 1975(B) | B/A | 1985(C) | C/B | 1988(D) | D/C |
|---|---|---|---|---|---|---|---|
| Cash | 1.9 | 10.0 | 5.2 | 20.3 | 2.0 | 27.5 | 1.4 |
| Demand deposits | 3.9 | 19.7 | 5.1 | 35.8 | 1.8 | 46.8 | 1.3 |
| Time deposits | 13.0 | 85.1 | 6.5 | 278.1 | 3.3 | 339.0 | 1.2 |
| Trust assets | 1.4 | 10.4 | 7.2 | 39.4 | 3.8 | 50.3 | 1.3 |
| Insurance | 3.6 | 21.4 | 5.9 | 88.7 | 4.1 | 145.4 | 1.7 |
| Securities | 7.4 | 31.9 | 4.3 | 109.4 | 3.4 | 175.1 | 1.6 |
| Total (T) | 31.2 | 178.5 | 5.7 | 571.7 | 3.2 | 785.1 | 1.4 |
| Personal disposable income (I) | 22.1 | 108.7 | 4.9 | 216.8 | 2.0 | 299.0 |  |
| I/T | 1.4 | 1.6 |  | 2.6 |  | 2.6 |  |
| Savings ratio % | 15.1 | 22.8 |  | 15.6 |  | 21.4 |  |

*Note:* Amounts are at the end of calendar year.
*Source:* BOJ, Flow of Funds Accounts.

## Financial internationalization

Another important change was the internationalization of the economy and finance. As a result of Japan's performance in the fast growth period, Japan became the second largest economy in the free world in terms of GNP and came to account for a major share of foreign trade as well as of financial transactions. If such a large country as Japan were to allow high barriers to foreigners' access to continue, then surely damage would be done to the development of international transactions in general.

The beginning of the internationalization of Japan's economy in the early 1970s was due to these circumstances. On the financial side, this meant a substantial increase in foreign lending, which centred on the overseas affiliates of Japanese financial institutions, and also meant a noticeable increase in the number of foreign banks that entered Japan. The number of foreign banks in Japan increased from 14 in 1960, to 18 in 1970, 63 in 1980, and 83 in 1989. Investment in the Japanese stock market was already substantial in the second half of the 1960s, but funding by non-residents in the Japanese market began in 1970 with the approval of yen-denominated bond issues (*samurai* bonds). Residents' investment in foreign securities was deregulated in 1972.

Internationalization of finance accelerated in the second half of the 1970s, partly as a consequence of the floating exchange rate system. Under the floating rate system, foreign exchange swap (spot and forward) transactions are important as a means of hedging exchange risks. If the interest rates and business practices in domestic financial markets are inconsistent with those of overseas markets, then the interest rate arbitrage transactions which link the financial and foreign exchange markets both at home and abroad will not occur smoothly, and the floating rate system cannot work effectively.

Internationalization of financial markets was also furthered by the structural changes in the flow of funds. Japan's financial institutions reacted to the decline in loan demand by domestic corporations in part by considerable expansion of syndicated loans abroad, particularly yen-denominated syndicated loans. In order to strengthen the basis for such business, the city banks opened overseas branches in major financial centres, as did the long-term credit banks and the trust banks. In addition, these institutions established affiliates abroad in order to deal with securities and the leasing business, and acquired local financial institutions in foreign countries. The foreign banks in Japan too saw the scope of their business activities grow and diversify. The foreign banks joined the underwriting syndication for government bonds and, since 1984, have distributed and dealt in them.

As internationalization of finance progressed, the flow of funds across national borders became increasingly active, requiring updating of the legal framework. In 1980, the Foreign Exchange and Foreign Trade Control Law (Law No. 228 of 1949) was completely revised and cross-border transactions became entirely free, in principle. This deregulation further encouraged rapid growth in the international flow of funds.

As the presence of Japanese financial institutions in the world financial markets expanded and active cross-border flow of funds became more common, it was unavoidable that discrepancies would emerge between financial practices in Japan and abroad. Since 1983, a series of meetings, such as the Japan–US Yen–Dollar Committee, the Japan–UK Financial Consultations and the Japan–West Germany Financial Consultations, were held. These meetings reflected foreigners' requests that Japanese financial practices be changed in order to conform with practices in Europe and the United States. The issues discussed in these consultations were very broad and included regulations on interest rates, segmentation of business, and regulation of financial activity across borders. The foreigners' objectives were not in general national treatment but rather deregulation from the viewpoint of reciprocity.

The internationalization of finance thus helped promote financial liberalization in the domestic economy. But more important causes of financial deregulation within Japan were to be found in internal factors.

### Changes in financial structure

The most striking domestic development was the contraction of over-borrowing by the corporate sector. Since the net fund shortage of the corporate sector declined in the second half of the 1970s, that sector's reliance on outside financing also declined. The share of financing of corporate businesses in total funding declined from 53 per cent in the period 1970–4 to 34 per cent in 1980–4, recovering somewhat to 36 per cent in 1985–8 (see table 2.3a and b). Within the environment of reduced dependence on outside funding, non-financial firms contributed to financial internationalization by expanding such financing routes as international bond issues.

The reduction in outside funding was at the expense of bank borrowings. The share of bank lending declined from 60 per cent in the period 1970–4 to 45 per cent in 1980–4, although a sharp recovery was observed in 1985–8. The major reason for this decline in reliance on bank borrowings was the feeling on the part of manufacturing firms that the banks would not retaliate if the firms reduced the level of compensating balances that had to be held in order to maintain relationships.

However, another feature of the financial system in the fast growth period remained unchanged. This was the predominance of indirect finance, which remained despite the prediction that the large-scale flotation of government bonds would increase the ratio of direct finance. The reduction of indirect finance has not been particularly noticeable.

*Table 23* (a) Demand for funds by sector (percentages); (b) Supply of funds by sector (percentages)

| (a) | Corporate business sector | Personal sector | Public sector | External sector |
|---|---|---|---|---|
| 1970–4 | 53 | 18 | 20 | 9 |
| 1980–4 | 34 | 14 | 36 | 16 |
| 1985–8 | 36 | 16 | 15 | 33 |

| (b) | Corporate business sector | Personal sector | Public sector | External sector |
|---|---|---|---|---|
| 1970–4 | 24 | 60 | 9 | 7 |
| 1980–4 | 16 | 64 | 8 | 12 |
| 1985–8 | 23 | 47 | 7 | 23 |

There was a tendency to decrease indirect finance until the early 1980s, but indirect finance increased again in the late 1980s. This means that a growing share of securities has been purchased by institutional investors and investment trusts. Therefore, it is hard to say that the predominance of indirect finance is being reduced gradually.

The other two features of the financial framework of the fast growth period, over-lending and the maldistribution of funds, also changed. As mentioned above, over-lending was closely related with over-borrowing. The chronic and excess reliance of the city banks on BOJ lending declined gradually. The BOJ's lending to the city banks increased slowly owing to the application of a credit ceiling system. Moreover, BOJ lending became a useful tool for very short-term adjustments in the financial markets. When the BOJ wished to make a large adjustment in total outstanding central bank credit, it generally used operations in the bill discount market.

As participants in the interbank markets diversified, the function of those markets changed. During the fast growth period, the interbank markets adjusted for the maldistribution of reserves among Japanese banks, all of which engaged in retail banking. But, after 1975, the city banks, the long-term credit banks, the trust banks, the foreign banks, and the securities firms alike became either borrowers or lenders in response to new financial needs, so that the interbank markets became a locus of wholesale banking.

After 1975, the regulated monetary framework of the fast growth period came into conflict with the changing needs and developing technologies of financial engineering. In order to reconstruct and to stabilize the financial system, it was necessary to reconsider existing regulations and systems in the light of the needs of the new era.

## Flow of funds analysis

The most distinctive indicator of the changes in the Japanese financial structure after the first oil crisis was the dramatic change in the flow of funds. A numerical expression of this indicator may be found in the flow of funds accounts by using the 'net surplus position' of the various sectors.

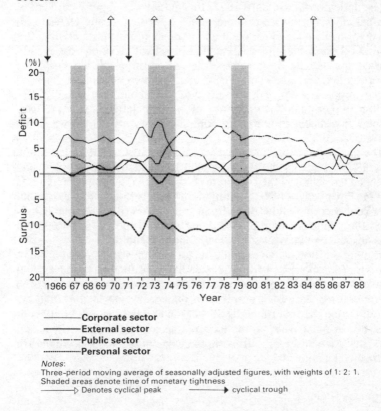

*Figure 2.1* Sectoral deficits and surpluses (per cent of nominal GNP)
*Source:* BOJ, *Chosa Geppo*, June 1989.

Figure 2.1 shows the net surplus (lending) or deficit (borrowing) of each economic sector as a proportion of nominal GNP each year. The figure shows that the personal sector had a continuous, stable and large surplus which was about 10 per cent of nominal GNP. This ratio reached a peak in 1972, due to increased personal interest in housing. But the ratio rose again after the first oil crisis because inflation had reduced the real value of financial assets and had made households save more. In contrast, both the corporate and the public sectors had deficits of funds. But the behaviour of the deficit sectors changed markedly, with 1974 marking a major turning point.

During the fast growth period and the early 1970s, the corporate sector's high level of investment for plant and equipment caused the largest deficit of funds. Until 1971, this deficit was about 7 per cent of nominal GNP, but it rose to more than 10 per cent during 1972–1974. The investment demand for plant and equipment fell substantially after the first oil crisis, and this decline, combined with cost-cutting, greatly reduced the deficits of the corporate sector. In 1978, the corporate sector's deficit was almost nil. Therefore the deficit of funds re-emerged for the corporate sector, but amounted to only about 3 per cent of GNP. In 1988, the corporate sector again increased net deficit of funds reflecting new investment in plant and equipment, most of which was from overseas.

The public sector, on the other hand, had a very small deficit in the early 1970s, but this deficit expanded tremendously after 1974 and exceeded the deficit of the corporate sector by 1975. Thereafter, deficits of about 7 per cent of GNP continued. In 1984, a slight decline to about 5 per cent occurred under the influence of severe fiscal trenchment. In 1988, the public sector recorded a net surplus due to favourable tax revenues and government's efforts to reduce spending.

The net position of the external sector is simply the current account position of Japan viewed from the standpoint of foreign countries, and is the inverse of the net position of all domestic sectors put together. The external sector showed a surplus on two occasions in the 1970–85 period: during the first oil crisis of 1973–4 and the second oil crisis of 1979–80. In other periods, the external sector had deficits. In recent years, the external sector is growing to be one of the major borrowers in the financial market.

### Corporate finance

Until the early 1970s, the corporate sector was desperate for funds. Now its surplus of cash is one of the major factors behind the extraordinary outflow of capital from Japan since 1984. Furthermore, funds are being raised to invest not only in new plant and equipment, but also in financial instruments as the corporate sector strives to boost overall profits.

The corporate sector's liquidity increased markedly following the export boom of 1984–5, which resulted in record profits. The more active financing activities of the corporate sector also received a boost from financial deregulation following the Japan–US Yen–Dollar Committee Accord reached in early 1984.

As a consequence, the growth of financial assets has increased faster than the growth of physical assets in the corporate sector. This growth in corporate assets has continued while overall corporate sector borrowing has increased, highlighting the drive to boost earnings from financial activities. In particular, there has been a large increase in foreign currency investments, which account for almost one-third of the total, and a big shift of funds from deposits under the interest rate regulation in favour of unregulated deposits. Much of these funds have flowed into high-risk/high-return investment, which represents a significant shift in behaviour on the part of Japanese corporate investors.

Since 1985, profit making from active fund management has been of increasing importance to overall corporate businesses. *Zaiteku* (financial management technique) has taken hold, with corporate treasurers keen to maximize financial revenues. The word '*zaiteku*' was first coined in 1985, following the rapid rise in financial speculation by many big firms. For many treasurers, this involves taking deposits out of low-interest time deposits in the banks and putting them into money market instruments. Some argue that this tendency is ultimately self-defeating, as it will reduce new plant investment, thus jeopardizing the long-run viability of the nation's industrial base. Many entrepreneurs reply that effective management of surplus cash helps raise corporate profitability overall, especially when their main line of business is unsatisfactory.

The fact is that fund management has taken hold, although there are very real concerns that senior or top management is not fully aware of the risks that have been incurred with some investments. The surplus cash position of the corporate sector is evidenced by the surge of funds in *tokkin* or special investment trusts.

The continuing deregulation of Japan's financial markets has resulted in a wider variety of instruments for corporate funding and asset management techniques which provide attractive rates of return. Even though new demand for investment funds for plant and equipment has been at a low level since the appreciation of the yen began in late 1985, new borrowings from banks and capital markets have continued.

By early 1987, the short-term prime rate, which is the city banks' best lending rate, was cut to 3.375 per cent. For many big firms, even cheaper funds could be raised offshore through convertible bond issues or bonds with warrants attached. Such new issuing activity remained strong for most of 1987 and 1988. With the alternative of cheap offshore fundings, around half of all fundings since 1986 were made outside Japan. There has been substantial diversification of currencies as well. In fact, most currency funding was denominated in US dollars, although with currency uncertainty, particularly from the mid-1980s, many corporations opted for other currencies.

Along with these developments, the corporate sector's deployment of surplus funds has been moved from bank deposits into a wide variety of instruments, both domestic and international. The largest companies are increasingly trading on their reputation to raise funds cheaply in one market for reinvestment in another. In these circumstances, the number of Japanese companies establishing offshore finance subsidiaries has risen continuously since 1985. Typically based in London, these subsidiaries trade a variety of instruments in different markets. Most companies taking this step are engaged in foreign trade and, utilizing offshore finance subsidiaries, can increase their range of financing options, as well as match foreign exchange risks.

For much of 1986, profiting from *zaiteku* activities was comparatively straightforward. The yen was moving up against the US dollar and domestic and international interest rates were declining, which caused the stock market to rise. This situation changed during 1987, however, when currency markets and domestic interest rates were hard to predict. As a result, companies that had profited from earlier trends found it difficult to maintain their position in the tougher investment climate of 1987. Short-term interest rates had begun to move upwards, creating havoc in Japanese bond markets and also clouding the short-term outlook for the stock market. Nervousness increased greatly in the wake of speculation about heavy losses.

In September 1987, a medium-size company, Tateho Chemical Industries, suffered a heavy loss from securities investments and nearly went bankrupt. Disclosure of the company's difficulties temporarily affected domestic and international bond markets. The Ministry of Finance (MOF) stepped in to conduct an investigation. The authorities were keen to limit the fallout from this incident and there were strong denials that more companies would also be posting heavy losses from poor securities investments.

For a time the difficulties of Tateho Chemical also resulted in heavy foreign selling of Japanese stocks. But, even with the enormous publicity that was given to the incident, the shift to *zaiteku* seemed irreversible. More adept financial investments have been an integral part of corporate management in the United States and Europe for many years. Now Japanese companies are following and it has become an important part of companies' operations.

The proportion of funds raised through overseas markets more than doubled from 8.1 per cent in 1980 to 17.5 per cent in 1985. The drive to offshore funding has been in response to easier issuing terms and, for many companies, the need to offset the foreign exchange risk stemming from foreign trade and earnings. This move to offshore funding has also been fuelled by the growing sophistication of swap and future transactions.

Against the backdrop of the steady drift offshore for funding, there has been progressive relaxation of domestic bond issuing conditions. In the convertible bond market, there has been a sizeable reduction in unsecured bond issues, together with a number of other changes, such as broadening the discretion of the underwriter in setting coupon rates, and a lengthening of maturities to ten years.

For straight bond issues in Japan there has been some relaxation of the restrictions on which groups can borrow from the market, and an easing of conditions for totally unsecured bonds, together with a lengthening of maturities. With easier access to capital markets, the corporate sector has increased its reliance on bank borrowings to less than one-third of funding requirements with a corresponding rise in the issuance of securities, which now exceed 30 per cent of financing needs.

The shift of corporate sector borrowings away from commercial banks received an additional impetus when commercial paper (CP) was approved in November 1987. Initially, about 180 companies were quali- fied to issue CPs. CPs may be issued with a term of one to six months and in an amount not less than ¥100 million. Issuing companies are in principle required to obtain a back-up line from banks. But for the forty largest companies and the power companies this is optional. CPs are sold through either banks or securities firms. In November 1988 or a year from its inception, CP outstanding reached to ¥8.2 billion, 70 per cent of which were issued by the trading companies. In April 1989, CP outstanding exceeded ¥10 billion.

Since 1988, corporate businesses have been active in expanding investment for plant and equipment. Statistics indicate that new invest- ment in plant and equipment in all industries other than financial services increased 28.7 per cent in 1988 compared with a 5.4 per cent growth in 1987. As a result, the corporate sector's fund deficit is growing vigorously for the first time since 1975 (see figure 2.1).

**Public finance**

Until 1964, no government bonds were issued in line with the stricture of the Public Finance Law (Law No. 34 of 1947). This formed a key part of the Dodge Plan imposed on Japan to overcome the post-war inflation. The Dodge Plan was named after the head of the US Economic Mission, Joseph Dodge, who in 1949 recommended maintenance of a balanced budget. Without the need to finance a budget deficit through household

savings, these savings could be directed towards financing the reconstruction of industries. In view of Japan's poor credibility at that time,
this step was essential to achieve basic financial efficiencies in Japan.

The principle of balanced budgets was maintained until 1965, when
government bonds were issued to make up for declining tax revenues.
After that 'construction bonds' were issued for public works and, in
1975, 'deficit-covering bonds' were floated. Once the government dis-
covered how easy it was to issue bonds to finance new programmes,
bond issuance quickly became commonplace.

Japan's fiscal policy has created a massive accumulation of public
debt since 1975, which the MOF is trying to bring under control (see
figure 2.2). The 'debt service ratio' exceeded 20 per cent of the total
budget in fiscal 1986, indicating the strain placed on fiscal policy. In
addition, government bonds outstanding represented 43.2 per cent of
GNP in 1987. Thus debt servicing has increased 10 per cent annually
and exceeded the annual expenditure for social security in 1987. By the
end of March 1988, total government debt outstanding had reached
¥151.8 billion, with 60 per cent financed through bonds. But the fears
that such a high level of government bond issues might crowd out
corporate business from the bond market have proved to be illusion, due
to the excessive liquidity in the corporate sector and its easy access to
alternative financing, especially in the 1980s.

The government maintained a restrictive fiscal policy since the late
1970s, after a significant increase in government spending in the wake
of the two oil crises sparked fears that growing debt would be almost
impossible to manage. During the period 1972–5, for example, general
budget expenditures increased by an annual average of 22.5 per cent.
Such a high rate of growth was maintained until 1980, when the budget
increase was cut to 5.1 per cent. Since then, the budget has been
progressively tightened.

For this purpose there have been various administrative reform
measures aimed at making the various bureaucracies more efficient.
Ceilings have been put on budget allocations for most ministries, with a
10 per cent cut each year during the first half of the 1980s. The budget
for the fiscal year 1987 planned for a 0.02 per cent rise in spending,
which was the lowest for thirty-two years. However, government budget
growth rate rose again to 4.8 per cent for 1988 and to 6.6 per cent for
1989 (see table 2.4).

The most notable feature of the government budgets during the 1980s
is that, following the spending spree of the 1970s, bond issues exceeded
20 per cent of total budget expenditures for nearly ten years. In the
budget for the 1987 fiscal year, however, this ratio slipped back below
the 20 per cent level for the first time since the budget began to grow in

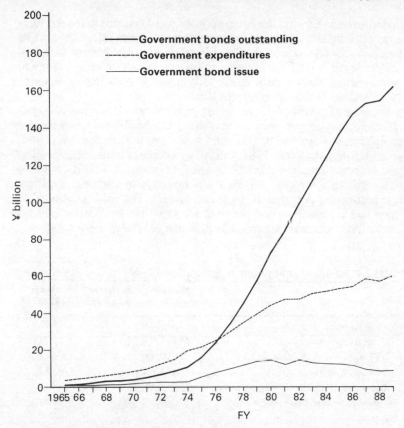

*Figure 2.2* Trend of government expenditures and government bonds
*Source:* BOJ, *Economic Statistics Annual.*

the late 1970s. In the 1989 fiscal year, bond issues to total budget ratio were estimated to be 11.8 per cent (see table 2.1).

It is obvious that the government's financial position improved markedly after the 1987 fiscal year and turned to surplus in 1989. This is attributable not only to the government's best efforts to reduce expenditures but also to favourable tax revenues reflecting the steady expansion of business activities since late 1986.

The real point of interest in the budget-setting process is not the general budget, which will remain under pressure for some time to come, but the so-called 'second budget', the Fiscal Investment and Loan Programme (FILP) managed directly by the MOF's Trust Fund Bureau. The FILP effectively operates as a bank within the government. The

Postal Savings Service, the largest pool of retail deposits in the world, is compelled by law to deposit for investment all funds raised through its nation-wide network with the Trust Fund Bureau. The bulk of the funds utilized through the FILP are used to finance the activities of a range of government financial institutions such as the Export–Import Bank of Japan and the Japan Development Bank.

In spite of steady pressure on the government budget and the considerable cuts in construction spending, the MOF has maintained a significant increase in the FILP and a 22.2 per cent increase was budgeted for the fiscal year 1987, following a 6 per cent rise in 1986. The rate of increase budgeted for 1987 was the highest since 1978. In terms of total budgets for 1987, the FILP was budgeted to reach ¥27.1 billion: one half of the government's general budget. The FILP continued to grow and increased by 9.4 per cent for 1988 and by 9.3 per cent for 1989. These increases are much higher than general account budgets.

*Table 2.4* Outline of government budget for fiscal 1989

| | *Millions of yen* | *% change from FY88* | *% change FY87–FY88* |
|---|---|---|---|
| General Account.............................................. | 60,414,200 | ( +6.6) | ( +4.8) |
| General expenditures.................................... | 34,080,500 | ( +3.3) | ( +1.2) |
| NTT proceeds.............................................. | 1,300,000 | ( 0.0) | ( – ) |
| Debt servicing.............................................. | 11,664,900 | ( +1.3) | ( +1.6) |
| Tax grants allocated to local governments... | 13,368,800 | (+22.6) | ( +7.1) |
| Fiscal investment and loan programme............ | 32,366,600 | ( +9.3) | ( +9.4) |
| **Debt** | | | |
| New government bond issues........................... | 7,111,000 | (–19.6) | (–15.8) |
| Budget deficit-covering bonds...................... | 1,400,000 | (–55.6) | (–36.7) |
| Construction bonds...................................... | 5,690,000 | ( 0) | ( +3.1) |
| Rollover bond issues........................................ | 15,203,900 | ( +4.8) | ( –7.7) |
| **Breakdown of general expenditures** | | | |
| Social welfare................................................. | 10,847,800 | ( +4.5) | ( +2.9) |
| Public works.................................................. | 6,197,400 | ( +1.9) | (+19.7) |
| Education and science..................................... | 4,862,800 | ( +0.1) | ( +0.2) |
| Defence.......................................................... | 3,892,700 | ( +5.2) | ( +5.2) |
| Official development assistance...................... | 740,000 | ( +5.9) | ( +6.5) |
| Foodstuff control (subsidies and others).......... | 415,300 | ( –7.3) | (–17.1) |
| Relief measures for small businesses............... | 189,800 | ( –2.8) | ( –1.1) |

*Source: The Japan Economic Journal*, 28 January 1989.

Chapter three

# Financial products, interest rates, and financial deregulation

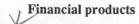

## Financial products

### Bank deposits

Recently, a wide range of financial products have grown in the process of financial deregulation. Among others, bank deposits are traditionally the most popular financial products held by households and business firms. They serve as a means of payment and as a means of saving for the short and medium term. There are three main types of deposits (i.e. current accounts, savings deposits, and time deposits), all of which are offered not only by commercial banks but also by other depository institutions.

Current accounts are payable on demand, by means of cheques drawn on the account and payable through the bank, or by means of promissory notes or bills of exchange which are payable at the bank. Thus they are mostly used by business firms as a form of payment. Current accounts bear no interest according to the provision of the Temporary Interest Rate Adjustment Law (TIRAL: Law No. 181 of 1947). In recent years, current account holders have been trying to reduce the balances they hold as much as possible.

In Japan savings deposits are also payable on demand. They are different from current accounts in that they are paid at the presentation of a passbook and a registered seal or by means of cash cards through automated teller machines (ATMs) or cash dispensers. Savings deposits are also used for automatic transfer services such as payroll credits, pension and dividend payments, and public utility charge debits, taxes and insurance premiums and instalment credit payments. Savings deposits are held mainly by individuals or households. In recent years, savings deposits have been used in connection with other financial products, such as *sogo* (composite) accounts, swing services, and transferable savings deposits and medium-term government bonds.

Time deposits are deposits for which the term of the deposit is fixed

31

and which cannot be withdrawn during this period unless one accepts a penalty. The rate of interest paid depends on the maturity of the deposits, which range from three months to three years. New products involving regular time deposits have been developed either by altering the method of interest payments or by combining them with other financial products. Examples of such alterations include maturity-designated time deposits, government bond deposit accounts, and public bond *sogo* accounts.

In addition to the traditional type of time deposits, there are new types of time deposits free from interest rate regulation. They include the CDs and non-negotiable large-sum time deposits. The money market certificates (MMCs) are also new products, but the rate of interest on these products is not free but is set a certain percentage point lower than that of the CDs. In addition, there are restrictions concerning minimum deposits, length of maturity, etc. These restrictions, however, have been eased.

Other than the deposits described above, there are two types of deposits worth noting. They are the foreign currency deposits and the non-resident yen deposits. Foreign currency deposits are offered by the authorized foreign exchange banks. The types of deposits offered are similar to those of local yen deposits (i.e. current, savings, and time deposits). The terms are left to negotiation between the bank and the depositor. Interest rates on such deposits do not fall within the jurisdiction of the TIRAL. Non-resident yen deposits are ones received by the authorized foreign exchange banks from non-residents. Interest rates on deposits by foreign governments, foreign central banks, and supranational organizations have been exempt from regulation since 1980.

## *Postal savings*

Postal savings are deposits offered by the Postal Savings Service for individual small savings. There is an account limit per depositor, which was increased from ¥3 million to ¥5 million in April 1988, and will be further increased to ¥7 million in January 1990. There are several types of postal savings deposits, including regular savings, fixed-amount savings, time deposits and instalment savings. Fixed-amount savings are unique financial products offered by the Postal Savings Service, and comprised 90 per cent of total postal savings in March 1989.

The fixed-amount savings may either be withdrawn at any time after having been on deposit for six months, or may continue on deposit for up to ten years if there is no need for withdrawal. The interest rate that applied on the date of deposit applies for the entire period of deposit, and interest is compounded semi-annually. For most deposits with regulated rates of interest, the interest rates are usually set so that it is advantageous to have longer-term deposits. The postal savings other than the fixed-amount postal savings correspond to the deposits offered by private depository institutions.

## Trusts assets

The trust accounts offered by the trust banks may be divided into two general classes according to the type of asset to which the funds invested are applied when the original deposit was made. These two types of trusts are called money trusts and non-money trusts. Among money trusts, the securities investment trust is of a special character and will be discussed later. The other types of money trust include ordinary money trusts, loan trusts, special-purpose trusts, and pension trusts.

An ordinary money trust is one that accepts funds in the form of money and invests them in loans, bills discounted, securities, and other deposits. The return on the funds in trust is then paid to the trust owner in the form of money at a rate according to the amount and the maturity of the trust at the time that the trust is dissolved. Distribution of the dividends is accounted for twice a year according to an expected dividend rate and depends on the performance of management and investments of the funds. The expected dividend rate is not under the jurisdiction of the TIRAL.

A loan trust is a type of ordinary trust, but authorized under the Loan Trust Law (Law No. 195 of 1952). Under a loan trust, a trust bank issues beneficiary notes and invests the funds so accumulated primarily in term loans. The returns are then distributed in proportion to the investment of principal with rights to benefits allocated according to holdings of beneficiary certificates. Dividends are paid semi-annually according to the expected dividend rate. A new type of loan trust was instituted in June 1981: the 'big' account. This account is exclusively for the use of individuals.

Special-purpose trusts differ from ordinary money trusts and loan trusts in that the client (i.e. the depositor) has specific control over the funds. For example, in the case of a loan, the client specifies the borrower, amount, interest rate, and collateral. Thus, the return on a special-purpose trust depends on the actual performance of the investment that is made after deduction of the trustee fee. Special-purpose trusts have grown rapidly since the late 1970s, due to fast expansion of the securities markets and advantageous tax treatment.

The pension trust is a pension fund whose management and investment has been undertaken by a trust bank or life insurance company. There are two types: the Tax Exempted Pension Plan and the Employees' Pension Plan. The former was initiated in 1962. This plan involves the grant of special privileges with respect to the tax laws and is deemed beneficial as an element of public policy. The latter dates back to 1966. This pension is organized as part of the National Welfare Pension System. The plan manages the welfare pension fund established by corporate businesses along with a portion of the funds accumulated under the government-managed welfare pension insurance scheme.

A securities investment trust is a type of money trust but with the funds invested in limited types of securities. There are two types of securities investment trusts. The first type is stock investment trusts, which began in 1951 with the enactment of the Securities Investment Trust Law (Law No. 198 of 1951). The second type is the public and corporate bond investment trusts introduced in 1961.

The stock investment trust concentrates the investment of its funds in equities, although bonds, bank deposits, money trusts, and call loans may also be used. Stock investment trusts are further divided into two types. One is the unit-type investment trust in which the funds are treated as a unit for the purpose of investment, liquidation, and distribution of earnings. The other is the open-ended investment trust under which extra funds may be added voluntarily, even after the trust fund has been established.

Public and corporate bond investment trusts restrict themselves to investing almost wholly in public and corporate bonds and do not involve equities. Excess funds are invested in call loans or bills discounted. As with stock investment trusts, there are two types, unit-type trusts and open-ended trusts, according to whether funds may be added after the original fund was established. Typical open-ended funds include the *chukoku* fund (medium-term government bond fund), *rikin* fund (interest earnings funds), and large-unit public and corporate bond investment trusts. Typical of unit trusts are non-distributed-dividend government bond funds. All of these have been developed by securities firms in recent years in their competition with banks to develop new financial products.

*Public bonds*

Public bonds are certificates of indebtedness issued by the government, municipalities or public corporations. They include long-term government bonds, medium-term government bonds, short-term government bills, municipal bonds and government-guaranteed bonds (see table 3.1). Traditionally, public bonds have been sold to investors through securities firms but since April 1983 banks have been permitted to sell newly issued public bonds according to the provision of the new Banking Law. Since June 1984, commercial banks have been allowed to deal in outstanding public bonds.

*Table 3.1* Classification of public securities*

| Type of bonds | Term | Form | Underwriting or public offering |
|---|---|---|---|
| Long-term government coupon bonds | 6, 10, 15, 20 years | coupon | Underwriting by syndicate |
| Medium-term government discount bonds | 5 years | discount | Underwriting by syndicate |
| Medium-term government coupon bonds | 2, 3, 4 years | coupon | Public offering in principle |
| Treasury bills | less than 6 months | discount | Public offering |
| Financing bills | usually 60 days | discount | Underwriting by the BOJ |
| Municipal bonds | 10 years | coupon | Public offering or private placement |
| Government-guaranteed bonds | 10 years | coupon | Underwriting by syndicate |

*Note:* *Excluding non-marketable government bonds.

Government bonds are issued within the limit established by the National Diet for each fiscal year and are used to cover payments from the general account of the government and to raise funds in order to pay maturing debt. Construction bonds or 'Article 4 bonds' are issued under the provision of Article 4 of the Public Finance Law (Law No. 34 of 1947). The proceeds are used for public works projects such as roads, harbours, and housing construction. Another type of government bond is the 'special bond' issued under the special bond flotation laws enacted in specific years; such bonds are also called 'deficit bonds', since the proceeds are used to finance deficits in the general account.

Non-marketable types of inscribed government compensation bonds also exist, though these are of minor importance. Examples include farm bonds, war-bereaved family bonds, repatriation bonds, and non-interest special benefit bonds.

Long-term government bonds of ten years' maturity with fixed rate coupons form the major share of government bond issues in Japan. Such bonds are issued every month, and issue amounts are divided into two portions, the market portion and the portion purchased by the Trust Fund Bureau of the Ministry of Finance (MOF). The market portion is under-written by the syndicate for underwriting securities, which consists of commercial banks, insurance companies, and securities firms. The government bond underwriting contracts are signed between the under-writing syndicate and the Bank of Japan (BOJ), as the agent of the government.

Medium-term government bonds consist of two types. The first are called 'government discount bonds', the maturity of which is up to five years. These types of bonds were first issued in 1972 in an attempt to promote the purchase of government bonds by individual investors. Currently they are issued, in principle, six times per year in the odd-numbered months. They are issued through the underwriting syndicate as are the long-term government bonds. Another bond is 'medium-term coupon bonds', the maturity of which ranges from two to four years. This type of bond was first issued in 1978 as a means of diversifying the types of government securities offered and thus of smoothing their sale in the market. They are mostly issued through public auctions but a certain portion is issued through fixed-rate private placements or through the Trust Fund Bureau.

Short-term government bills are also classified into two types; the financing bills (*seifu tanki shoken*) and the treasury bills (*tanki kokusai*). The financing bills, which were formerly called 'treasury bills', are intended to finance temporary shortages of funds of the government. They are issued three times a week within a limit established by the National Diet and are redeemed either within the fiscal year or within a calendar year. They are usually of sixty days' maturity and are in discount form. Since the rate of interest on the financing bills is fixed at a level below the BOJ's discount rate and short-term money market rates, virtually all the amounts issued are subscribed by the BOJ.

The treasury bills (TBs) are issued in discount form with a maturity of six months or less. They have been issued since February 1986 to smooth the redemption and refunding of the huge number of government bonds coming due in 1985 and thereafter. TBs are roll-over bills and the BOJ is prohibited from underwriting them. They are floated through public auction and are expected to be short-term money market instruments for institutional investors.

Municipal bonds (*chihosai*) are defined as long-term liabilities of municipalities such as prefectures, cities, towns, and villages. These bonds are issued either through public offering or private placement, the latter based on underwriting by the financial institutions in the local area. These debts are in the form of securities or certificates of indebtedness. The yield to subscribers of the municipal bonds has been fixed at the same level as for government-guaranteed bonds since 1981.

Government-guaranteed bonds are those issued by public corporations or public utilities, and which have a government guarantee on principal and interest payments. They are issued by public offering and are subscribed and underwritten by underwriting syndicates composed of banks and securities firms. The yield to subscribers is set only slightly above that of long-term government coupon bonds.

Public bonds also include external bonds, either issued in Japan by official non-residents or those issued outside Japan. The former includes the foreign currency issues (so-called '*shogun* bonds') and yen-denominated issues ('*samurai* bonds'), but the larger share is in yen-denominated bonds, mostly floated through public subscription. Most *samurai* bonds are floated by supranational organizations, foreign governments, and foreign government agencies. The first one was issued by the Asian Department Bank in 1970. The foreign currency bonds have been issued since 1955. They are issued outside Japan, and include foreign currency bonds and yen-denominated bonds (Euroyen bonds). The Euroyen bonds have been issued since 1977 but issue to residents was not allowed until March 1984.

## Corporate bonds and commercial paper

Corporate bonds are divided into financial bonds, industrial bonds, and external bonds which are issued overseas. Corporate bonds are divided into straight bonds, convertible bonds, and warrant bonds. Issuers of these bonds are financial institutions and corporate businesses in the private sector.

Financial bonds in straight form are issued by only six financial institutions, including three long-term credit banks, the Bank of Tokyo, the Norinchukin Bank, the Shokochukin Bank, and the National Federation of Credit Associations, which qualified only recently. They are issued in the form of coupon bonds or discount bonds. Maturities range from one to five years. The term of issue for these bonds is determined by taking into consideration the issuing conditions on long-term government coupon bonds. Individuals and institutional investors are the major purchasers. Financial institutions, particularly city banks, used to be major purchasers, but their role has declined since 1965. Commercial banks and mutual banks are not allowed to issue straight bonds, but they have been permitted to issue convertible bonds since April 1987.

Industrial bonds are issued by corporate businesses other than the financial institutions. Within the industrial bonds, there is a distinction between ones issued by the nine power companies and ones issued by other companies. All the power company bonds are floated through public subscription but other industrial bonds are floated through either public subscription or private placement. Industrial bonds must be secured against the issuing companies' plant and equipment for the principal and interest payments. However, power companies and certain other companies of the highest credit standing are released from this requirement. The rates of interest depend on the ranking of the company which is, in turn, based on the size of the company measured by net worth. However, issuing conditions are now starting to be based on credit-ratings of rating institutions.

Convertible bonds are financial or corporate bonds which allow conversion of a bond into the stock of the issuing company. A holder of these bonds may either hold them as bonds or convert them into stock. Conversion may be made at any time within a certain period after the issue date. The rate of interest is determined primarily by securities firms or managers of underwriting syndicates on the basis of a standard rate which takes into consideration market conditions. Convertible bonds are not subject to collateral requirements.

An innovation in the field of convertible bonds are similar instruments called 'warrant bonds', i.e. bonds that give the holder the right to buy new stock of the company. The holder has the right to request a new issue of stock from the issuing company for a certain proportion of its holdings, and also has the right to buy new stock at the price determined at the issue of the warrant bonds. Warrant bonds were first permitted under a revision of the Commercial Code (Law No. 48 of 1899) in 1981. Warrant bonds attract many investors because these holders have the privilege of buying new stock in the issuing company without losing bonds currently held.

External bonds are also issued by the private sector, usually without collateral. The guide-lines for private sector yen-denominated issues have been gradually eased since 1984. Euroyen bond issues by corporate businesses have been permitted since 1984. Japanese companies are very active in floating Eurobonds in foreign currency in the form of straight bonds, convertible bonds, or warrant bonds. In recent years, about 50 per cent of corporate bonds have been external bonds.

Commercial papers (CPs) are short-term papers issued by the prime industrial corporations since November 1987. No collateral is required, but severe restrictions are imposed. CPs maturities must be more than one month but not more than six months. Denomination must be more than ¥100 million. In principle, the issuing companies need bank guaranties or back-up lines for CPs, but these requirements are optional for power companies and the forty largest companies. CPs are issued through commercial banks or securities firms.

## Stocks

Stocks are a means of indicating the share rights of stockholders of a corporation and are considered to be securities that are freely negotiable. Stocks are also widely bought by individual investors primarily as a means of making capital gains. The proportion of stocks held by individuals has been declining continuously since 1960, and stood at 23.6 per cent in March 1988.

Capital increase occurs through the issue of new stocks to be purchased and the issue of new stocks without compensation. For the issues of new stocks to be purchased there is a further distinction among three types, those for which the rights to purchase the new stocks are allocated among existing stockholders, those for which the rights to purchase new stock are allocated among specified parties, and those for which the funds are gathered from the general public. In earlier years, the common practice in Japan was to issue at par value to the existing stockholders, but in recent years issuance at market prices to the general public has become the most common.

*Insurance*

The types of insurance sold in Japan include not only life and non-life insurance sold by insurance companies, but also various types of mutual aid insurance, agricultural co-operatives insurance, and postal life insurance.

Life insurance is of three varieties. The first is insurance against death, which pays insurance money in the case of death of the insuree during the period of the contract; the second is pure endowment insurance which pays insurance money so long as the insuree survives for a specified period of time; and the third type combines the characteristics of other two types. Each of these three types includes several sub-types.

In addition, many new types of insurance having special conditions concerning casualty, injury, and sickness have been developed. In recent years, savings-type insurance contracts have been popular because of investors' increased sensitivity to interest rates. Group insurance has also been conspicuous as corporate businesses seek better welfare protection for their employees. The insurance premiums are based on the expected mortality rates and estimated rates of return for investing premium income; determination and change of premium rates falls within the jurisdiction of the MOF.

Non-life insurance includes various types of contracts including fire insurance, marine insurance, and automobile insurance. In recent years, automobile insurance has accounted for 60 to 70 per cent of total insurance. In previous years, maturity of insurance contracts was one year or less, and the premiums were not subject to return after the expiration of the contract. However, in recent years, insurance contracts with savings provisions for the return of premium payments have been growing. The rates of premiums are established by the casualty insurance premium calculation committee or the automobile insurance premium calculation committee, and are charged by the individual companies subject to approval by the Minister of Finance.

**Interest rates**

*Regulatory structure*

Before deregulation, each type of interest rate was given a niche in the total structure, so that relationships between the various types of interest rates were supposed, in principle, to be permanent. For this reason, when any kind of interest rate was changed, the whole structure of interest rates had to be altered. Since lower interest rates were intended, there was strong pressure to change the interest margin.

Since 1947, the TIRAL has set the maximum limits for interest rates of private financial institutions, the TIRAL regulates rates of interest on deposits and lending in commercial banks and other financial institutions, including insurance companies. Interest rates on postal savings are decided by the Postal Savings Law (Law No. 144 of 1947) and those on lending by government financial institutions are under regulation by the individual laws on which these institutions are incorporated.

In the 1950s and 1960s, under the TIRAL, government policy attempted to fix the rates of interest on deposits and lending of financial institutions at a low level. Since 1970, however, flexibility has been granted in the interest rate regulation on bank deposits. Restrictions over lending rates have remained at a high level.

Large banks call for deregulating all interest rates, but repeal of all regulations at one time would create confusion in financial markets. For the time being, therefore, the Research Committee on the Financial System has been proposing that attempts should be made to increase the flexibility of interest rates, in order that the level of interest rates may change as much as possible in response to the demand and supply of funds, while at the same time existing regulations should be maintained as far as necessary.

*Interest rates on deposits*

As for rates of interest on deposits, the TIRAL sets the ceiling for deposits of commercial banks and other financial institutions. Those interest rates on deposits subject to regulation under the TIRAL include time deposits, current deposits, and deposits for tax payment. Foreign currency deposits have been exempted from the regulations since September 1974. The CDs and non-negotiable large-sum time deposits have been also exempted since May 1979 and October 1985, respectively. As for the interest rates on other deposits including MMCs, more detailed guide-lines are provided by the BOJ for every kind of deposit. Interests rates actually applied are determined by the individual institution within the guide-lines but, in fact, they correspond to the ceilings of the guide-lines.

Financial institutions other than banks also offer the same type of deposits as banks. Their ceilings are also fixed under the TIRAL. However, financial institutions for small businesses such as credit associations and credit co-operatives are allowed to apply interest rates that are 10 to 25 basis points higher than the ceiling for commercial banks' deposits.

Interest rates on postal savings are determined by Cabinet Order following the recommendation of the Committee on Postal Service in accordance with the Postal Savings Law. The rates on postal savings are higher than the rates on savings deposits of the commercial banks. This means that postal savings have advantages over the commercial bank deposits, a situation to which the banks object.

Interest rates on bank deposits used to be fixed at a relatively low level. For instance, interest rates for one-year time deposits remained unchanged at 5.50 per cent for a period from April 1961 to April 1970. In April 1970, however, a formula for determining the interest rate for bank deposits was introduced to facilitate flexible changes in the interest rates. Now interest rates on deposits move with changes in market rates though the rates remain low.

Since 1979, new types of deposits which are largely free from interest rate regulation have been introduced, including CDs, foreign currency deposits, non-resident yen deposits, MMCs, and non-negotiable large-sum time deposits. MMCs are not entirely free from regulation; interest rates on MMCs must be 75 basis points less than the average CD issuing rate published weekly by the BOJ. Current rates are shown in table 3.2.

*Short-term lending rates*

Although the TIRAL applies to a wide range of financial institutions, its control over lending rates is limited to those of the banks, the Norin-chukin Bank, and the insurance companies. Even in these cases, only lending with a term of less than one year and an amount of more than ¥1 million are under its jurisdiction. Interest rates for other forms of lending are free from regulation of the TIRAL.

At present, the legal ceiling on lending rates is fixed at a relatively high level. Within this ceiling, individual banks determine their own interest rates. Of these rates, the short-term prime rate, which is applied to the discounting of bills with the best credit standing and of the same nature, used to be linked to the official discount rate of the BOJ. In February 1989, the commercial banks introduced a new short-term prime rate formula; the new rate is one percentage point higher than the average cost of funding, including transaction accounts, regulated time deposits, open market borrowing, and interbank borrowing. Commercial banks raised the short-term prime rate from 4.25 per cent to 4.875 per cent in June 1989.

*Table 3.2* Interest rates on bank lending and deposits (as of 3 July 1989)

| | Current rates % | | Statutory ceiling % |
|---|---|---|---|
| Bank lending | | | |
| short-term prime rate | 4.875 | | 15.00 |
| long-term prime rate | 6.00 | | 15.00 |
| Bank deposits | | | |
| current deposits | 0 | | 0 |
| savings deposits | 0.38 | | 0.38 |
| three month time deposits | 2.04 | | 2.04 |
| six month time deposits | 3.20 | | 3.20 |
| one year time deposits | 3.95 | | 3.95 |
| two year time deposits | 4.20 | | 4.20 |
| MMC for less than one year | 4.63 | CD rate – | 0.75 |
| MMC for more than one year | 4.88 | CD rate – | 0.50 |
| super MMC for six months | 4.00 | CD rate – | 1.25 |
| super MMC for one year | 4.50 | CD rate – | 0.75 |
| loan trusts for two years | 4.40 | | 4.40 |
| money trusts for two years or more | 4.25 | | 4.25 |
| Postal Savings Service | | | |
| regular savings | 1.80 | | 1.80 |
| time deposit for six months | 3.20 | | 3.20 |
| time deposit for one year | 3.95 | | 3.95 |
| fixed amount savings (6 months to 10 years) | 4.174 ~ 5.513 | | |

*Source: Nihon Keizai Shinbun, 4 July 1989.*

## Long-term lending rates

With regard to long-term lending rates, which the TIRAL does not regulate, the long-term credit banks fix the long-term prime rate which reflects the coupon rate of financial bonds. The trust banks also determine the long-term prime rate for their own loan trusts. The two types of long-term prime rates are usually at the same level, but, while the former is a fixed rate, the latter is a floating rate that is altered to reflect changes in the monetary situation. The long-term prime rate was raised from 5.7 per cent to 6.0 per cent in July 1989.

Interest rates for housing loans are held to a relatively low level under the government's housing policy. Interest rates for newly extended housing loans change when the long-term prime rate is changed. Introduction of such a system was suggested by the Research Committee on the Financial System in 1973, because housing loans are a form of finance for households.

Until mid-1983, interest rates for housing loans were at an exclusively fixed rate. However, because the term for housing loans was very long, it was possible that banks' funding costs could surpass the agreed rate of interest. Therefore, the floating rate was applied to housing loans from May 1983. Customers may now choose fixed or floating rates, whichever is preferred.

Before the Second World War, the call market was the entire money market. Since 1960, however, money markets have developed rapidly. At present, *gensaki* (since the early 1960s), bill discount (since 1971), dollar call (1972). CDs (1979), yen BAs (1980), offshore deposits (1986), and CPs (1987) also form money markets. Interest rates on money markets are all exempted from the TIRAL.

*Rates of interest on bonds*

Although the issuing terms for most bonds are included in the regulated interest rate structure, the issuing terms for certain bonds have been deregulated. For medium-term government coupon bonds, a public tender formula was adopted in 1978 when these bonds were issued for the first time. In the original auctions, the buyers would bid on the overall yield for the securities; since August 1979, the coupon rate on the bonds has been set prior to the auction, and the buyers have bid on the price.

Unlike the issuing terms for new bonds, the secondary market yields on outstanding bonds are formed in the open market and change in response to demand and supply. This was largely true earlier, but was extended by the formation of the huge secondary market in government bonds and the easing of regulations concerning the sale of government bonds held by banks. The most interesting facet of recent developments in the secondary markets is the strengthened influence on the formation of secondary market bond yields brought by the internationalization and deregulation of securities markets and the extension of trading in securities by the banks.

Current yields of bonds are shown in table 3.3.

*Pressure on the regulated interest rate structure*

After mid-1970, with the expansion of open markets for both short-term and long-term assets, a clear yield curve developed in the open markets. This yield curve for free market assets came to influence the structure of regulated interest rates, including short-term ones. The yield curve implied by the structure of regulated interest rates was always upward sloping. As a result, in the final stages of monetary tightness, when expectations of falling interest rates were common, the upward-sloping yield curve of regulated interest rates was entirely different from the downward-sloping yield curve of free interest rates.

*Table 3.3* Money market interest rates and bond market yield (as of 3 July 1989)

|  | *Rates of interest or yields (%)* |
| --- | --- |
| Money markets | |
| Call loan, collateralized and unconditional | 4.96875 |
| Call loan, uncollateralized and overnight | 5.21875 |
| Bill discount (three months) | 5.40625 |
| CDs, new issue (three months) | 5.475 |
| *Gensaki* in securities (three months) | 5.375 |
| BAs in yen (sixty to fifty-nine days) | n/a |
| CPs (three months) | n/a |
| JOM in yen (three months) | 5.53125 |
| Bond markets | |
| FBs (three months) | 5.2515 |
| TBs (sixty days) | 5.000 |
| Government bonds with coupon (ten years) | 5.174 |
| Municipal bonds (ten years) | n/a |
| Government-guaranteed bonds (ten years) | 5.151 |
| Financial bonds with coupon (five years) | 5.100 |

*Source: Nihon Keizai Shinbun,* 4 July 1989.

The inconsistency between regulated and open market rates led to a shift of funds from interest-regulated assets into free-rate assets, such as *gensaki* and medium-term government bond funds. This shift of funds meant nothing less than 'disintermediation', i.e. a decline in the ability of depository institutions to attract money. Consequently, the banks were no longer able to continue relying on borrowing at regulated rates. They had no choice but to deposit interest rates and to supply depositors with new types of deposits that guaranteed higher yields.

In 1980, the securities companies introduced medium-term government bond funds. When these began to attract smaller deposits from small businesses and households, there occurred a gradual deregulation on minimum amounts and maturities of CDs in depository institutions. In 1985, MMCs were introduced. MMCs were of a smaller denomination than CDs but had interest rates which moved in parallel. In the same year, there was a deregulation of interest rates on non-negotiable large-sum time deposits. The minimum denominations of these deposits were substantially lowered in 1987 and 1988. The pressure on financial institutions by the regulation of interest rates was one reason for the change in the structure of regulated rates and was important in influencing and contributing to the deregulation of interest rates.

**Progress of financial deregulation**

The introduction of the new Banking Law (Law No. 59 of 1981) contributed to the expansion and deregulation of financial markets. In May 1984, the Japan–US Yen–Dollar Committee and the MOF released reports simultaneously on internationalization of the yen and deregulation of financial markets. These reports presented a concrete programme for deregulation of the financial system.

Deregulation measures taken so far are classified as deregulation of interest rates on deposits, deregulation of domestic financial markets, promotion of access for foreign financial institutions to Japan's markets, and deregulation of Euroyen transactions. As a result of these measures, internationalization of the yen has made considerable progress, and Tokyo has become one of the world's major financial centres.

*Deregulation of interest rates on deposits*

Deregulation of large-sum deposits has progressed markedly since 1979. Because deregulation of interest rates on deposits in a drastic way might result in difficulties for the banks, deregulation is proceeding gradually, starting with deregulation of interest rates on large-sum deposits. In principle, ceilings on interest rates by type and maturity of deposits are set by an announcement from the Minister of Finance and by guide-lines of the BOJ, under jurisdiction of the TIRAL. The deregulation of interest rates has proceeded through the contraction of areas subject to these regulations.

The first step in the deregulation of interest rates took place with the approval of the issuance of negotiable certificates of deposits (CDs) in May 1979. Interest rates on CDs are free from regulations. Initially, the minimum amount for CDs was ¥500 million and permissible maturities ranged from three to six months. In spring 1985, money market certificates (MMCs) were introduced with a minimum amount of ¥50 million. In October 1985, interest rates on non-negotiable large-sum time deposits of more than ¥1,000 million were exempted from regulation. The minimum amount of these deposits gradually decreased, and by April 1989 minimum amounts were ¥50 million for CDs, ¥20 million for non-negotiable time deposits, and ¥10 million for MMCs (see table 3.4). Also, other limitations on these deposits, such as acceptable maturities, were relaxed. With deregulation, the proportion of such deposits has steadily increased and currently accounts for more than 50 per cent of domestic deposits at the city banks (see table 3.5).

*Table 3.4* Process of interest rate deregulation

| Dates | Certificates of deposits | | Large-sum time deposits | | Money market certificates | | |
|---|---|---|---|---|---|---|---|
| | Deposit units | Terms | Deposit units | Terms | Deposit units | Terms | Interest rates |
| May 1979 | ¥500m | 3–6 mths | – | – | | | |
| Apr. 1985 | ¥100m | 1–6 mths | – | – | ¥50m | 1–6 mths | CD rates –0.75% |
| Oct. 1985 | | | ¥1000m | 3 mths – 3 yrs | | | |
| Apr. 1986 | | 1 mth – 1 yr | ¥500m | | | 1 mth – 1 yr | |
| Sept. 1986 | | | ¥300m | | ¥30m | | |
| Apr. 1987 | | | ¥100m | | ¥20m | 1 mth – 2 yrs | CD rates –0.75% for one year or shorter items; CD rates –0.5% for longer than one year items |
| Oct. 1987 | | | | 1 mth – 2 yrs | ¥10m | | |
| Apr. 1988 | ¥50m | 2 wks – 2 yrs | ¥50m | | | | |
| Nov. 1988 | | | ¥30m | | | | |
| Apr. 1989 | | | ¥20m | | | | |
| Oct. 1989 | | | ¥10m | | | | |

*Source: Tokyo Business Today*, October 1988.

## Deregulation of banking business and new financial products

The past few years have been characterized by the rapid development of new financial products and the diversification of operations by financial institutions. The needs of corporate businesses and households are being reflected not only in the deregulation of interest rates on deposits, but also in a widening variety of financial products offered by life and non-life insurance companies, securities firms, and other financial institutions. In addition to those which have been developed by financial

*Table 3.5* Share of deposits with deregulated rates of interest*

|  | March 1986 % | March 1987 % | March 1988 % | March 1989 % |
|---|---|---|---|---|
| City banks | 16.2 | 25.4 | 39.5 | 52.4 |
| Regional banks | 9.6 | 13.7 | 21.3 | 32.3 |
| Mutual banks** | 8.6 | 16.5 | 22.3 | 31.3 |
| Credit associations | 2.2 | 3.6 | 9.5 | 16.2 |

*Notes:* *Including CDs, MMCs, large-sum time deposits, and foreign currency deposits.
  **Mutual banks converted into commercial banks in February 1989 are not included in
    regional banks, but in mutual banks.
*Source: Nihon Keizai Shinbun*, 1 January 1989 and 18 April 1989.

institutions, a growing number of financial products are being introduced in co-operation with other business firms.

Further, in 1983, the commercial and other banks were granted permission for distribution of newly issued public bonds, including government bonds and, in 1984, the banks began dealing bonds in the secondary markets. Through the diversification of financial products, the banks have been able to respond to an increasingly broad range of customers' needs. Also, the Research Committee on Financial System, is conducting research on basic issues that might affect the financial system, such as the segregation between the commercial banks and the long-term financing institutions.

Foreign banks and securities firms in Japan are becoming more active each year, and the number of branches and representative offices is increasing. In 1985, nine foreign banks set up trust banking subsidiaries in Japan to handle corporate pension funds and conduct other business. By June 1989, twenty-eight foreign securities firms and twenty-two securities affiliates of foreign banks received permission to open branches engaging in the securities business in Japan. Foreign banks and securities firms opened branches dealing in government bonds as members of the underwriting syndicate. In May 1988, foreign regular members of the Tokyo Stock Exchange increased from six to twenty-two firms.

## Deregulation of financial markets

Measures are being taken to diversify and to increase the flexibility of short-term financial markets through deregulation and internationalization. Over the past several years, many deregulation measures have been taken, including the issuance of CDs, a lifting of limitations on the conversion of foreign currencies into yen in 1984, the introduction of MMCs in 1985, the establishment of Japan offshore markets in 1986, and approval of commercial paper (CP) in 1987. As a result of these measures, money markets have grown substantially. These measures have also strengthened the funding ability of foreign financial institutions.

In addition to deregulation in the domestic markets, deregulation of the Euroyen market is also proceeding, further internationalizing the yen. The MOF is taking various measures to expand the Euroyen market. Euroyen bond markets for residents and non-residents have expanded yearly since 1984 as deregulation measures, including the relaxation of Eurobond qualification standards, the diversification of products, and the deregulation of other aspects, have proceeded. This has stimulated the use of the yen in international capital transactions, and further internationalization of the yen is anticipated.

### Background of financial deregulation

The accumulation of financial assets has made households increasingly careful in their selection of financial products, thus expanding the need for deregulated interest rate accounts and diversified financial products. The balance of accumulated assets is outpacing the nominal rate of academic growth, reflecting changes in the structure of the economy. The accumulated assets of households are expanding faster than income as the ageing of the society increases retirement savings needs. Moreover, households are paying more attention to return on investment in choosing financial products. Consequently, the proportion accounted for by means of deposits is decreasing as the shares in stocks, bonds, and investment trusts increase.

International and domestic capital movements are becoming more active as the Japanese economy assumes an increasingly important role in the world. Expansion of her economy has made Japan the world's largest holder of financial assets, and acquisition of foreign securities is increasing continuously. Bond issues of foreign firms in Japan and of overseas subsidiaries of Japanese firms are showing rapid growth. These activities have expanded rapidly since 1980 when the revised Foreign Exchange and Foreign Trade Control Law (FEFTCL: Law No. 228 of 1949) simplified procedures and deregulated capital transactions. Increased capital flows have brought about a linking of the domestic and international capital markets and have contributed to further deregulation and internationalization of the Japanese financial markets.

In recent years, financial transactions have become more sophisticated and diversified with the introduction of advanced techniques of data processing and communication. Along with the progress in such technology, cash dispensers and other equipment have come into wide use. Recently, banks have developed services that use even more advanced information and telecommunications technology, such as automatic transfers from savings deposits to time deposits (the so-called swing service). Other advances include home and corporate banking systems used for deposits and remittances that link customers with financial institutions. Tests have also begun on 'card shopping' services using IC (integrated circuit) cards. Through the development and introduction of such sophisticated technology, financial institutions are moving to meet the diversified needs of households and corporate customers in domestic and overseas markets.

*Government bond explosion and expansion of securities markets*

As huge amounts of government bonds have been issued continuously, the primary and secondary bond markets have made progress in their consolidation and expansion. At the same time, financial products tied to government bonds have increased over the past ten years. The total amount of government bonds outstanding reached nearly ¥160 billion in March 1989.

In order for the nation's economy to accommodate the large volume of government bonds, a flexible revision of bond issue conditions reflecting market values has been taking place. Additionally, there has been a diversification of the types and methods of government bond issues, with medium-term bonds being issued on a public-bid basis.

Long-term government bonds, which constitute the bulk of government bonds, are mainly underwritten by the government bond syndicate. The city banks, which are the core of this syndicate, underwrite a large volume of the government bonds. In 1983, in order to promote bond holdings of households, banks were allowed to begin distribution of government bonds at their banking offices and, in 1984, banks were permitted to engage in the dealing business. Consequently the secondary market for government bonds has expanded, becoming the key factor in Japan's capital markets.

Additionally, government bonds themselves have become an effective instrument for savers, and the development of new products has expanded to include new accounts that combine time deposits with government bonds. The expansion of a deregulated government bond market has had a major influence on regulated financial markets and has become an important factor in furthering financial deregulation.

To expand the securities-related services provided by banks, further financial deregulation is needed. The banking and securities industries are segregated in Japan, as in the United States, and under this legal framework they have played their own role in each field of business. Recent changes in domestic financial markets, however, have led to increasing competition between banks and securities firms, particularly in money markets and government bond markets. Although it is natural for both banks and securities firms to wish to protect their own preserve, efforts to promote deregulation in the future will see banks and securities firms merging into similar areas of business. Equal access should be established.

For many years, certain forms of savings were exempted from income tax up to a certain amount per person. This measure proved to be an assistance to financial asset accumulation. Such tax exempt savings instruments included *maruyu* (bank deposits up to ¥3 million per person), *marutoku* (public bonds up to ¥3 million per person), postal savings which were limited to ¥3 million per person, and property formation accounts which were limited to ¥5 million. In April 1988, these tax exemptions were abolished except for fatherless households and senior citizens. As a result of the tax reform, a 20 per cent uniform tax was imposed on interest earned from bank deposits, postal savings, and government bonds, and increased securities investments.

With continuing deregulation of interest rates on large-sum time deposits, developments towards deregulation of interest on smaller sum deposits are also to be made. In order to accomplish this, a review of the postal savings system is essential because postal savings account for one-third of all personal deposits in Japan. In June 1989, banks and the Postal Savings Service introduced so-called 'super MMCs' with a minimum amount of ¥3 million. The minimum amount was reduced to ¥1 million by April 1990 and will be reduced to ¥100,000 by 1992.

It is notable that, in June 1988, the Extraordinary Council to Reform Public Administration (*Gyokakushin*) submitted a recommendation to the government to privatize the Postal Savings Service with a view to putting it on an equal footing with private sector financial institutions so that deregulation of interest rates on deposits will be furthered.

## Financial innovation

### New financial products

Financial innovations became quite numerous after 1975. The 1950s and 1960s saw such innovations as the direct crediting of payrolls into individual bank accounts and the automatic transfer of public utility charges from these accounts. These innovations reduced the costs to firms of paying wages and salaries or collecting fees.

In 1972, the '*sogo* (composite) account' was introduced. The *sogo* account is a savings account with a credit facility collateralized by a time deposit. By using such an account, the depositor may borrow money at a cost of only 25 basis points above the interest earned on the time deposit without cancelling the time deposit. The introduction of *sogo* accounts was the result of the increased usage of automatic transfer services for public utility charges.

Progress in financial innovation was slow until the end of the 1960s. Moreover, the types of financial innovation centred on those which eased the technological limitations of financial transactions or which attempted to lower the cost burden to customers. But the regulations and customs which ruled the fast growth period – that is, interest rate regulations, segregation of business fields of financial institutions, foreign exchange control, and the principle of collateral requirements – were appropriate to the economic and financial structure of that time, and thus these regulations were not particularly costly for corporate businesses or households.

For example, interest rate regulations assured an upward-sloping yield curve, and thus stabilized the profits based on maturity transformation. Market segmentation and foreign exchange control restricted overseas participants' entry into the various financial markets within the country and thus assured all the profits to the financial institutions which participated. This system worked to the particular advantage of financial institutions and was one of the major factors that assured the predominance of indirect finance. In the world of indirect finance, even small banks with poor management could gain the same benefits or opportunities for transactions as those gained by large banks, while small lenders had the opportunity to invest funds profitably.

Collateral requirements helped channel funds towards fixed investments because they favoured borrowers offering tangible collateral. Thus the regulations and customs of the fast growth period were an effective means of achieving growth based on high levels of investment, even in an environment of relatively little accumulation of financial assets. The costs of such regulations and customs were not particularly high, and hence there was very little incentive for financial innovations seeking to circumvent regulations.

However, the situation changed in 1973. Since then, government bonds were issued in volume, and open financial markets for both long-term and short-term assets developed. As financial assets accumulated, both corporate businesses and households became more sensitive to the profitability of their assets. Under the floating rate system, there were stronger incentives for swap transactions for the purpose of risk-hedging, as well as for yen-denominated international transactions.

These changes manifested themselves in the altered behaviour of corporate businesses, households, and the government with respect to financial transactions. In order to improve the efficiency of financial transactions, there was a greater need to employ transaction methods that did not limit interest rates or participation. As needs changed, the opportunity cost of interest rate regulations and exchange controls rose, and higher opportunity costs raised the latent demand for financial innovations that sought to circumvent the regulations. These movements on the demand side meant new profit opportunities for banks, securities firms, and other suppliers of financial products.

It was possible for these suppliers to raise their profits through their function as intermediaries in the financial markets, and by developing new types of financial instruments with a higher rate of return. Moreover, technological progress accelerated these trends; the remarkable progress of computers and telecommunication technology lowered the costs of acquiring market information and of transmitting and processing market transactions. These technical developments reduced the costs of supplying financial innovations and contributed to a substantial expansion of profit opportunities.

After 1975, therefore, there were higher costs associated with the constraints imposed by the regulations of the fast growth period. As a result, new types of financial innovation attempting to circumvent these regulations became numerous. Typical examples are: the '*chukoku* fund' which is an investment trust circumventing interest rate regulations by means of medium-term government coupon bonds carrying the market rate of interest, investments in foreign securities, and foreign currency deposits abroad.

Financial innovations by financial institutions seeking to circumvent regulations encouraged the authorities to react by easing or discontinuing regulatory requirements. Each innovation led to the next. This interdependence meant that the framework of the financial system of the fast growth period had to change.

Deregulation of interest rates on deposits began mainly because of the large-scale issues of government bonds and a substantial expansion of the *gensaki* market. Although the *gensaki* market had existed since the late 1960s, it jumped in size around 1975 due to the increased volume of government bonds. Many corporations came to hold surplus funds, which they sought to invest efficiently. One method was to shift funds from three to six month time deposits into the unregulated *gensaki* market.

An innovation for smaller transactions was the *chukoku* fund which offered liquidity, but also higher yields than short-term time deposits. These innovations reduced the ability of banks to collect deposits and caused a rapid decline in the banks' share *vis-à-vis* other financial institutions. The decline also reflected the shift of funds into postal savings which offered more attractive yield.

The banks, of course, sought to maintain a stable business environment for themselves and reacted with financial innovations of their own. In 1979, banks introduced CDs. In 1980, the regulation-free ¥3 million per person ceiling on foreign currency deposits was repealed. In 1985, banks introduced the money market certificates (MMCs), whose interest rates were linked to those of CDs, but were available in smaller denominations.

## Expansion of power for each industry

The new financial products supplied during the process of financial innovation have intensified competition between the banks and securities firms. As a result, there has been a partial relaxation of the segmentation of business between the two types of institutions. For example, banks may now offer financial products that are linked to government bonds, and may also supply government bond transaction services to their customers. This implies a reduction in the regulations that prohibited banks from engaging in the securities business.

The debate about the legality of the power of banks to engage in the securities business resulted in a very clear statement in the new Banking Law, concerning the types of securities operations in which commercial banks may participate. The commercial banks were permitted to engage in placements connected with the underwriting of government bonds, in distribution, and in dealing business.

Distribution of long-term government bonds began in April 1983 and of medium-term government bonds in October of the same year. Dealing began in June 1984. The banks have also introduced innovations, such as the government bond linked time deposit account, which divides the funds that a depositor places with a bank between a time deposit and government bonds, and thus pays a higher yield. Yet another product has developed in order to enhance liquidity by combining the government bond deposit account with a *sogo* account.

The securities firms were much more aggressive. In 1984, they developed a combined product, which linked *chukoku* funds with savings deposits, in co-operation with credit associations. This made it possible to transfer funds freely into and out of savings accounts, although there was a minimum balance requirement for the accounts. This meant that the *chukoku* funds became *de facto* an asset that could be used to settle payments, even though the settlements had to travel through saving accounts.

In addition, securities firms obtained permission to make loans to customers without limitations on the use of funds when the loans were collateralized by government bonds. When such loans were first permitted in 1984, they were done on a case-by-case basis, but, since 1985, the only constraint is an upper limit on such loans. Thus, commercial banks have made a partial entry into the securities business, while securities firms have made a partial entry into the banking business. Regulations segregating banking and securities business have been eased.

The segregation of long-term and short-term financing, and the segregation of banking and trust businesses continue to be debated. The commercial banks are exerting pressure for deregulation and repeal of such regulations on the grounds that the maturity structures of their assets and liabilities are becoming imbalanced, and that entry into growing areas such as pension trust management would be desirable. On the other hand, the long-term credit banks and the trust banks point to the merits of specialization and segregation, and they seek to continue the existing regulations.

In December 1987, the Research Committee on Financial System approved the Report submitted by the Sub-Committee on System Issues. This report suggested that Japan's segregated financial system should be reviewed from the viewpoint of financial deregulation and internationalization. For example: (a) bond issues should be allowed not only to the long-term credit banks and specialized foreign exchange banks, but also to the commercial banks; (b) trust business should not be limited to the trust banks; (c) banks and securities firms should be allowed to enter other areas of business through subsidiaries; (d) the specialized foreign exchange bank system should be re-examined; and (e) the mutual banks should be allowed to convert to commercial banks.

*Repeal of foreign exchange controls*

Pressure for the repeal or deregulation of foreign exchange controls gained strength with the increased incentives for international financial transactions that accompanied the shift to the floating rate system in 1973. Foreign exchange controls had been gradually eased since 1977, and the revised FEFTCL deregulated in principle all capital transactions in 1980. In 1984, the Report of the Japan–US Yen–Dollar Committee was released and extensive measures for the internationalization of finance were adopted, including easing regulations on Euroyen transactions.

The easing of controls was to be carried out with a consideration of the equilibrium between various regulations in the domestic market and the Euroyen markets. For example, Euroyen lending by Japanese banks was liberalized in the case of short-term lending, but deregulation of long-term lending to resident borrowers was put off because of the principle of segregation between short-term and long-term financial business. Concerning the segregation between banking and the securities industry, the MOF Report of 30 May 1984 states that 'the international business of Japanese banks and securities firms will be treated flexibly in accordance with the progress of deregulation and internationalization, keeping in mind the principle of segregation in the banking and securities business'.

In the process of deregulation, it could well be that the competitiveness of Japanese banks in the Euromarkets may be constrained. In this sense, the current situation is a period of transition toward a state of much greater deregulation or complete repeal. In 1984, the restriction on the conversion of foreign currencies into Japanese yen was repealed. This step allowed Japanese banks to raise yen funds by acquiring long-term foreign currency deposits. Such transactions would allow the circumvention of regulations segregating long-term and short-term finance. In 1985, foreign banks were permitted to enter into the trust business. It is quite possible that pressure to relax regulations in this area will come from domestic commercial banks, given the potential profitability of pension trust management.

*Repeal of collateral requirements*

The practice of collateral requirements has also been affected by internationalization. In the long-term bond market, there was a relaxation of the conditions for uncollateralized securities issues in 1984. This was done to bring Japanese practices into conformity with the eased guidelines for the issue of Euroyen securities by resident borrowers. In the short-term money markets, uncollateralized call money transactions were introduced in 1985.

In addition, interest rates on interbank time deposits were completely deregulated under the same conditions that applied to interest rates on large-sum time deposits. Together with this, there was a major expansion in the opportunities for uncollateralized interbank trading. The possibilities for expansion of uncollateralized trading depend upon the costs which must be incurred in order to ensure safety of the transactions.

**Impact of financial deregulation and stabilization policy**

*Financial innovation and banking industry*

Deregulation and internationalization of the financial system will have important influences on the banking industry. Rates of return in banking will surely be reduced by deregulation of interest rates on deposits, because the deregulation will raise the cost of funding. Moreover, the deregulation of interest rates will promote competition and will lead to a decline in lending rates. As a result, the spread between lending and the deposit rates will shrink.

However, reduction in the spread between deposit and loan rates will not necessarily lead to a fall in the profitability of the banking system. The net effect of deregulation is not clear. When banking becomes more diversified, there will be the potential for economies of scope, and hence an increase in the rates of return. For example, when a single office is able to carry out both deposit and securities business, then the unit costs of conducting the two types of businesses will fall. By use of appropriate and flexible techniques for balance sheet management, there will be increased opportunities to earn returns not possible under a regime of regulated interest rates.

Bank profits will also be assisted considerably by advanced technology in computer and telecommunications. There are, of course, some disadvantages to such technology, such as the huge investments necessary for the mechanization of financial business and the great risks associated with it, along with the increase in the optimal size of banks. On the other hand, joint development of communications systems among financial institutions is not impossible, and such co-operation would lower the costs to the financial institutions and raise the rates of return. In particular, the joint networks of automated teller machines (ATM) have lowered the cost of such networks to individual banks.

The savings from these joint activities cannot be ignored. In the area of firm banking and home banking, mechanization has clear merits when compared with the cost of offering the same sorts of service with labour instead of capital. Thus deregulation will not necessarily have only negative effects on bank returns but rather, because of the positive effects, may even raise bank profitability.

Risk, however, is another matter. There are four types of risk which financial deregulation may increase: credit risk, liquidity risk, interest rate risk, and foreign exchange risk. As banks enter the long-term finance and international finance area, they naturally will face investment opportunities with higher credit risk. With the deregulation of interest rates, an expansion of spread-lending is expected. This will pass the interest rate risk on to the borrower, but will also raise credit risk from the viewpoint of the bank.

Liquidity risk and interest rate risk are basically a matter of maturity mismatch between assets and liabilities. Because maturity transformation is the hub of the banking industry, it will be impossible to eliminate these kinds of risk. But for banks that face regulation on the maximum maturity of deposits due to the regulation concerning segregation of long-term and short-term banking business, liquidity risk is currently on the rise. Moreover, as deregulation of interest rates goes on, fluctuation in borrowing costs will also rise, and interest rate risk will rise with it.

The increase in the share of funding in domestic markets has raised interest rate risk, and this growing dependence on unstable market funds simultaneously implies an increase in liquidity risk. As CD issuing becomes more flexible and as the bankers' acceptance (BA) market expands, these trends will be accentuated. Foreign exchange risk will also rise with the expansion of assets and liabilities in foreign currency and with the expansion of foreign exchange dealing.

Thus, it appears likely that deregulation will increase the risk in the banking business, but it is also necessary to recognize that deregulation will stabilize some aspects. Two factors are at work. First, deregulation will raise the various types of risk for banks. At the same time, the ability of the banks to cope with these risks will be strengthened. In establishing the balance between the two factors, an important aspect is the creation of a financial futures market; such a market may allow banks to hedge interest rate risks at comparatively low cost.

Thus, other factors will still work to raise bank returns and to lower bank risk, while the changes in the financial system will simultaneously work to lower bank returns and to raise bank risk. That is to say, financial deregulation will expand the degree to which banks have a free hand in their operations. Just how deregulation and internationalization will change the stability of the banking business will depend on the degree of risk aversion in banks. In short, deregulation and internationalization will not necessarily lead to either a rise or a fall in bank failures.

*Financial stability and deposit insurance*

The changes in the financial system will not necessarily destabilize individual banks, but arriving at conclusions about changes in the stability of the financial system as a whole is very difficult. The financial regulations during the fast growth period were introduced to maintain stability in the financial system. Since these regulations have been eased or repealed, it is necessary to consider what other policies for ensuring stability could replace the regulations that restricted competition.

In order to maintain financial stability, regulatory authorities may put banks under balance sheet control and surveillance. Once any bank faces difficulties, proper relief measures are required in order to prevent a chain reaction of bank failures. The public safety net, which comprises both the lender of the last resort function and also the deposit insurance system, has a potent effect in ensuring the stability of the financial system. In 1965, the BOJ extended an emergency loan of ¥23,400 million without collateral to the ailing Yamaichi Securities Co. Ltd. However, as the public safety net is improved, expanded, widened, and made more flexible, the possibility of moral hazard only grows. The public safety net should be available only for the purpose of maintaining the stability of the financial system.

In 1971, the government enacted the Deposit Insurance Law (Law No. 34 of 1971) in accordance with the recommendations of the Research Committee on Financial System. This report, which was concerned with the state of the financial system in general, thought it desirable to introduce appropriate levels of competition into the financial markets in order to increase efficiency. As part of the proposal of reform, measures for depositor protection would be necessary and the deposit insurance system was one of these measures. Thus a deposit insurance corporation was established in 1971.

Currently, Japan's deposit insurance system contains two organizations, the Deposit Insurance Corporation (DIC) and the Savings Insurance Corporation for Agricultural and Fisheries Co-operatives (SICAFC). The DIC is capitalized at ¥450 million, with the government, the BOJ, and private financial institutions each contributing one-third of the capital. The participating institutions are the city banks, the regional banks, the long-term credit banks, the trust banks, the specialized foreign exchange bank, the mutual banks, the credit associations, the credit co-operatives, and the labour credit associations. The type of deposit liabilities to be insured are yen-denominated regular deposits, instalment savings, and money in trust. The rate of premiums is currently 0.008 per cent. Insured amount was originally ¥3 million, but was increased to ¥10 million in 1986.

The SICAFC was established in 1973, with paid-in capital of ¥300 million. The government, the BOJ, and the Norinchukin Bank contributed ¥75 million each and the remainder was subscribed by the credit federations of agricultural and fisheries co-operatives. Since the SICAFC was modelled on the DIC, the types of deposit insured, the rate of premiums, and insured amounts are quite similar to those of the DIC.

So far both the DIC and the SICAFC have never experienced payoff of deposits because no bankruptcy of financial institution was recorded during the post-war period in Japan. Problem banks were merged with healthy banks before bankruptcy.

# Part II

# Financial markets

Chapter four

# Short-term money markets

## Call and bill discount markets

Short-term money markets or, more simply, 'money markets', are those in which debt instruments maturing within a year are traded, while long-term markets or capital markets are those in which debt with maturities of over one year are traded. Money markets are divided into two parts: interbank markets and open markets. The former are the markets in which only financial institutions may participate. The interbank markets include the call market and bill discount market. The open markets include the *gensaki* (RP) market, certificate of deposit (CD) market, treasury bill (TB) market, financing bill (FB) market, bankers acceptance (BA) market, and the commercial paper (CP) market. The money markets have been growing very rapidly as signified in table 4.1 and figure 4.1.

The interbank markets are the main fields in which the Bank of Japan (BOJ) carries out open market operations for the purpose of monetary control. And it is from these markets that the effects of interest rate policy spread to other markets through arbitrage relationships. If the FB market becomes the core of the money markets in the future then it will be possible to conduct open market operations in FBs which may strengthen the influence of the BOJ over liquidity in the market.

### Call market

In the pre-war era, the call market was the only money market. At that time, however, the call market included not only very short-term lending but also slightly longer-term or fixed period transactions such as over-the-month lending. In May 1971, lending over one month or more was shifted to the newly established bill discount market and the call market reverted to its real role of short-term transactions. As a result, Japan's call transactions are very similar to federal fund transactions in the United States. In November 1988, terms of all loans were again

Table 4.1 Outstanding amounts of money markets

| | End of 1970 | | End of 1975 | | End of 1980 | | End of 1985 | | End of 1988 | |
|---|---|---|---|---|---|---|---|---|---|---|
| | ¥bn | % | ¥bn | % | ¥bn | % | ¥bn | % | ¥bn | % |
| Interbank markets: | <1.8> | <75.0> | <7.1> | <79.8> | <12.2> | <57.0> | <31.7> | <47.4> | <96.4> | <57.5> |
| Call market | 1.8 | 75.0 | 2.3 | 25.9 | 4.1 | 19.2 | 5.1 | 7.6 | 16.9 | 10.1 |
| Bill discount market | – | – | 4.4 | 49.4 | 5.7 | 26.6 | 14.7 | 22.0 | 15.3 | 9.1 |
| Tokyo dollar call market | – | – | 0.4 | 4.5 | 2.4 | 11.2 | 11.9 | 17.8 | 14.2 | 8.5 |
| Japan offshore market | – | – | – | – | – | – | – | – | 50.0 | 29.8 |
| Open markets: | <0.6> | <25.0> | <1.8> | <20.2> | <9.2> | <43.0> | <35.2> | <52.6> | <71.1> | <42.5> |
| Gensaki market | 0.6 | 25.0 | 1.8 | 20.2 | 4.5 | 21.0 | 4.6 | 6.9 | 7.4 | 4.4 |
| CD market | – | – | – | – | 2.4 | 11.2 | 9.7 | 14.5 | 16.0 | 9.5 |
| BA market | – | – | – | – | – | – | – | – | – | – |
| CP market | – | – | – | – | – | – | – | – | 9.3 | 5.6 |
| FB market | – | – | – | – | – | – | 10.3 | 15.4 | 21.2 | 12.7 |
| TB market | – | – | – | – | – | – | – | – | 2.0 | 1.2 |
| Foreign CDs and CPs | – | – | – | – | – | – | 0.7 | 1.0 | n/a | n/a |
| Euroyen market | – | – | – | – | 2.3 | 10.8 | 9.9 | 14.8 | 15.2 | 9.1 |
| Total | 2.4 | 100.0 | 8.9 | 100.0 | 21.4 | 100.0 | 66.9 | 100.0 | 167.5 | 100.0 |

Source: BOJ, Economic Statistics Annual 1980 and 1988.

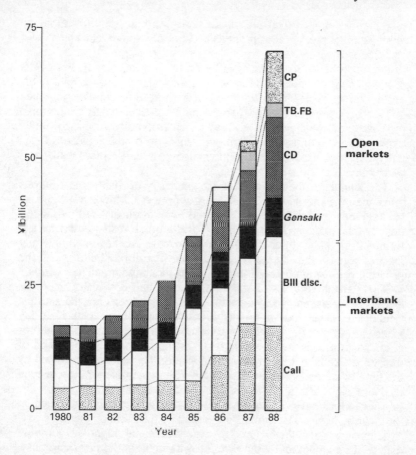

*Figure 4.1* Expansion of money markets
*Source: Nihon Keizai Shinbun,* 26 March 1989.

extended to six months, while the bill discount market was also expanded to include one week to three week transactions. Therefore, currently the two markets are quite similar to each other, although bill transactions require promissory notes or bills of exchange.

The call market comprises lending and borrowing institutions, including depository institutions, securities firms, and securities finance companies, other than money market brokers or intermediaries. For collateralized call transactions, the money market brokers may act as dealers trading on their own account but, in fact, their function is closer to that of brokers who only bring together demand and supply in the market. For non-collateralized transactions, introduced in July 1985, the money market brokers act simply as brokers and do not take any risk on transactions.

Among others, city banks have by far the largest share as borrowers of funds in the call market. They take 50 to 60 per cent of the total funds in the market. This share has been on a slight downward trend since 1975. The shares of foreign banks and long-term credit banks have increased because they have gradually increased borrowing in the inter-bank markets in order to supplement long-term funds. Securities firms and securities finance companies also gradually increased their borrowing.

The lenders in the call market are generally depository institutions other than the city banks. The largest suppliers of funds are the trust banks, credit associations, the National Federation of Credit Associa-tion, and the financial institutions for agriculture, forestry, and fisheries. Regional banks traditionally had a large role but are no longer net lenders because their liquidity position has deteriorated along with the growing volume of underwriting of government and municipal bonds.

There are three types of call transactions; half-day loans, uncondi-tional call loans, and fixed-date loans. Half-day loans are the shortest type of call loans and are repaid within the day of the loan. Half-day loans include morning loans and afternoon loans. Morning loans are for cases when a bank needs funds early in the morning for purposes of transfer of funds to local areas or cash needs. These loans are repaid by the time of settlement at the clearing house, which is at 1.00 p.m each business day. Afternoon loans are for funds that are necessary for transfer to local areas or for other purposes after the daily settlement at the clearing house. These funds are repaid by 3.00 p.m on the same day.

Unconditional call loans are, in principle, repaid on the day after the date of the transaction by the time of settlement at the clearing house. However, if neither party of the transaction indicates a desire for repay-ment of the loan, it is automatically extended. In addition, there is a type of morning repayment call loan which is repaid at 9.00 a.m in the morn-ing following the day of transaction. Currently, unconditional call trans-actions account for 70 to 80 per cent of the total call transactions.

Fixed-date loans are those which are outstanding for a fixed period that is more than two days including the day of the transaction. Tradi-tionally, such periods ranged from two days to seven days, but, from August 1985, two-week loans and three week loans were added. Further, one month to six month loans were added in November 1988. Fixed-date call loans are always repaid in a lump sum on the due date, and pre-payments are not permitted. Fixed-date transactions account for 20 to 30 per cent of the total call transactions.

Traditionally, call transactions require collateral, although un-collateralized call loans bearing a higher rate of interest have been available since July 1985. Collateralization was introduced when un-collateralized call loans caused a great financial panic in 1927. In principle, government bonds were used as collateral for such purposes. Since call transactions are large, the amounts of collateral are also very large. In order to reduce the trouble of collateral transfer and to reduce risk as well, several schemes have been devised, such as the substitute certificate system and the depository certificate system.

## Bill discount market

As the bill discount market was a spin-off from the call market in 1971, the two markets are similar. However, bill discount transactions have longer maturities than call transactions. Bill discount transactions do not require any additional collateral as the bills serve as collateral. The BOJ also participates in the bill discount market, as do financial institutions and money market brokers.

In the bill discount market, the city banks are the largest borrowers of funds or sellers of bills, accounting for 80 per cent of market trans-actions. Foreign banks are the second largest borrowers in the market, but take only 5 per cent of the funds. In the bill discount market the largest lender or buyer of the bills is the BOJ which is active in bill buying operations. Other large lenders include the credit associations and their national federation, the trust banks, and the financial institu-tions for agriculture, fisheries, and forestry.

There are two types of bills that are eligible for transactions in the bill discount market. The first type consists of bills of various sorts, includ-ing credit-worthy industrial bills, trade bills, credit-worthy accommo-dation bills, and yen-denominated usance bills for exports and imports. The second type consists of bills of exchange, or so-called 'cover bills', which are prepared and accepted by borrowing banks. By means of these bills, financial institutions bundle a number of other eligible bills and use them as collateral. Most transactions are in the form of cover bills because the accompanying bills are not necessarily in round numbers.

According to term, bill transactions are classified as one to three week bills, one to six month bills and resaleable bills. The one to three week bills are a new type of transaction introduced in November 1988. These bills were established in response to the growing need for shorter-term transactions and to help open market operations of the BOJ. Re-saleable bills may be resold one month after their original dates of issues.

It should be noted that the BOJ operates directly in the bill discount market, both buying and selling, and adjusting the level of its lending in order to smooth out seasonal or irregular movements in the bill discount market or call market. In addition, these markets feel the direct impact of monetary policies. For example, when the BOJ wishes to reduce the growth of the money supply or total credit, it will purchase smaller amounts of bills relative to the shortage of funds in the market or take a more strict attitude toward lending.

## *Gensaki* (RP) Market

A *gensaki* transaction is a contract in which there is a prior promise either to repurchase or to resell the same securities as originally transacted after a fixed time and on a fixed date, just like repurchase agreements in the United States. Although *gensaki* transactions are securities buying and selling, they are virtually short-term lending and borrowing with the securities functioning as collateral. However, there are many other motivations for their use. For example when the *gensaki* rate is lower than the interest rate on the securities concerned, bondholders may sell their bonds in the *gensaki* market and then reduce the book values of these bonds.

It is generally agreed that the *gensaki* market developed spontaneously in the early 1960s, when securities firms sold excess bonds with repurchase agreements to small- and medium-sized financial institutions. Until 1979, this market was the only open and free market in which anyone could participate although individuals were later excluded. Currently, participants include securities firms, financial institutions, corporate businesses, government financial institutions, and non-residents (such as foreign investors). Among the buyers of *gensaki* or lenders in the market, the trust banks have the largest share at 20 per cent.

Trading volume declined in the *gensaki* market when the CD market was created in May 1979, although it has been growing again in recent years. The establishment of the CD market meant that the short-term open money market was no longer limited to the *gensaki* market and, as a result, the share of corporate businesses in the *gensaki* market declined after 1980. Foreigners' participation in the *gensaki* market was liberalized in the same year. Since 1980, the share of foreign investors in the *gensaki* market has risen and currently stands at around 8 per cent. Foreigners' transactions in this market concentrate on interest rate arbitrage transactions which link overseas interest rates, *gensaki* rates, and foreign exchange swap costs.

The largest bond sellers or *gensaki* borrowers in the market are bond dealers, primarily in securities firms. The share of bond dealers in the market is 60 to 70 per cent because securities firms sell bonds as a means of financing inventories of securities, although foreign currency loans (impact loans) and the financing systems for the circulation of public and corporate bonds are also used. Insurance companies and the city banks are also regular borrowers in the *gensaki* market. In the market's early years, the BOJ regulated the total amount of *gensaki* that could be sold by banks, but, with the growth of the market and the large-scale flotations of government bonds, these regulations were lifted between October 1978 and May 1980.

There are three types of *gensaki* transactions: own-account *gensaki*, consignment *gensaki*, and direct *gensaki*. An own-account *gensaki* is a transaction in which a securities firm sells a bond in its possession with a repurchase agreement; such transactions are carried out for the purpose of funding. At present, *gensaki* transactions are an important method of financing of securities firms' inventories. Regulations on the totals outstanding of own-account *gensaki* were imposed in 1978 in order to ensure the safety of the market and the sound management of the securities firms.

Consignment *gensaki* are repurchase agreements under which the bondholders other than securities firms carry out a *gensaki* transaction through securities firms. That is, the borrower will sell securities with a repurchase agreement to the securities firms, and then the securities firms will sell the very same securities with the very same date on its own account to another buyer in the market, such as a corporate business or a financial institution with excess funds. Such transactions do not cause a change in the balance of securities inventories in the securities firms. The upper limits on total outstandings in consignment *gensaki* have been introduced since May 1974.

A direct *gensaki* is a transaction between a bank or other financial institution with surplus funds and a buyer such as a corporate business. Own-account *gensaki* has about 70 per cent of total and consignment *gensaki* has about 30 per cent. But data for direct *gensaki* are not available.

### Certificate of deposit (CD) market

The CD market was established in May 1979, when depository institutions were allowed to issue CDs for the first time in Japan. It is obvious that CDs are modelled after ones in the United States. Initially there were restrictions on minimum amounts, length of maturity, and total ceiling for each institution, but these constraints have been gradually eased (see table 3.4).

The original regulation held the issue of CDs to 10 per cent equivalent of the net worth of the issuing institutions, or 10 per cent equivalent of yen-denominated assets of the issuing bank in the case of foreign banks. By April 1987, this limit was raised to 300 per cent equivalent of the net worth or yen-denominated assets and in October 1987 was finally abolished. The minimum denomination was lowered from the original ¥500 million to ¥50 million by April 1988. The maturity period was originally limited to between three and six months, but was expanded to a period of between two weeks and two years by April 1988.

This liberalization was a response to the needs of depository institutions, which were suffering from a decline in market share, and also to the need for more efficient funds management by corporate businesses. As a result of such deregulation, the CD market has developed very rapidly and is currently one of the largest money markets in Japan. In order to develop the market further there is a need to lift remaining restrictions. Another problem is a need to change the form of negotiability from registered securities to a bearer form which is transferable with endorsement.

In the primary market, city banks currently have the largest share of the issues outstanding at 50 to 60 per cent, followed by the regional banks, the mutual banks, the credit associations, and foreign banks. The primary market is the hub of activity in the CD market, and there are no restrictions whatsoever on which investors, that is, depositors, may purchase CDs. Corporate businesses, individuals, residents, and non-residents may all be purchasers. Although there are no statistics available on the amounts purchased, it is believed that the largest purchasers are corporate businesses, followed by public mutual aid co-operatives and municipalities.

CDs not only have unregulated rates of interest but also are negotiable instruments. There are no controls on who may participate in the secondary CD market but an official designation is required. Firms designated to participate or to act as intermediaries include money market brokers, depository institutions other than the issuer, and firms related to depository institutions, such as factoring companies, leasing companies, and credit-guarantee companies. Securities firms have been permitted to operate in the secondary CD market since June 1985. When the secondary market was formed, the money market brokers were major intermediaries, but since then the depository institutions and their affiliated companies have been more important.

There are two types of transaction in the secondary market: unconditional and conditional. Unconditional purchases and sales occur when CDs are bought or sold outright through brokers. Conditional purchases and sales or so-called CD *gensaki* use the same technique as with *gensaki*, so that the CDs are purchased or sold with the promise to be repurchased or resold after a specified period which is usually less than one month. The brokers are seeking buying and selling orders and then matching sellers and buyers. Currently, most CD transactions are conditional.

The secondary CD market has developed gradually since the fall of 1980, with the money market brokers in the centre of the transactions. In the early period, there was about ¥100,000 million of monthly turnover but there was a huge increase after fiscal 1981. Both depository institutions and their affiliates followed the money market brokers in actively seeking such business. By the end of 1985, the monthly trading volume had reached ¥10 billion. There has been another large increase in transactions since the securities firms were permitted to participate in the CD market.

Reasons for such a remarkable increase in the secondary CD market include the search for new profit opportunities on the part of the money market brokers in the light of the slow-down of expansion of the interbank markets and the desire to diversify business on the part of depository institutions in order to compensate for the narrowing spread of interest rates. In addition, the growth of the secondary market has been assisted by the *de facto* shortening of the maturities of transactions through the use of CD *gensaki*, which enables circumvention of the earlier constraint on maturity of issue. Both the primary and secondary CD markets have achieved stable development over the past decade.

### Financing bill (FB) and treasury bill (TB) markets

Short-term government paper which include financing bills (FBs) and treasury bills (TBs) are rather unusual debt instruments issued by the Ministry of Finance (MOF). The MOF has consistently been opposed to any rapid development of the market for short-term government papers whereas the BOJ is keenly in favour because of a need for an effective monetary policy.

### *FB* (seifu tanki shoken) *market*

FBs, which were called 'treasury bills' before 1986, have rather a long history, but secondary markets have not developed for these bills because of insufficient supply. So far, almost all issues have been taken up by the BOJ. Since May 1981, the BOJ has often tried to sell FBs in its possession to financial institutions through money market brokers but market inventory soon disappeared when their maturity came up. However, there has been a steady increase in the market balances of FBs in recent years, with ¥4.2 billion in December 1975, ¥11.8 billion in December 1980, and ¥21.2 billion in December 1988. Maturities are limited to sixty days. The FBs are issued at a premium of one or two points above the official discount rate and, while included as part of the short-term money market, are captive financing for the MOF from the BOJ. In the near future, it is thought likely that they will be offered more widely for distribution.

## *TB* (Tanki Kokusai) *market*

TBs have been issued since February 1986 with a maturity of less than six months and a minimum denomination of ¥100 million. The MOF issued ¥1.0 billion in fiscal 1985 and ¥4.1 billion in fiscal 1986. The narrowness of this market in Japan is in clear contrast to the case of the United States, where the TB market is one of the largest short-term money markets. By December 1986, Japanese TBs on issue totalled ¥2.1 billion. By mid-1987, this had fallen to ¥1.9 billion, or less than 2 per cent of the total short-term money market. Dealing in TBs is restricted to banks and corporate businesses.

TBs are issued in discount form and on a tendering basis. Tendering for TBs is done through a large number of institutions, including 89 securities firms, all city banks, long-term credit banks, trust banks, regional banks, mutual banks, a number of life and non-life insurance companies and a limited number of foreign banks in Japan. There is sufficient demand for short-term government paper, but the MOF's determination to limit the impact of short-term interest rates on the government's long-term debt policy has stifled the development of this market.

## Bankers' acceptance (BA) market

The market for yen-denominated BAs was established in June 1985 as one of the measures agreed to at the Japan–US Yen–Dollar Committee in May 1984. The market was expected to promote diversification and internationalization of Japan's financial markets. The yen-BAs are yen-denominated fixed-term bills of exchange which are accepted by banks but were originally issued by exporters or importers for payment of foreign trade transactions.

The BA market is in principle an open, free-rate of interest, short-term money market in which financial institutions, corporate businesses, non-residents, and others may freely participate. At present, however, those who are permitted to bring bills directly to the market are limited to the authorized foreign exchange banks that have accepted the bills. In addition, in the secondary market for yen-BAs, there was originally a restriction that participants would be only depository institutions, money market brokers, and the affiliates of financial institutions. In

April 1986, however, permission for participation by securities firms was granted.

The conditions on eligibility of yen-BAs are that (a) they must be accepted within thirty days after loading on board ship; (b) the date of maturity must be within six months after loading, with the addition of mailing days; and (c) the bills must be of over ¥100 million in denomination. These bills are all eligible for discounting by the BOJ.

In spite of bright expectations, the yen-BA market has not been successful. Immediately after its inception, the yen-BA market stood at ¥70,000 million, but declined to ¥3,100 million by the end of July 1988. The reason for the failure is that most large borrowers, such as the big manufacturers and trading companies, can obtain cheaper funds through other markets. The authorities argue that the deregulation of interest rates will spur the development of the yen-BA market. However, more to the point would be the reduction of the stamp duty which has limited the usefulness of the market for most likely borrowers.

## Commercial paper (CP) market

The CP market, established in November 1987, is the newest among the money markets. CPs are obviously modelled after CPs in the United States, but several restrictions have been imposed since their inception.

CPs are promissory notes with maturity ranging from one month to six months. CPs are issued on a discount basis with minimum face amounts of ¥100 million. For the time being, about 180 corporations are qualified to issue CPs, but most of them are required to furnish bank guarantees or back-up lines in advance. Only forty of the largest corporations and power companies are exempted from this requirement. In December 1988, the MOF increased the number of qualified companies from 180 to 450 if they are granted top rating or AA rating and have a net worth of ¥55,000 million. CPs are issued through depository institutions or securities firms. Brokers in the CP market are banks, securities firms, and money market brokers.

The CP market has continued to grow rapidly. By the end of August 1988, eighty-four corporations have issued CPs and the market balance stood at more than ¥5 billion. The development of this market will bring with it a potent force for change in domestic capital markets and it may provide the key to unlocking the difficulties that continue to surround the corporate bond markets in Japan. In November 1988, the BOJ decided that CPs would be subject to its open market operations. In January 1988, the MOF allowed non-residents to issue CPs in Japan under the same regulations as Japanese firms.

71

Chapter five

# Foreign currency and Euroyen markets

### Foreign exchange markets

Japan's foreign exchange markets take place in Tokyo and Osaka, but the predominant share of market transactions, say 99.8 per cent, are concentrated in Tokyo. As in New York and London almost all transactions are carried out over the telephone and there exists no bourse for foreign exchange as in some countries on the European continent. Participants in the market include the authorized foreign exchange banks including foreign banks, the foreign exchange brokers, and the Bank of Japan (BOJ) which operates to stabilize the market.

Since its reopening in July 1952, the Tokyo foreign exchange market has been ever-expanding alongside a steady deregulation of foreign trade and capital transactions with foreign countries and the growth of the nation's economy. There were, of course, many changes and disruptions over this period, such as the Nixon shock in August 1971, by which the convertibility of US dollars into gold was suspended, and the shift from a fixed to a floating exchange rate system. The Smithsonian Agreement in December 1971, enabled a temporary return to a fixed rate system, but finally gave way to floating rates in February 1973.

Throughout these years, there was a steady internationalization of both the system and the transaction practices in the foreign exchange markets. These changes were very important in promoting an active exchange of funds between Japan and foreign countries. Among major changes were the entire revision of the Foreign Exchange and Foreign Trade Control Law (FEFTCL), which took effect in December 1980. The principle of the new law is that every transaction would be permitted unless specifically prohibited, in contrast to the previous law which prohibited every transaction unless specifically permitted.

Another major change was the repeal of the actual demand principle, under which an underlying actual transaction was necessary in order for individuals or corporate businesses to conduct a forward exchange transaction with an authorized foreign exchange bank. This change was made in April 1984. Some other changes include repeal of regulations on conversion of foreign currency into yen in June 1984, and the introduction of international broking by foreign exchange brokers and direct transactions among domestic banks in February 1985.

These developments have made the Tokyo foreign exchange market one of the most important foreign exchange markets in the world, along with New York and London. During 1985, total transaction volume in the Tokyo foreign exchange market stood at $1.4 billion, including spot, forward, and swap transactions (which was 125 times the amount traded in 1970 just before the Nixon shock). In 1988, total transaction volume in the Tokyo market increased 13.1 per cent to $5.4 billion.

There are two types of transactions on the foreign exchange market, depending on the delivery of the funds: spot and forward transactions. Spot transactions in most cases are those in which the delivery of the funds is made on the second business day after conclusion of the contract, though there are also spot transactions in which delivery is made on the day of transaction or the following business day. Forward transactions, on the other hand, are transactions in which delivery of the funds is made at a certain date in the future defined from the second business day after conclusion of the contract.

In analysing the form in which foreign exchange transactions occur, it is possible to distinguish between outright transactions and swap transactions. Outright transactions are those in which the foreign currency is either sold or bought outright, while swap transactions are those in which the foreign currency is simultaneously bought and sold but with different dates of delivery. For example, one might sell US dollars and buy yen spot and simultaneously buy US dollars and sell yen forward.

In the Tokyo foreign exchange market, yen–dollar transactions form the largest portion of trading because of the large share of foreign transactions carried out in US dollars. However, due to the internationalization and diversification of Japan's foreign exchange transactions, a growing volume is being conducted in German marks and Swiss francs. During 1988, yen–dollar transactions were 79.5 per cent of the total and remainders were in other currencies.

By type of contract, the growth of swap transactions has been the largest. This reflects the growing level of interest arbitrage transactions and the fact that foreign exchange banks are covering the largest portion of forward transactions with customers through swap transactions. Of the yen–dollar transactions carried out during 1988, 35.5 per cent were spot transactions and 64.5 per cent were forward and swap transactions.

The BOJ from time to time carries out foreign exchange operations or so-called 'market intervention'. This is done by buying and selling foreign currency in order to stabilize the foreign exchange market and to

73

maintain orderly conditions. In such intervention, the BOJ acts as agent for the Ministry of Finance which is in charge of the 'Foreign Exchange Fund Special Account'.

These operations were introduced in April 1963 as part of the expansion of margins of exchange rate fluctuation under the Bretton Woods Agreement to plus or minus 0.75 per cent from the IMF parity. Having experienced several large fluctuations of international currency conditions over the past decades, the BOJ currently follows the actual developments in the markets and undertakes market intervention when it feels it necessary in appropriate volume and at the appropriate time. Since the Plaza Agreement of September 1985, the BOJ has market intervened quite frequently in co-operation with major countries in the world (see figure 5.1).

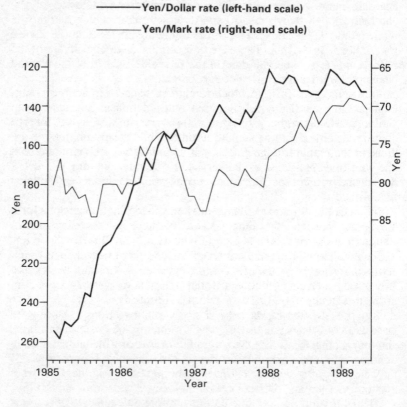

*Figure 5.1* Recent trend of foreign exchange rates
*Source:* BOJ, *Chosa Geppo*, May 1989.

The growth of foreign exchange trading in Tokyo has been dramatic. Two rounds of deregulation of foreign exchange controls, initially in 1980 and again in 1984, laid the ground for the growth in foreign exchange dealing which now rivals New York in terms of daily trading volumes. The growth has acted as a magnet to the foreign banks, eager to expand their foreign exchange trading capacities in Tokyo, so that they can round out their international currency trading services.

Much of the growth in foreign currency trading has been fuelled by the exchange rate volatility of the 1970s and 1980s, combined with the removal of many restrictions. In the mid-1970s, for example, when domestic controls were much stricter, the yen–dollar exchange rate moved by an average of 9 per cent annually. The other factor influencing present developments is the attractiveness of the yen as a reserve currency. During 1983–8, the use of the yen as a reserve currency has increased from 4.9 per cent to 7.0 per cent and may continue to grow in the future.

## Short-term foreign currency market (Tokyo dollar call market)

'Tokyo dollar call market' is a foreign currency market in which the authorized foreign exchange banks may borrow or lend foreign currency funds among themselves over relatively short periods of time. While the dollar call market is not directly tied with the foreign exchange market, the former nevertheless facilitates the foreign currency funding operations of the foreign exchange banks and has been an important factor in the development of the foreign exchange market.

Tokyo's dollar call market is relatively young. The market was established in April 1972 under regulation of the FEFTCL. Originally, there was a limit of six months for the maturity of transactions, but, with the revision of the FEFTCL in December 1980, the maturity of transactions was deregulated and currently no limit is imposed.

The dollar call market was originally used as a place to adjust for a temporary shortage or excess of foreign currency funds. In recent years, however, it has also functioned as a place either to borrow or to lend foreign currency funds on hand. During 1988, total turnover in the dollar call market stood at $1.9 billion indicating the huge growth during the past decade. Even now, overnight and other very short-term funds are the major part of the market but the proportion of relatively long-term funding has risen to around 15 per cent.

The participants in the Tokyo dollar call market are the authorized foreign exchange banks, including foreign banks and the foreign exchange brokers. At present, non-residents are not permitted to participate. Transactions in the market take the form of lending or borrowing transactions and thus differ from the deposit transactions in the

75

Euromarket, but they are identical in being non-collateralized. Although the dollar call market has the word 'dollar' in its name, there are no restrictions on the currencies which may be transacted. In fact, however, most of the transactions are denominated in US dollars.

Market transactions are made through brokers, whose functions are the same as the brokers in the foreign exchange market. The minimum transaction value is $100,000 or equivalent, and delivery of funds is generally made to the foreign currency deposits of the transacting banks on the business day following the transaction. The Tokyo dollar call market has experienced dramatic growth since its inception in 1972. By 1981, the balance exceeded the size of the call market in yen and exceeded the bill discount market. The dollar call market is of considerable importance to the regional banks and other smaller financial institutions which have no offices overseas or only limited access to US dollar funds. They constitute the most active borrowers through this market, and the city banks are the most active lenders because they have a much greater volume of dollar funds.

### Japan offshore market (JOM)

One of the major developments in Japan's financial markets since the deregulation process began is the establishment of the Japan offshore market (JOM), which has been in operation since December 1986. The JOM was modelled on International Banking Facilities (IBF) in the United States. Deposits in offshore accounts are not subject to interest rate regulation, deposit insurance, reserve requirements, and withholding tax on interest payments. However, offshore transactions in the JOM are not exempt from local taxes, and duties are still levied on transactions. With the entire process of financial deregulation in Japan, the authorities tried to limit the adverse impact on the domestic market which stemmed from the development of the offshore market, which was underscored by the tight controls.

The offshore banks which may open offshore accounts are limited to the authorized foreign exchange banks who have approval from the Minister of Finance. When the JOM was established 181 banks including sixty-nine foreign banks participated in the market, but market participants increased to 187 (including seventy-three foreign banks) by December 1988. Foreign exchange brokers help conclude transactions among offshore banks.

Participation in the dealings transacted through the offshore market are limited to non-resident banks domiciled overseas, including the overseas branches of Japanese banks and securities firms, foreign corporations, including overseas subsidiaries of Japanese corporations, and foreign governments and agencies. Excluded from direct access to the market are residents, individuals, and overseas branches of Japanese non-financial corporations.

A basic feature of the operation of the offshore market is that it is limited to 'out-out transactions'. To comply with such a regulation, the authorized foreign exchange banks with offshore accounts have to ensure that the counterparties to any transactions are non-residents, and that any funds transacted through the market are used outside Japan. Another constraint on the market's expansion is that transactions processed through this market are still subject to local taxes and stamp duties, a clear disincentive to channel deals through the Tokyo market rather than through other markets such as Hong Kong or Singapore, which offer more favourable tax treatment. In addition, securities issued by non-residents cannot be held in offshore accounts.

Even with the regulations presently in place, the JOM has grown steadily since its establishment on 1 December 1986. In fact, by the end of June 1989, total outstanding assets of the market stood at $461,800 million. Of this figure, $211,200 million equivalent were denominated in yen, with other currencies' assets making up the balance. The bulk of the funds in the offshore market are ones deposited in offshore accounts primarily by Japanese banks for management by their overseas branches. Soon after the launch of the market, Japanese banks began to provide syndicated loans through their accounts held in the market, although the level of activity has been subdued in line with the weak demand for syndicated loans in recent years.

The main interest in accessing the market came from the large Japanese banks engaging in arbitrage transactions by monitoring interest rate movements in the Euroyen, call and bill discount markets, together with the cost of yen funding by selling US dollars in the foreign exchange market. As a result, interbank transactions accounted for most of the activity in the market. The initial growth of the JOM has been achieved by Japanese banks transferring funds to their offshore accounts, but the very low level of lending channelled through the market is seen as an indication that the market still lacks depth and cannot realistically be justified.

The MOF is under pressure to remove certain constraints surrounding the JOM, especially in terms of tax treatment, but the power of the Taxation Bureau of the MOF is such that little ground will be given unless there is a complete revision of Japan's taxation system. Some argue that the present organization of the JOM is a transitional form and that further steps will be taken in the future to liberalize activities in the market.

### Euroyen market

Euroyen are yen-denominated deposits held by depository institutions located outside Japan. The Euroyen market is a part of the Euromarket. Euroyen markets are formed in London, Singapore, Hong Kong, New York, and other places, but the London market is considered the most important, having about a 60 per cent share.

According to data compiled by the Bank for International Settlements (BIS), Euroyen outstanding were equivalent to $2,700 million at the end of 1977. However, the outstanding level of Euroyen grew to $115,674 million equivalent (¥19.2 billion) by the end of March 1989, due to the rapid growth of interest arbitrage transactions and to the increases in yen-denominated Japanese exports, yen-syndicated loans, and Euroyen bonds.

The reasons for the rapid growth of the Euroyen market in recent years include the relaxation of regulations and guidance over Euroyen transactions. Euroyen transactions are free from domestic regulations and rules of transactions such as legal reserve requirements, interest rate regulations, and collateral requirements. Euroyen transactions are also advantageous in their tax treatment, for example, in the absence of withholding tax on interest. In addition, the accumulation of know-how and concentration of information concerning international financial transactions enables diversification of risks and lower costs and also ensures a high degree of efficiency and competitiveness in international transactions.

Because of these advantages the Euroyen market is not simply a place for interest rate arbitrage or earning profits on spread, but rather a substitution for certain domestic financial transactions, i.e. a 'parallel market'. Indeed, one may view it as one of the open markets of the financial system. Thus, authorized foreign exchange banks have increased their dependence on the Euromarkets for yen financing in recent years. Fund transfers from overseas branches of Japanese banks to their main offices in Japan have increased tremendously, particularly after the swap limitations on conversion of foreign currency into yen were lifted in June 1984.

The Euroyen transactions are divided into two groups: primary transactions and secondary transactions. The primary transactions are the inflow of yen funds into the Euroyen market in the form of deposits from non-residents and overseas branches of Japanese banks. The secondary transactions are the outflow of yen funds from the Euroyen market to other non-residents in the form of Euroyen CDs, Euroyen lending, Euroyen impact loans and Euroyen bonds. Euroyen CDs and non-residents Euroyen bonds have been liberalized since December 1984 and resident Euroyen bonds since April 1985.

Naturally, Japanese banks have the largest share in Euroyen transactions: an overall share of about 70 per cent, including about 40 per cent of funds borrowed and 80 per cent of funds lent. The remainder is carried by foreign banks, foreign monetary authorities, and foreign non-financial corporations. The important characteristics of Euroyen transactions are that there are no collateral requirements and no restrictions on maturity. Transactions may be either direct or through brokers, but the largest portion is carried out through brokers. Delivery of yen funds is carried out on the business day following the contract day.

Chapter six

# Securities markets

## Capital and securities markets

A major portion of the capital market is the securities market, consisting of the bond market and the stock market. In the financial structure of the fast growth period that favoured indirect finance, the securities markets remained underdeveloped. After 1975, however, the securities markets grew quite rapidly under the influence of the large-scale flotations of government bonds and the internationalization of finance. In addition, new types of bonds such as convertible bonds, warrant bonds, '*samurai* bonds' and '*shogun* bonds' have been developed as a result of financial deregulation and innovation.

It has been pointed out that securities markets were broadened and deepened. These developments resulted from the expanded flow of funds through the securities markets, particularly through the government bond market. In fact, the ratio of total securities outstanding to nominal GNP rose from 45.5 per cent at the end of 1970 to 115.8 per cent at the end of 1988 (see table 6.1). There was also a diversification of financial assets in the market, such as medium-term government bonds, along with an expansion of investors from banks to institutional investors, individuals, and non-residents.

At the same time, flows of funds across international boundaries increased. This is particularly true since the revision of the Foreign Exchange and Foreign Trade Control Law (FEFTCL) in December 1980. A large part of the transfer of long-term funds is carried out on an uncovered basis, including foreign securities investments and overseas bond flotations by residents, and domestic securities investments and yen-denominated securities flotations by non-residents. There are many factors related to such transfers of funds, but the most important ones seem to be interest rate differentials and exchange rate fluctuations.

In addition, there has been an unclear distinction between the commercial banks and the securities firms with respect to government bond business, and conflict and competition have become more serious. Com-

*Table 6.1* Outstanding amounts of securities

|  | 1970 | | 1980 | | 1985 | | 1988 | |
|---|---|---|---|---|---|---|---|---|
|  | ¥bn | % | ¥bn | % | ¥bn | % | ¥bn | % |
| FBs and TBs | 2.3 | 7.1 | 14.0 | 7.5 | 13.7 | 4.4 | 21.2 | 5.0 |
| Government bonds | 3.2 | 9.6 | 67.3 | 36.3 | 135.2 | 43.4 | 156.8 | 36.9 |
| Municipal bonds | 1.5 | 4.4 | 16.8 | 9.0 | 20.9 | 6.7 | 20.0 | 4.7 |
| Public corp. bonds | 6.0 | 17.9 | 25.3 | 13.7 | 26.6 | 8.5 | 21.1 | 5.0 |
| Financial bonds | 6.2 | 18.6 | 25.8 | 13.9 | 41.6 | 13.4 | 54.5 | 12.8 |
| Industrial bonds | 3.0 | 9.1 | 10.2 | 5.5 | 18.4 | 5.9 | 34.7 | 8.2 |
| Equities | 9.8 | 29.4 | 20.2 | 10.9 | 35.6 | 11.4 | 50.0 | 11.8 |
| Commercial paper | – | – | – | – | – | – | 14.6 | 3.4 |
| SITBC | 1.3 | 3.9 | 5.8 | 3.2 | 19.3 | 6.2 | 51.6 | 12.1 |
| Total (A) | 33.3 | 100.0 | 185.4 | 100.0 | 311.3 | 100.0 | 424.3 | 100.0 |
| GNP (B) | 73.1 | | 235.8 | | 321.2 | | 366.5 | |
| A/B % | | 45.5 | | 78.6 | | 96.9 | | 115.8 |

*Note:* Amounts are at the end of calendar year.

Securities denominated in foreign currencies are not included.

SITBC stands for Securities Investment Trust Beneficiary Certificates.

*Source:* BOJ, Flow of Funds Accounts.

mercial banks have been permitted to distribute newly issued long-term and medium-term government bonds since April 1983, and have been permitted to deal in outstanding government bonds since June 1984. On the other hand, securities firms have been allowed to make loans having deposited government bonds as collateral since June 1983, though with certain limits and on the basis of individual contracts only.

## Primary market

Securities markets are usually divided into two parts, the primary market and the secondary market. The primary market comprises essentially the issuers and the subscribers. Also important are intermediaries who are go-between issuers and subscribers, carrying out issuing procedures and using their offices to facilitate the issue. The intermediaries include underwriters and trustees.

Underwriters are firms that agree to purchase either the entire amount or a portion of the new issues from the issuer for the purpose of selling them, or agree to purchase whatever may be left of the issue if it is undersubscribed. Underwriters may ask other firms to sub-underwrite the original portion. Article 65 of the Securities and Exchange Law (Law No. 25 of 1948) prohibits underwriting business to financial institutions other than the securities firms, with the exception of government bonds, municipal bonds, and government-guaranteed bonds. As a result, corporate securities are underwritten by securities firms only.

There are two types of trustees, trustees for subscription and trustees for collateral. The trustees for subscription are entrusted by the issuer to take care of the necessary clerical work concerning the subscription of an issue of corporate bonds. The trustees for collateral administer the collateral that is attached to a collateralized bond on behalf of the bond-holder. Usually the long-term credit banks and the trust banks are permitted to be trustees for subscription, while trustees for collateral require licences from the appropriate authorities. In fact, client banks of the issuers play the role both of trustees for subscription and trustees for collateral.

*Secondary market*

Secondary securities transactions are divided into two parts, transactions at the stock exchanges and transactions at the securities firms or so-called 'over-the-counter' transactions. In the pre-war period, stock exchange transactions had a very strong speculative character. In the post-war period, however, exchange transactions came to occur through spot trading on a cash basis. In addition, over-the-counter transactions in listed stocks are prohibited, in principle, in order to facilitate transactions through fair price formation. For these reasons, transactions of outstanding stocks came to be concentrated at the stock exchanges.

The stock exchanges are corporations organized by member firms in conformity with the Securities and Exchange Law. The purpose of these organizations is to create the market places necessary for securities transactions. Membership in stock exchanges is limited to securities firms. Currently there are eight exchanges in Japan, i.e. in Tokyo, Osaka, Nagoya, Kyoto, Hiroshima, Fukuoka, Niigata, and Sapporo. The Tokyo Stock Exchange has more than 80 per cent of the total trading volume of all exchanges, and the Osaka Exchange has 15 per cent.

Transactions in non-listed stocks or those in odd lots are carried out bilaterally with individual customers at the offices of securities firms. Along with the post-war boom in equities there has been a sudden increase in the amount of transactions in non-listed stocks, and as a result the need grew to organize this trading. The response to this need was the establishment in 1961 of a second section of the stock exchanges, jointly listed by the stock exchanges in Tokyo, Osaka, and Nagoya.

In the Osaka Stock Exchange, the stock futures market and the Nikkei Stock Price Index futures market were created in June 1987 and in September 1988, respectively. The Tokyo Stock Exchange added the

Tokyo Stock Exchange Price Index (TOPIX) futures market in September 1988.

In the field of bond transactions, with the exception of the markets for government bonds, convertible bonds, and warrant bonds, there was no need to concentrate the market. Hence, the share of the bond trading on the stock exchanges was small and most transactions were made over-the-counter. For large-lot trading in government bonds a large-lot transactions system was introduced in 1979. This reform was aimed at improving the method of price formation and notification. In October 1985, the bond futures market was also added to the Tokyo Stock Exchange.

In the case of bonds, over-the-counter trading is generally permitted, even for listed bonds, and about 95 per cent of the trading volume in bonds is over-the-counter. To help determine prices for over-the-counter trading, two indices are used. a daily index including about twenty securities with large trading volumes and a weekly index published every Thursday, which includes about 230 representative bonds chosen according to maturity and interest rates.

## Corporate bond markets

Corporate bonds are classified into financial bonds and industrial bonds depending on issuer. These bonds are also classified as straight bonds, convertible bonds, and warrant bonds. Straight bonds are traditional forms of issues. Convertible bonds have been issued by industrial corporations since 1970, and by commercial banks since 1987. Some corporations have also issued warrant bonds since 1981.

Battles over regulations surrounding the domestic corporate bond markets are symptomatic of the broader dispute between the securities firms and the commercial banks within Japan's financial system. As the banks are prohibited from underwriting all but public bonds, the securities firms act as lead-managers to negotiate the terms of the proposed issue with the proposed issuers. The banks, especially long-term credit banks, are increasingly vocal in their opposition to this regime, arguing that, even though they do all of the issue preparation, they are unfairly prohibited from acting as lead-managers, a position reserved for the securities firms.

Given the overwhelming size of the government bond issuing programme, domestic issues of straight bonds by the corporate sector, excluding the electric power companies and Nippon Telegraph and Telephone Corporation (NTT), are modest, accounting for just 0.5 per cent of all domestic bonds issued in 1986. This has more to do with the absolute size of the government borrowing programme and its growth than to the size of the corporate borrowing programme.

Smaller companies are usually unable to tap domestic markets. So with increasing regularity they have tapped the Swiss market, where the minimum limit on the size of offerings is small, while larger corporations go to Euromarkets. The pressure of the move offshore and the implications for the domestic corporate bond market resulted in the securities firms (via the Securities and Exchange Council, an advisory body to the Minister of Finance) lobbying hard for a relaxation of the restrictions on domestic bond issues in an attempt to bring some of the offshore borrowing back onshore. This is but the latest development in a long-running dispute surrounding the domestic bond market.

Another major development in the bond markets is the gradual erosion of the collateral requirement for industrial bonds in recent years. In the early part of this century, most domestic bond issues were unsecured, but, after a spate of bankruptcies in 1927, the underwriters demanded stiff collateral requirements. However, by the early 1970s, the corporate sector was beginning to press for approval to be able to issue unsecured bonds. Naturally, they had the full support of the securities firms. The long-term credit banks countered, arguing that the collateral requirement ensured that investors were adequately protected from possible loss incurred by default.

This issue was discussed throughout the 1970s. In 1977, the Securities and Exchange Council released a report supporting unsecured bond issues. The debate heated up the following year when Sears Roebuck, a US retailer, announced that it intended to seek approval to issue unsecured yen bonds in Tokyo. In mid-1978, Ito-Yokado, a Japanese retailer, issued an unsecured bond in the United States. This bond issue helped bring foreign pressure on the Japanese government as it was clear that Japanese companies had open access to US capital markets, but foreign companies could not obtain the same access to Japan.

In late 1978, Matsushita Electric announced that it also intended seeking approval to make an unsecured domestic bond issue. The Industrial Bank of Japan (IBJ), the leading long-term credit bank, was asked to draw up a set of proposals to resolve the impasse. The IBJ did so by putting forward suggestions that allowed only a highly restricted number of Japanese companies to issue unsecured bonds in the domestic market. In the following year, Sears Roebuck and Matsushita Electric were successful in issuing unsecured bonds, but Matsushita's bonds were in the form of convertible bonds.

In 1982, Dow Chemical sought approval to tap the market through an issue of unsecured bonds, which issue was approved after some delay, thus setting the scene for further change. Subsequently, Japanese companies of equal or better credit standing, which could not tap the domestic unsecured market, were in a position to move. A campaign headed by the securities firms was launched to liberalize issuing conditions. This included a halving of the minimum net worth required by an issuing company to ¥55,000 million, but even so the number of Japanese companies that could tap this market was limited to an estimated seventy. In January 1985, TDK, a Japanese electronic appliance manufacturer, became able to issue the first unsecured straight bonds in Tokyo.

With the growing volume of external issues, the securities firms began a further lobbying campaign in 1986, alarmed by the drift of Japanese borrowers overseas. An overhaul of issuers' qualification was made, with final agreement between the securities firms and the banks being reached in early 1987. The new criteria will approximately double the number of companies that can access this market to around 170 which is still a far cry from complete liberalization. An estimated 330 companies will be able to issue convertible bonds, almost double the number that were allowed to issue such bonds previously. In November 1988, the Ministry of Finance (MOF) increased the number of companies authorized to issue unsecured straight bonds from 180 to 280. To qualify, the applicant had to be rated A and have a net worth of ¥33,000 million. Now the number of companies qualified to issue convertible bonds has been increased from 330 to 480. The company must be rated BBB or higher and have a net worth of ¥33,000 million or more.

In order to develop the unsecured bond market, a bond rating system is essential. Bond ratings have been used in Japan for several years, although primarily for foreign borrowers seeking to tap the yen-denominated non-resident bond (*samurai* bond) market. There are now five rating agencies in Japan, of which three are Japanese and two US. Moody's and Standard & Poor's were the first agencies recognized for rating Euroyen issues, private placement, and *samurai* bonds. The Japan Bond Research Institute is also active in rating *samurai* issues. Competition became more intense in early 1986 with the decision also to admit the Japan Credit Rating Agency and the Nippon Investors Service. However, it is commonly argued that Japanese investors are unfamiliar with the role of bond and company ratings in determining prices.

## Public bond markets

At the time of the first major post-war flotation of government bonds in 1966, the Tokyo and Osaka stock exchanges reopened bond trading in order to promote the development of bond markets. Since then the markets have grown very rapidly, particularly since 1975. The biggest contribution to the growth of the markets came from the large-scale flotations of government bonds and an easing of the resale regulations on government bonds held by commercial banks. The government bond market is now the second largest market for government debt in the world after the United States. During fiscal 1988, the government floated ¥8.8 billion of the medium- and long-term bonds and the out-standing balance stood at ¥159.1 billion in March 1989.

A massive increase in government spending in the 1970s to offset the recessionary impact of the first oil shock has resulted in Japan's gross government debt relative to GNP exceeding that of all OECD member countries except for Italy. In fiscal 1971, government bond issues slightly exceeded ¥1 billion; by 1979, they topped ¥13 billion. In the late 1970s the potentially adverse impact of the unrestrained increase in government spending became a major point of debate, not only over the issue of crowding-out, but also because of the latent inflationary pres-sures stemming from such a large and continued growth in government spending.

By 1980, the turning point had been reached. In fiscal 1980, bond issues as a proportion of the government budget financing declined to 32.6 per cent from 34.7 per cent the preceding year, and there has been a progressive reduction since then (see table 2.1). The reduction in new bond issues lowered the ratio of bond issues to the government budget to less than 25 per cent by 1985. In fiscal 1988, the government had planned to issue ¥8.8 billion of bonds, down 15.8 per cent from the previous year's initial budget, but actual issuance was ¥1.3 billion further less than planned due to favourable tax revenue reflecting business expansion. Therefore, the government planned to issue only ¥7.1 billion in bonds for fiscal 1989, which would be the largest reduction compared with the previous year's initial budget.

The preferred method for issuing government bonds is through the large bond syndicate originally formed in the late 1960s. Tenders are usually restricted to shorter-term public offerings. The standard practice is for the Bank of Japan (BOJ), as the agent of the Minister of Finance for government bond issues, to meet with the lead-managers of the underwriting syndicate to determine issuing conditions for the forth-coming bond issue. The head of the syndicate is the chairman of the Federation of Bankers Association of Japan, a position which rotates among a limited number of the city banks headquartered in Tokyo.

Usually, proceedings are smooth, although during periods of rapidly changing conditions in bond and capital markets it can take some time for agreement to be reached. The syndication system has been a very profitable arrangement for the banking sector for much of the 1980s, and has helped offset the losses incurred in 1979 and 1980 when the BOJ quickly raised interest rates, leaving the banks with sizeable losses on their recently acquired bond holdings. The general downward trend of interest rates during the 1980s made the banks very reluctant to accept any reduction of their share in the syndicate.

Bond trading in Japan is dominated by dealing in government bonds, which has steadily expanded to reach over 90 per cent of all dealing during 1988. Almost all of this is handled through the over-the-counter market. Dealing in government bonds has expanded from approximately ¥3,271 billion in 1982 to ¥5,544 billion in 1987, with declining interest rates fuelling trading during 1986 and 1987. Such a sharp increase in trading activity is unlikely to be maintained at the same pace. In fact, trading volumes during 1988 stood at ¥4,175 billion.

Apart from interest rate volatility, trading has been boosted by the decision to give banks full dealing power. While giving banks full access to dealing, the MOF has also progressively expanded the power of commercial banks and other financial institutions to distribute government bonds they underwrite. In 1982, the new Banking Law and the amendments to the Securities and Exchange Law permitted banks to deal in government bonds in some circumstances, but it was not until April 1983 that approval was given to distribute the public bonds, including long-term government bonds, government-guaranteed bonds, and municipal bonds. It was subsequently decided to allow banks also to deal in outstanding medium-term government bonds from June 1984.

Securities firms have tried to market government bonds aggressively to individual investors but with limited success. By the end of March 1986, for example, individuals accounted for only 12.1 per cent of all holdings of the long-term government bonds, although a further portion is held through the highly successful *chuki kokusai* (medium-term government bond) funds which the securities firms began marketing from 1979. Medium-term government discount bonds are much more popular, with individual investors holding over 60 per cent of those bonds on issue.

Public bonds other than government bonds are quite limited, particularly their trading. Municipal bonds, for example, account for only around 2 per cent of all bonds issued domestically, with corporate bonds approximately equal.

## Non-resident bond (*samurai* bond and *shogun* bond) markets

The formation of the yen-denominated bond (*samurai* bond) market for foreign issuers or non-residents was one of the landmarks in the internationalization of the Tokyo market. Progress was slow after the first public issue by the Asian Development Bank (ADB), made in December 1970, but growth in the 1980s has been remarkable. In addition, the dollar-denominated bond (*shogun* bond) market for foreign issuers or non-residents was opened in 1985.

Growth since 1985 has been rapid in sharp contrast to the 1970s, when the authorities kept the *samurai* bond market under close control, severely limiting its expansion. Initial caution was a reflection of the fact that the authorities were keen to limit the impact of yen-denominated bond issues on the balance of payments. More recently, the aim has been to isolate developments in the Euroyen market from affecting the domestic deregulation process, an aim that has proved impossible to achieve.

### Yen-denominated non-resident bonds (samurai bond and daimyo bond)

The first *samurai* bond issue by the ADB in 1970 was followed by two private placements, one by the World Bank and the other by the Inter-American Development Bank. The approval of the MOF for the ADB issue represented as much Japan's traditional dominance over the ADB as its responsibility for the expansion of the bank's capital base. The authorities were cautious in allowing market expansion initially and restricted the borrowers to sovereign entities with close relationships with Japan.

Hence, the market was not opened for corporate borrowers until 1979, when Sears Roebuck issued unsecured bonds, taking advantage of the authorities' embarrassment over the reciprocity issue between Japan and US capital markets. Issues by foreign corporate borrowers were sparse and up to 1982 there were only three issues: by Sears Roebuck, Dow Chemical, and NCR.

By the mid-1980s, the level of new issues had flagged severely, causing the authorities further embarrassment. In 1985, for example, there were only thirty-five issues, raising ¥1.1 billion, which fell in 1986 to just twenty-one issues raising ¥590,000 million – well below the level of activity in the late 1970s. The test of the market's viability came with the explosion of activity on the Euroyen market where issuing conditions and, more importantly, timing are much more flexible. Consequently, borrowers have switched from the *samurai* bond market, where it can take three months from the time an initial action is made to when the issue is completed.

Another difficulty with the *samurai* bond market was the lack of liquidity which caused an additional cost to tapping the market. To help circumvent this problem, the authorities put pressure on the four largest Japanese securities firms to develop a secondary market which they undertook to do in 1986. In a bid to give the market additional depth, it was decided in February 1987 that, along with the four largest securities firms, ten medium-sized firms would also endeavour to develop the secondary market to increase liquidity and hence cut borrowing costs. But this move, similar to the initial steps undertaken by the four largest, had only a marginal impact on new issues.

Innovation was made in the market in 1987. In the light of the extraordinary success of the Euroyen market, the World Bank was allowed to issue a so-called '*daimyo* bond'. This bond, a hybrid between the *samurai* and Euroyen bonds, may point the way the authorities intend to allow the market to develop in the future. These bonds, of which by mid-1987 there had been two issues, both by the World Bank, are issued in Tokyo and listed on the Luxemburg Stock Exchange. Issues of the World Bank are not subject to withholding tax and the bonds can also be cleared through either Cedel or Euroclear.

The permission for the World Bank, the pre-eminent supranational borrower, to issue on such favourable terms may eventually be extended to other similar organizations such as the ADB, although the authorities have yet to signal their views. However, as it is still less competitive than the Euroyen market. The *samurai* market is likely to remain the domain of supranational organizations and sovereign borrowers, especially Asian borrowers.

## *Foreign currency non-resident bonds* (shogun *bonds*)

The principal variation of the *samurai* bond is the so-called '*shogun* bond', which is a foreign currency bond issued in Japan. The *shogun* bond market was opened in August 1985 by the World Bank and was originally limited to supranational organizations and foreign governments only. However, tax revision in the United States in 1986 stimulated interest in issuing these securities. The US government allowed US corporations to issue bearer bonds abroad without fear that these issues would violate US tax laws. In addition, rules for *shogun* issues were eased, waiving the requirement that the capital to assets ratio be higher than 30 per cent for corporations with an AA rating or better or corporations with an A rating and assets of over $1,500 million.

The first *shogun* issue by a private corporation was made by the Southern California Edison Company in October 1985. Issues have been sparse since, totalling less than $1,000 million annually. The major handicap was that, like the *samurai* issue, the registration period for *shogun* issues was comparatively long and the documentation requirements were onerous. Both of these difficulties were partly overcome during the first half of 1988, once the MOF had obtained Diet approval for streamlining, which gave these issues greater flexibility, although still not enough if they are to compete successfully with the Euroyen market.

**Euroyen bond market**

The first Euroyen bond was floated in 1977, with a ¥10,000 million offering by the European Investment Bank, lead managed by Daiwa Securities Co. Until 1983, there were only ¥420,000 million worth of issues made. Although Japanese companies were unable to access the market, Ito-Yokado made a ¥5,000 million private placement with the government of Kuwait, taking advantage of a loophole in the regulations. A limited number of similar issues followed. Along with deregulation in early 1984, foreign corporations with an A rating or better were allowed to tap this market. Minimum maturities of five years were required and a 180-day 'frozen period' was installed as related later.

When the first Euroyen bonds were issued in 1977, as with the *samurai* bond market, Japanese authorities were extremely concerned about allowing the market to develop, largely because too fast growth might have had severe repercussions on Japan's balance of payments. Therefore, usually only one issue in a quarter was allowed and tight limits were set on the amount of any one issue. The Euroyen market appeared destined to remain a backwater of Japan's capital markets but strong pressure from the US government changed the situation.

To force Japan to liberalize its capital market, the US government brought considerable pressure to bear as part of the Japan–US Yen–Dollar Committee proceedings. Debate over liberalizing the Euroyen market became a notable feature of the argument between the two countries. Thus, non-Japanese corporations rated A or better were allowed to issue yen-denominated bonds in the Euromarket after 1 December 1984. The decision proved to be the catalyst not only for much of the subsequent financial deregulation in Japan but also for unleashing Japan's securities firms into the international market.

Demand among international borrowers for yen is still limited because only an estimated 12 per cent of Japan's imports and 36 per cent of its exports were denominated in yen in March 1988. Due to a weak demand for yen, many of the new issues in the Euroyen market have been swap driven, with Japanese banks eager to get access to long-term yen funds to even out their mismatched portfolios in Japan. Market activity has also been driven by the needs of Japan's institutional investors which have fuelled an extraordinary variety of innovative issues, such as 'heaven-and-hell bonds' and 'survival bonds'.

In the early stage, the MOF tried to mitigate the impact of the Euroyen market on domestic financial markets by forcing its domestic institutions to delay buying Euroyen paper for 180 days after the initial issue, a ruling that was easily circumvented by simply holding the paper overseas for such a period. The MOF subsequently reduced the 'frozen period' to ninety days. Even though the level of activity on the Euroyen market has been and will probably continue to be swap driven with the market's rapid expansion, despite the impact on domestic market developments.

The spectacular growth of the Euroyen market followed in April 1985, when the MOF approved dual currency bonds, zero coupon bonds, deep discount bonds, and floating rate notes. With most of these novel structures driven by swap deals, the arbitrage opportunity between Euroyen bond rates and Japan's long-term prime rate underpinned much of the activity. The flexibility of the Euroyen market for issues contrasts sharply with the severe restraints on domestic bond issues. When the domestic markets will be liberalized depends heavily on the trade-offs that the long-term credit banks in particular can obtain from the MOF.

The rapid growth of the Euroyen market resulted from several causes including, particularly, innovation. One of the most popular instruments in the Euroyen market has been the dual currency bond which is issued in yen and carries a yen coupon, although the redemption is usually made in US dollars. The borrower may obtain low-cost financing without any foreign exchange risk, with the principal and the coupon converted to a foreign currency. The investor assumes the currency risk, although this is partly compensated for as these issues offer yen income at a higher rate than straight yen bonds.

Other innovations included the reverse dual currency bond, the first of which came to the market in 1986. This variety is purchased and redeemed in yen, with interest paid in US dollars. The split dual currency bond gave investors a low yield in the initial years but a much higher yield in the late years of the bond, with a part of the principal repayment in yen and the balance in a foreign currency, typically US dollars. The heaven-and-hell bond was linked to stock market movements, with the investor taking a position on either a rise or a decline in the equity market. The rise in equity markets for much of 1986 made these instruments particularly attractive. There were a number of variations on this theme. The only limit to the level of innovation is the attitude of the MOF.

## Stock market

### Primary market

New equity issues for capital increase are classified into four cases: offerings to shareholders, public offerings, allocations to related parties, and conversions from convertible bonds. In the case of public offerings, new issues are sold to general investors, directly or indirectly. In other words, new issues are sold by the issuer itself or through underwriting by the securities firms. The traditional method of new stock issue for capital increase was allocation to shareholders at par value.

Public offerings at market price began in 1969, and, although they receded temporarily after the oil crisis in the fall of 1973, they rose again after 1975. Currently, about one-half of equity flotations in the market are market-value issues. Such issues have become the norm for capital increase. These issues are useful in strengthening the capital base of a corporate business because the difference between the market price and the par value may be retained within the corporation as capital reserves. This is why corporations prefer market-price issues.

It is possible, however, for market-value public subscriptions to occur when stock prices are high. Since the procedures for capital increase are time-consuming, it is possible that the market price falls to the subscribers' price at the point of payment and thus disappoints the expectations of investors. For this reason, the Securities and Exchange Council is considering a policy that will improve the use and strengthen the benefits of market-price public offerings.

One problem with the primary stock market was the prohibition on firms with equities registered on the over-the-counter market from carrying out public subscriptions for capital increases. This makes it difficult for small- and medium-sized firms which do have good prospects, but which are not listed on the stock exchange, to raise funds. To cope with this problem measures were adopted in November 1983, to ease the standards for over-the-counter registration and to permit public offerings for capital increases.

## Stock exchanges

The stock exchange, where market prices are formed, is the centre of secondary markets for securities. The Tokyo and Osaka stock exchanges trace their origins to the stock exchange legislation of 1878. It took some time for the markets to become established and much of the early trading was in bonds, both government and corporate. Also, since much of the industrial sector was organized around '*zaibatsu*' which had their own bank at the centre, industry's need for external financing was limited. However, between the First and Second World Wars a number of the *zaibatsu* firms began to issue stocks, although the bulk of funds for investment came from bond issues.

In August 1945, trading on the stock exchange was suspended and did not resume until May 1949. Under the control of the Supreme Commander of Allied Powers (SCAP), fundamental changes were made to Japan's securities trading system. The most important change was a measure to separate the banking and securities business. This was implemented in the Securities and Exchange Law (Law No. 25 of 1948) modelled after the Glass-Steagall Act of 1933 in the United States. As part of post-war change, the stock exchanges were re-established in 1949 as independent non-profit exchanges, futures trading was banned, margin trading was eventually introduced and subsequently new legislation was introduced controlling the establishment of investment trusts.

Even though Japan has eight stock exchanges, nearly all of the transactions are written through the Tokyo Stock Exchange. In 1988, the Tokyo Stock Exchange carried out 86.1 per cent of all transactions by volume and 85.8 per cent by value. Osaka was a distant second, with 9.7 per cent of trading by volume and 10.4 per cent by value, followed by Nagoya with just 3.8 per cent of trading by volume and 3.4 per cent by value.

Tokyo, Osaka, and Nagoya have first and second section markets, with the first section being for larger corporations, and the second section for comparatively smaller companies. Listing criteria on the second section is slightly easier than on the first section. As of 30 June 1989, there were 1,135 stocks listed on the first section of the Tokyo Stock Exchange, with 453 second section stocks and 112 foreign section stocks. In Osaka, there were 814 first section stocks and 284 second section stocks. In Nagoya there were 419 first section stocks and 104 second section stocks. Nearly all of the first-section stocks in both Osaka and Nagoya are listed on the first sections of more than one exchange, although slightly more than one-quarter of stocks on the main board in Tokyo do not have a second listing in either Osaka or Nagoya.

All trading must be done through regular members of the exchanges. Brokers' commission on transactions in Japan's stock markets are still fixed, making Japan the only large stock market world-wide that refuses to consider switching to negotiated commissions. In their fight against the move to negotiated commission the Japanese firms have been joined by the foreign firms active in Japan; the foreign firms are pleased to see rates pegged at comparatively higher levels than those operating in other major markets in Europe or the United States as this helps offset the higher operating costs in the Tokyo market.

The Japanese securities firms are also more insulated because they have enjoyed the significant expansion of activity of their investment trusts, which have seen a large inflow of new funds flowing in over the past few years. Along with the steady reduction in commissions, it was also decided to reduce the amount of the commission retained by member firms for processing transactions on behalf of non-members. Formerly, this was set at 27 per cent, although it was reduced to 20 per cent in 1987.

*Over-the-counter (OTC) market*

Japan's OTC market, with only 207 companies traded as of April 1989, is a small market compared with the stock exchanges. After languishing in the backwater of the securities markets in the early 1980s, it has taken on a new lease of life, although with only limited success so far. New listings have been active since 1985, and the indications are that it will remain buoyant for the medium-term, although the burst of new activity could easily decline.

The OTC market likes to model itself on the NASDAQ market in the United States, which boasts over 4,000 actively traded companies. A more appropriate comparison for the OTC market in Japan may be the unlisted securities market in London. Historically, Japan had a very active OTC market which was subject to extensive trading excess. Before the Second World War, trading on the main board was mainly in futures with the OTC market functioning more as a spot market.

With futures trading outlawed after the war, OTC trading was more in stocks not listed on the exchanges. Partly as a means of cleaning up this market, the authorities asked the major exchanges to establish a second trading section in 1961, which assumed the bulk of the OTC market stocks, leaving a small number of mostly sickly stocks out in the cold. At present there are large differences between the OTC market and the second section in the stock exchanges. For example, companies with a net worth of only ¥200 million are permitted on the OTC market, compared with ¥1,000 million for the Tokyo Stock Exchange listing (¥500 million for Osaka and Nagoya, and ¥300 million for other stock exchanges).

Most companies going to the OTC market do so with the ultimate aim of up-grading to the second section of the stock exchanges, which marks a major point of contrast with the NASDAQ in the United States. One of the reasons for the smaller size of the OTC market in Japan is the fact that companies regularly up-grade to the second section. An important aspect of listing on the OTC for smaller companies is that the value of the listing can be used as collateral for lending, which can also help to reduce funding costs.

*Regulation of the securities markets*

It is essentially important to help develop the securities market and to protect investors' interests. For this purpose, the Securities and Exchange Law was implemented in 1948, and since then this law and related regulations have been the general framework of regulation of the securities market in Japan. In addition, there has been administrative guidance by the MOF and voluntary restraints by the stock exchanges and the Securities Dealers Association of Japan. In recent years, the basic thrust on the regulatory side has been to promote the market conditions enabling the securities markets to fulfil their function through the price mechanism.

The BOJ has a small role in the regulation of the securities market. The Bank of Japan Law (Law No. 67 of 1942) stipulates, in the articles concerning operation of monetary policy, that the BOJ will adjust the conditions of lending which financial institutions carry out for securities firms. But the law lacks any specific prescriptions in this regard, so that the powers are not very effective.

However, the BOJ has some direct relationship with the securities markets through lending activities, based on provisions of the System of Collateral Receipt for Call Loan Transactions. Such operations occur in cases when the BOJ makes loans to money market brokers on the collateral of promissory notes issued by securities finance companies for call money. In such cases, the BOJ may decide, in consultation with the stock exchange and the securities finance companies, on changes in the assessment rate of standard collateral and the particular equities for which securities finance companies may demand the issue of collateral receipt.

The BOJ may also, if necessary, change the assessment rate of collateral that supports a money market broker's bill. In addition, the BOJ may issue guidance concerning the borrowing of call money in an effort to secure funding for securities finance companies. The BOJ may lend directly to securities finance companies. In order to smooth out the conditions in the bond market during 1964–5, when the securities markets were in severe depression, the BOJ carried out special lending to certain securities firms on the basis of Article 25 of the Bank of Japan Law. These measures were aimed at forestalling a financial collapse.

# Part III

# Financial institutions

Chapter seven

# Private depository institutions

## Classification and authorized foreign exchange banks

*Classification of financial institutions*

Japan's financial institutions, except for the central bank, are classified into three categories: private financial institutions (domestic), government financial institutions, and foreign financial institutions. Financial institutions are also divided by function into depository institutions and non-depository institutions.

An overall classification of financial institutions in Japan is shown in table 7.1. In recent years, growing competition among financial institutions has brought about major changes, including diversification, internationalization, and mechanization. Now, it is difficult to grasp the structural dynamics of financial institutions.

The private depository institutions have played the essential role in the historical development of the Japanese financial system. Among these institutions are the city banks, the regional banks, the trust banks, the long-term credit banks, the mutual banks, the credit associations, the credit co-operatives, the labour credit associations, the Shokochukin Bank, the Norinchukin Bank, and other financial institutions for agriculture, forestry, and fisheries. The mutual banks are currently being converted to regional banks. All depository institutions in the private sector are traditionally allowed to offer current accounts.

Although each type of depository institution is regulated by its respective laws, it is difficult to make very precise distinctions among them (see table 7.2). Since 1975, the distinctions have become ever harder to make. After 1975, there was an intensification of competition as the environment surrounding financial institutions changed with the reduction in the funding needs of the corporate sector. Each type of institution began to invade the turf of others. Diversification of business, including internationalization and business links in other areas became the basis of activities, as institutions sought stable profits and a stronger business base.

Table 7.1 Financial institutions in Japan (as of 31 March 1989)

**Depository institutions**

| Category | | Institution | (No.) | TA ¥1000m. |
|---|---|---|---|---|
| Private financial institutions | Commercial banks | City banks | ( 12) | 395,124 |
| | | Specialized foreign exchange bank | ( 1) | 26,106 |
| | | Regional banks | ( 64) | 160,547 |
| | Long-term financing institutions | Long-term credit banks | ( 3) | 78,715 |
| | | Trust banks | ( 7) | 70,896 |
| | Financial institutions for small businesses | Mutual banks | ( 68) | 58,715 |
| | | Credit associations | ( 455) | 77,931 |
| | | Zenshinren | ( 1) | 11,057 |
| | | Labour credit associations | ( 47) | 6,673 |
| | | National Federation of L.C.A. | ( 1) | 2,039 |
| | | Credit co-operatives | ( 418) | 21,049 |
| | | National Federation of C.C. | ( 1) | 2,965 |
| | | Shokochukin Bank | ( 1) | 12,185 |
| | Financial institutions for agriculture, etc. | Norinchukin Bank | ( 1) | 32,516 |
| | | Agricultural co-ops. | (3936) | 49,419 |
| | | Credit Federations of A.C. | ( 47) | 42,959 |
| | | Fisheries co-operatives | (1701) | 4,182 |
| | | Credit Federations of F.C. | ( 35) | 2,268 |
| Government financial institutions | | Postal Savings Service | ( 1) | 125,869 |
| | | Trust Fund Bureau | ( 1) | 214,812 |
| Foreign financial institutions | | Foreign banks | ( 83) | 21,858 |
| | | Foreign trust banks | ( 9) | 51 |

**Non-depository institutions**

| Category | Institution | (No.) | TA ¥1000m. |
|---|---|---|---|
| Private financial institutions | Life insurance companies | ( 25) | 97,083 |
| | Non-life insurance companies | ( 23) | 20,669 |
| | Mutual Insurance Federation of Agricultural Co-operatives | ( 47) | 16,296 |
| | Securities firms | ( 210) | 35,107 |
| | Securities finance companies | ( 3) | 7,972 |
| | Other finance companies | (n/a) | n/a |
| | Securities investment trust management companies | ( 12) | 52,533 |
| | Money market brokers | ( 6) | 33,614 |
| | Foreign exchange brokers | ( 7) | 24,468 |
| Government financial institutions | Export-Import Bank of Japan | ( 1) | 5,435 |
| | Japan Development Bank | ( 1) | 8,640 |
| | Overseas Economic Co-operation Fund | ( 1) | 5,008 |
| | Government finance corporations | ( 9) | 67,665 |
| Foreign financial institutions | Life insurance companies | ( 5) | 897 |
| | Non-life insurance companies | ( 37) | 278 |
| | Securities firms | ( 47) | 1,057 |

*Notes:* TA = total assets; n/a = not available. Mutual banks include banks converted to commercial banks in February 1989.

*Table 7.2* Legal limitations on depository institutions

| | Minimum paid-in capital ¥m. | Legal lending limit % of (X) | Qualification on borrower (B) or member (M) of institution |
|---|---|---|---|
| Commercial banks | 1,000 | 20 | none |
| Trust banks | 1,000 | 30 | none |
| Long-term credit banks | 10,000 | 30 | none |
| Specialized foreign exchange bank | 10,000 | 40 | none |
| Mutual banks | (L) 600 (O) 400 | 20 | (B) With 300 or fewer employees or ¥800m. or less capital |
| Credit associations | (L) 200 (O) 100 | 20 | (M) With 300 or fewer employees or ¥600m. or less capital |
| Labour credit associations | (L) 200 (O) 100 | 25 | (M) Labour unions, consumer co-operatives, etc. |
| Credit co-operatives | (L) 20 (O) 10 | 20 | (M) With five or fewer employees |

*Notes:* (B) qualification for borrower, (M) qualification for member, (L) in large cities, (O) in other areas. (X) net worth.

The credit associations, labour credit associations, and credit co-ops may receive deposits from and extend credit to non-members for up to 20 per cent of their total deposits or total credits.

Non-depository financial institutions include insurance companies, finance companies, securities firms, securities investment trust management companies, and money market/foreign exchange brokers. Insurance companies are becoming institutional investors in recent years. Securities firms have been promoting an indirect finance through their role as the primary institutions in the securities markets. The money market/foreign exchange brokers, on the other hand, have become even more active in the interbank markets and have aggressively increased new types of business such as handling CDs and CPs in the secondary market. Moreover, even 'non-banks' such as retail companies, have entered into financial services through such instruments as consumers loans.

One of the characteristics of the Japanese financial system is that government financial institutions have influential powers. Postal Savings Service has a network of some 24,000 post offices throughout the country. Postal savings are used for lending operations for the government financial institutions through the Trust Fund Bureau of the Ministry of Finance (MOF). The government financial institutions were established to implement public policy such as industrial development, foreign trade and economic co-operation, construction of houses, small businesses and agriculture.

A major change in Japan's financial system over the past decade has been the rapid growth in the participation of foreign financial institutions. Due to the rising capital flight beyond national boundaries, the pressure from foreign banks and securities firms to expand their presence in Tokyo has been intense. Growing stock markets and the progressive deregulation of the domestic financial system have given the foreign institutions a much stronger position than ever before, though still tiny compared with Japan's financial giants. Other than the banks and securities firms, foreign insurance companies, finance companies, and foreign exchange brokers are also penetrating into the Japanese market.

## Authorized foreign exchange banks

Authorized foreign exchange banks are an international aspect of financial institutions in Japan. These include not only Japanese banks in the private sector, but also government financial institutions and foreign banks operating in Japan. Financial institutions other than the authorized foreign exchange banks are not allowed to engage in foreign exchange business or to participate in the foreign exchange market, the Tokyo dollar call market, or the Japanese offshore market.

The authorized foreign exchange banks are composed of the specialized foreign exchange bank and other foreign exchange banks. The specialized foreign exchange bank was established under the Foreign Exchange Bank Law (Law No. 67 of 1954) and its main business is in foreign exchange transactions and foreign trade finance. At present, there is only one such bank, the Bank of Tokyo. Other foreign exchange banks are financial institutions having foreign exchange licences granted by the Minister of Finance under the Foreign Exchange and Foreign Trade Control Law (FEFTCL). In July 1988, the authorized foreign exchange banks included the specialized foreign exchange bank, all of the city banks, the long-term credit banks, the trust banks, the regional banks, and the foreign banks, most of the mutual banks, some credit associations, the Norinchukin Bank, the Shokochukin Bank, and the Export-Import Bank of Japan (see table 7.3).

There is no qualitative difference between exchange transactions carried out by the specialized foreign exchange bank and those carried out by other authorized foreign exchange banks. The only differences are that the specialized foreign exchange bank centres its activity on foreign trade finance and foreign exchange business, and that it gets some preferential treatment. This treatment includes deposit of the government's foreign exchange balances and the approval of overseas

Table 7.3 Foreign activities of financial institutions in Japan (as of 31 Dec. 1988)

| Type of financial institution | Total number of institutions | Foreign exchange banks | With foreign correspondents | With foreign rep. offices | With foreign branches | With foreign subsidiaries |
|---|---|---|---|---|---|---|
| Specialized foreign exchange bank | 1 | 1 | 1 | 1 | 1 | 1 |
| City banks | 12 | 12 | 12 | 12 | 12 | 12 |
| Long-term credit banks | 3 | 3 | 3 | 3 | 3 | 3 |
| Japanese trust banks | 7 | 7 | 7 | 7 | 6 | 6 |
| Regional banks | 64 | 64 | 56 | 32 | 13 | 3 |
| Mutual banks | 68 | 60 | 31 | 10 | 0 | 0 |
| Credit associations | 456 | 47 | 7 | 1 | 1 | 1 |
| Other Japanese banks* | 3 | 3 | 2 | 3 | 2 | 0 |
| Foreign banks | 82 | 82 | 82 | n/a | n/a | n/a |
| Foreign trust banks | 9 | 9 | 9 | n/a | n/a | n/a |
| Total | 705 | 288 | 210 | 69 | 38 | 26 |

Note: * The Norinchukin Bank, the Shokochukin Bank and the Export–Import Bank of Japan.
Source: MOF, Okurasho Kokusai Kinyukyoku Nenpo (International Finance Bureau Yearbook), 1989.

branches. In addition, the specialized foreign exchange bank has been allowed to issue bonds up to ten times its net worth in order to supplement yen funding. On the other hand its establishment of domestic branches is limited to the cities that are important for the purpose of carrying out trade finance and foreign exchange business.

## International operations

Japanese banks may carry out international operations if qualified as either a specialized foreign exchange bank or an authorized foreign exchange bank. Their international operations have grown tremendously over the past decade because of the progress of internationalization of the Japanese economy. Particularly after the liberalization of foreign exchange transactions under the revised FEFTCL, the types of international operations diversified rapidly owing to a series of deregulation measures. Japanese banks operated 513 overseas offices throughout the world in March 1989.

Foreign exchange banks carry out various types of international operations. In the domestic market, these include the sale, purchase, and remittance of foreign currency or travellers' cheques, foreign currency deposit transactions with individuals, the collection and settlement of payment for imports and exports, trade finance, extension of foreign currency loans, and exchange contracts for corporate businesses. In the international markets, they include loans extended to overseas subsidiaries of Japanese corporations, financing to foreign governments, underwriting and sales of Eurobonds, and transactions that use financial products centred in the Euromarkets.

Since 1980, foreign exchange banks are quite active in lending to residents through such instruments as foreign currency impact loans and Euroyen impact loans. Traditionally, 'impact loans' mean foreign currency loans made by foreign banks to Japanese companies. Until 1979, Japanese banks were unable to extend impact loans, but, since May 1979, they have been allowed to provide short-term impact loans and, since December 1980, long-term impact loans, both in foreign currencies. In addition, short-term Euroyen impact loans were approved in June 1984.

Lending by Japanese banks through their overseas branches to nonresidents, in either foreign currency or yen, is termed 'overseas locale lending'. Such lending started in the second half of the 1960s and was primarily to the foreign branches or locally incorporated subsidiaries of Japanese corporations. Overseas locale lending is a major portion of Japanese bank lending. Currently, about 80 per cent of total overseas locale lending is in foreign currencies.

Along with expansion of lending operations, Japanese banks have diversified their international activities into securities, trust, leasing, and other areas. Of these activities, they have taken a particularly active stance in international securities operations.

Much of Japan's exports and imports are denominated in foreign currencies. As a result, most of the international operations of Japanese banks is in foreign currencies and particularly in US dollars. It is therefore necessary for Japanese banks to raise foreign currency funds. The chief methods of doing this are borrowing from foreign banks, Euromarkets, and the Tokyo dollar call market.

Japanese banks have been very active in expanding their international network of branches, subsidiaries, and representative offices throughout the world. Currently forty-two Japanese banks have established 267 branches, 246 subsidiaries and 426 representative offices in foreign countries as specified in table 7.4. It should be noted that their subsidiaries include not only banking subsidiaries but also non-banking subsidiaries such as primary dealers in the United States and merchant banks in the United Kingdom.

*Table 7.4* Japanese banks' overseas offices by location (as of 30 June 1989)

| Location | Branches | Subsidiaries* | Representative offices |
|----------|----------|---------------|------------------------|
| North America | 97 | 60 | 90 |
| Latin America | 8 | 8 | 52 |
| Europe | 65 | 88 | 77 |
| Near East | 1 | 1 | 27 |
| Asia | 82 | 54 | 144 |
| Oceania | – | 21 | 34 |
| Africa | – | – | 2 |
| Others | 14 | 14 | – |
| Total | 267 | 246 | 426 |

*Note:* *Including non-banking subsidiaries.
*Source: Kinyu Zaisei Jijo*, 7 August 1989.

In July 1988, the Bank for International Settlements (BIS) established a framework on capital adequacy standards for international banks in order to maintain sound operations of international banking. The decision calls for banks to increase their ratio of net worth to risk assets to 8 per cent by 1992. Japanese banks have been given until the end of March 1993. In line with this decision, the MOF informed Japanese banks of definitive guidelines on the capital adequacy ratio in December 1988.

The guide-lines, covering forty-two Japanese banks which have overseas branches and subsidiaries, established the policy that accomplished capital should equal at least 7.25 per cent of total risk-weighted assets by 31 March 1991 and 8 per cent by 31 March 1993. The guide-lines also include definitions of assets and capital, as well as risk-weighted assets and off-balance transactions. Under these circumstances, Japanese banks put forth their efforts in order to increase their capital so that their ratios of net worth to assets would be improved. In fact, many Japanese banks have issued new stocks and convertible bonds in recent years.

In addition, operating performances have been very profitable and banks can increase their portion of earnings to be retained. As a result, most of the banks are already successfully exceeding the 7.25 per cent line which is allowed for a transitional period until 31 March 1993. It is certain that Japanese banks will clear an 8 per cent final standard by the end of March 1993.

## Commercial banks

Commercial banks including city banks, regional banks and the specialized foreign exchange bank occupy the major part of the financial system in Japan. The city banks and the regional banks are ruled by the new Banking Law (Law No. 59 of 1981), while the specialized foreign exchange bank is ruled by the Foreign Exchange Bank Law (Law No. 67 of 1948). The commercial banks have two functions. The first is to act as financial intermediaries by accepting deposits from the public and investing these funds either in loans or in securities. The second is to perform the function of handling current accounts and thus to perform a function of settlement of payments. The commercial banks also have an important influence over the business activities through the credit creation function. The banks' performance of these functions makes them indeed the pillar of the financial system.

### *City banks* (toshi ginko)

City banks are commercial banks headquartered in the largest Japanese cities and have nation-wide branch networks. Currently, there are twelve city banks. These are the Dai-Ichi Kangyo Bank, the Fuji Bank, the Sumitomo Bank, the Mitsubishi Bank, the Sanwa Bank, the Tokai Bank, the Taiyo-Kobe Bank, the Mitsui Bank, the Kyowa Bank, the Daiwa Bank, the Saitama Bank, and the Hokkaido Takushoku Bank. In practice, the Bank of Tokyo, which is a specialized foreign exchange bank, is also included in the city banks, resulting in a total number of thirteen city banks.

The city banks have been at the centre of the private financial institutions in Japan ever since the 1870s. Today they hold 20 per cent of the total deposits of all depository institutions and 50 per cent of the deposits of all banks (i.e. commercial banks, trust banks, and long-term credit banks) in the private sector. They also provide about 20 per cent of the credit needs of corporate businesses, and thus have an extremely large influence on the nation's economy. It is notable that the five largest city banks are not only the five largest in Japan but also the five largest in the world.

The lending of city banks goes in large part to large corporations. As far as domestic operations are concerned, more than 20 per cent of the total lendings of city banks were to corporations capitalized at over ¥1,000 million or more in March 1989. On the deposit side, about 50 per cent of total deposits were corporate deposits, and 90 per cent of these were large sum deposits of ¥10 million or more. In recent years, however, banks have seen a declining trend in loan demand from large manufacturing corporations, and have put efforts into developing business with small companies and individuals. In addition, there has been a conspicuous increase in international operations and securities business, and they have taken an aggressive attitude toward mechanization of their operations.

## *Regional banks* (chiho ginko)

Regional banks are commercial banks other than the city banks. Usually they have their head offices in large or medium-sized cities throughout the country and do most of their business in the prefecture in which the head office is located. Like the city banks, they are ruled by the new Banking Law. At the beginning of 1989 there were sixty-four regional banks, but the number increased to 132 a year later because all mutual banks are in the process of converting to commercial banks. Some of the regional banks are almost equal in size to smaller city banks, but the largest majority of the regional banks are of medium or small size.

The main borrowers from the regional banks are small and medium-sized firms in the area in which they are located, and more than three-quarters of regional bank lendings are to firms with capital of less than ¥100 million. Over one-half of the regional bank deposits are from individuals and about 60 per cent are time deposits, which are of one year or more in maturity. Because the regional banks have such a large share of stable deposits from individuals and because their main lending is for local firms in the area of their operations, they have a relatively easy fund position compared with the city banks.

Like the city banks, regional banks have also been undergoing a diversification of their business in recent years, but with respect to international operations, they have been late, relative to city banks, in establishing overseas offices. As a result, their international operations centre on trade financing, and exchange transactions that depend on correspondent relationships.

## Banking operations

The new Banking Law which became effective in 1982, establishes detailed provisions concerning the extent of operations in which commercial banks may engage. According to the provisions, there are four types of operations in which banks may engage: first, exclusive operations such as taking deposits or instalment savings and making loans, discounting bills, or engaging in domestic exchange transactions (Article 10); second, auxiliary operations (Article 10); third, securities business (Article 11); and fourth, other operations pursuant to laws (Article 12).

Conventionally, however, banking business is divided into six types: deposit, lending, domestic exchange, securities business, international operations, and other operations such as auxiliary and peripheral business.

Deposit operations are the most basic function of banks and for this reason were made the exclusive activity of banks, along with lending operations and domestic exchange operations. The types of deposit that banks may accept are divided into two major categories: term deposits, which have a determined length of deposit, and demand deposits, which have no determined length of deposit and which may be payable on demand of the depositor. The former include time deposits, instalment savings, and CDs, while the latter include current deposits, savings deposits, notice deposits, deposits for tax payments, and special purpose deposits.

Except for current account and special-purpose deposits, interest is paid on deposit accounts. The rates of interest paid on deposits must fall within the ceiling set under the provisions of the Temporary Interest Rate Adjustment Law (TIRAL), details of which are determined by guide-lines from the Bank of Japan (BOJ) that specify interest rates by the type of deposit. In fact, rates of interest paid by the banks are identical to limit in the guide-lines. As a result, there are no differences among banks in the rates of interest paid on deposits.

In recent years, however, banks have responded to growing demands from customers for higher rates of interest and have developed new types of deposits or financial products through tie-ups with other industries or through combining deposit accounts with government bonds in some form. There has also been a gradual approval of new types of financial product with free interest rates, i.e. those which are exempted from application of the TIRAL. These are primarily for large investors, and include non-resident yen deposits that are held by foreign governments, central banks, and supranational organizations, all foreign currency deposits, CDs, and large-sum time deposits. Interest rates of MMCs and super-MMCs are subject to the ceiling set by the Minister of Finance, which moves with the interest rate of CDs (see table 3.4). It is certain that there will be a gradual relaxation of this limitation.

Lending operations are integral parts of the credit-granting activities of commercial banks. There are two forms of lending: discount of bills and loans. The loans are further classified into loans on bills, loans on deeds and overdrafts. In March 1989, the respective shares by type of lending in the total lending were as follows: bill discounts, 8 per cent; loans on bills, 32 per cent; loans on deeds, 46 per cent; and overdrafts, 15 per cent. It is a recent trend that the share of overdraft is increasing, reflecting growing demand from corporate businesses.

The discount of bills is the purchase of an outstanding bill at its face value less the amount of interest that accrues by the maturity date. Most such loans are discount of trade bills, which are issued in order to settle the payment in commercial transactions, and usually are of about three months' maturity. The higher quality trade bills may be sold through the bill discount market or rediscounted with the BOJ or may be used as collateral for a loan from the BOJ.

Loans on bills are lendings on promissory notes issued by the borrowers to the banks as payee. Unlike discount of trade bills in which the bill discounted is one based on a commercial transaction, the bills for loans are issued for the purpose of borrowing money from the bank. Loans on bills are used to supply working capital to corporate businesses and are usually of three to four months' maturity. However, a roll-over of such bills is not uncommon, and hence the funds may be used for long-term working capital or equipment investment.

Loans on deeds require a lending certificate as evidence of indebtedness rather than a bill. These loans are often used for long-term lending, primarily as a means of lending for plant or equipment investment collateralized by real estate or for lending to municipalities or public corporations. In recent years, loans on deeds have been increasing, which reflects the expansion of consumer credit and housing loans.

Overdrafts are facilities that are concluded with holders of current accounts and that allow the payment of cheques issued above the level of the outstanding balance in the current account so long as this extra payment remains within a pre-arranged line and is repaid within a pre-arranged time. For banks, managing such credit is more difficult than managing discounts of bills or loans, and in addition they are not eligible for refinancing by the BOJ. Thus, Japanese banks have not been active in granting overdraft facilities. From the standpoint of borrowers, however, these facilities have several advantages. They are extremely convenient for borrowers who have a large turnover of funds through accounts.

For loans other than bill discounts, it is common practice to require collateral, either personal or physical, in order to assure the principal and interest payment of the loans. In recent years, banks are forced to extend credit without collateral, reflecting increased competition among lending banks.

Domestic exchange operation is business in which a bank acts as the intermediary for the remittance or the collection of funds between distant locations. There are four methods of sending funds through banks: ordinary remittance, telegraphic remittance, ordinary account transfer, and telegraphic account transfer. When these transactions are carried out between the branches of a single bank, the settlement is made through internal procedures of the bank on the books of the various branches; but, when the transactions are carried out with other banks, there is a rapid and centralized settlement of the exchange balances through the Nationwide Data Telecommunications System of All Banks in Japan (Zengin System).

## Securities operations

Securities operations seem the most important field of business for banks in the future. The permissible limits for banks to engage in securities operations such as underwriting and subscribing of new bonds, dealing in already issued bonds, and broking bonds with customers have been debated for many years, chiefly through interpretation of Article 65 of the Securities and Exchange Law. The new Banking Law clearly establishes that the banks may undertake securities operations concerning public bonds, that is, government bonds, municipal bonds, and government-guaranteed bonds. There are two categories of such business: underwriting through the syndicate and distribution of government and other public bonds, and the total underwriting, dealing, and broking operations in government and other public bonds.

The syndicate activities have been carried out by banks in their role as members of the government bond underwriting syndicate since 1965. Distribution of government bonds were recently permitted to the banks for the purpose of reducing the risk burden that accompanied the large-scale underwriting of government bonds. In 1983, distribution began with the selling of long-term government coupon bonds, government-guaranteed bonds, and publicly subscribed municipal bonds. In the same year, medium-term government coupon bonds, and medium-term government discount bonds were added to the list of eligible securities. Dealing in government and other public bonds has been permitted since 1984.

In addition to the securities operations mentioned above, the banks carry out other operations related to securities, such as securities investment operations, securities lending operations, trustee operations, and securities agent operations. These activities have been carried out by the banks for many years and are listed as specific types of auxiliary operations under the new Banking Law. It should be noted that financial institutions are able to invest in corporate bonds and stocks in their own accounts. However, investment in stocks is limited to 5 per cent of the respective corporation, as stipulated in the Anti-Monopoly and Fair Trade Law (Law No. 54 of 1947).

## Statements of conditions and incomes

The most important sources of funds for commercial banks are deposits, which provide about 76.3 per cent of total funding as shown in table 7.5. More than 60 per cent of total deposits are time deposits, and of those more than 80 per cent are for a period longer than one year. The large share of time deposits and particularly of time deposits of more than one year's maturity is a special characteristic of Japan's banking system. This helps to make possible the relatively long-term lending by Japanese banks.

In March 1989, 34.4 per cent of total time deposits were large-sum time deposits, which, though non-negotiable had their rates of interest deregulated in October 1985. The share of CDs in total liabilities was only 2.6 per cent in March 1989. The CDs had been introduced in order to combat the outflow of funds to the *gensaki* (RP) market and other open financial markets before the deregulation of interest rates on large-sum time deposits. It is thought that the shares of large-sum time deposits and CDs in the total funding of the commercial banks has been rising because the minimum amount for application of free rates to large-sum deposits is decreasing and CDs become smaller in minimum amounts and more flexible in maturity.

Lending, both through bills discount and through direct loans, has been the major asset for the commercial banks. Currently, the weight of lending in total assets is 54 per cent. Although lending to individuals has risen considerably in recent years, the largest portion of bank lending continues to go to corporate businesses. Breaking down lending to corporate businesses by industrial classification indicates that about 25 per cent continues to go to the manufacturing and construction industries, although this share has been declining in line with the shift of the nation's economy towards slower growth. The share going to wholesale and retail trade is the second largest, at 20 per cent. Among loans to non-manufacturing industries, there has been a prominent growth of lending to the service industries, from just under 6 per cent of total lending in 1975 to 14 per cent in March 1989.

Table 7.5  Financial figures of city banks and regional banks

| | City banks (13) | | Regional banks (64) | | Commercial banks (77) | |
|---|---|---|---|---|---|---|
| | ¥bn | % | ¥bn | % | ¥bn | % |
| Total assets | 421.2 | 100.0 | 160.5 | 100.0 | 581.8 | 100.0 |
| Cash and deposits | 88.4 | 21.0 | 12.1 | 7.5 | 100.5 | 17.3 |
| Call loans and bills bought | 10.8 | 2.6 | 8.0 | 5.0 | 18.8 | 3.2 |
| Securities investments | 44.9 | 10.7 | 29.2 | 18.2 | 74.1 | 12.7 |
| Loans and other lending | 215.9 | 51.3 | 98.5 | 61.4 | 314.4 | 54.0 |
| Total liabilities | 410.7 | 97.5 | 155.2 | 96.7 | 565.9 | 97.3 |
| Deposits and bonds issued | 308.6 | 73.3 | 135.4 | 84.4 | 444.0 | 76.3 |
| Call money and bills sold | 36.7 | 8.7 | 5.6 | 3.5 | 42.3 | 7.3 |
| Contingent liabilities | 30.0 | 7.2 | 3.3 | 2.1 | 33.5 | 5.8 |
| Net worth | 10.5 | 2.5 | 5.3 | 3.3 | 15.8 | 2.7 |
| Paid-in capital | 2.6 | 0.6 | 1.2 | 0.7 | 3.8 | 0.6 |
| Yield on loans and investment | | 6.40 | | 5.44 | | 6.13 |
| Cost of deposits and funding | | 6.03 | | 5.04 | | 5.76 |
| Profit margin | | 0.37 | | 0.40 | | 0.37 |

Note: Balance sheet items, from which overseas assets and liabilities are excluded, are as of 31 March 1989. Operating figures are for fiscal 1988.
Source: Federation of Bankers Associations of Japan, Analysis of Financial Statements of All Banks, August 1989.

The share of so-called 'front-line' payments reserves, including cash and funds on deposits, is currently 22.6 per cent of total deposits. The largest portion of these funds are required reserves that are deposited with the BOJ under the reserve requirement system. Second-line reserves, i.e. call loans and bills bought are only 4.2 per cent of total deposits.

The composition of assets and liabilities described above is reflected in the banks' income and expenses. Nearly 60 per cent of banks' current income is from interest on lending. The remaining 40 per cent comes from interest on securities, etc. The overall yield on risk assets (lending, call loans, and securities) was about 6 per cent in fiscal 1988. On the other hand, about 60 per cent of current expenses are interest payments on deposits. The total cost of funds (costs of deposits, securities, borrowing, and call money) during fiscal 1988 was 5.76 per cent (see table 7.5)

As a result, the overall profit margin, i.e. the difference between the total yield on risk assets and total cost of funds, was extremely narrow at 0.37 per cent. In recent years, there has been a conspicuous trend towards narrowing the overall profit margin due to a rise in the interest rate on deposits and the more flexible interest rates applied to these liabilities. On the other hand, profits stemming from international operations are growing and in the case of city banks, about 20 per cent of gross profits were generated from international operations for fiscal 1988.

## Long-term financing institutions

Long-term financing institutions include long-term credit banks and trust banks. The long-term credit banks were established under the Long-term Credit Bank Law (Law No. 187 of 1952) in order to develop long-term financing to industrial sectors. Trust banks are organized under the Banking Law and engage in trust business under the Law Concerning Joint Operation of Trust Business by Banks (Law No. 43 of 1943). They extend term loans as a result of investment activities of funds received with trust accounts.

### Long-term credit banks

Currently, there are three long-term credit banks (LTCBs): the Industrial Bank of Japan (IBJ), the Long-term Credit Bank of Japan, and the Nippon Credit Bank (formerly called Nippon Fudosan Bank). It should be noted that the LTCBs are authorized to issue financial bonds as a means of raising the long-term funds because they are substantially different in character from that of commercial banks. The LTCBs played an important role as institutions specializing in long-term finance during the fast growth period, but recently have developed new demands for funds in the domestic markets and international financial operations.

In the domestic markets, the LTCBs expanded their financing of the wholesale and service industries, which in recent years have had a strong demand for funds, and have entered businesses related to the demands of individuals for funding, through lending to private housing finance companies and consumer credit companies. In the international fields, just as city banks, the LTCBs have not only lent to the foreign operations of Japanese corporations but have also participated in international syndicated lending to foreign governments, public bodies, and corporations, as well as participating in the international securities business.

For the LTCBs, the main sources of funding are bond issues. The limit on bond issues is thirty times the bank's net worth. There are two types of bonds issued by the LTCBs, five-year coupon bonds and one-year discount bonds. In principle, these bonds are uninscribed, but, if the subscriber or the holder wishes, inscription may be carried out. Total outstanding in financial bonds issued by the LTCBs stood at ¥37.4 billion at the end of March 1989, equivalent to 50 per cent of total liabilities. But deposit balance is small since there are some restrictions on the types of deposits that the LTCBs may accept. Thus outstanding total deposits other than CDs were 25.3 per cent of total liabilities at the end of March 1989.

Lending activities of the LTCBs are mainly focused on lending for plant and equipment and for long-term working capital, discount of bills, guarantee of debts, and acceptance of bills. There is, however, a restriction that the total supply of short-term working capital by the LTCBs may not exceed the amount of deposits.

The securities-related operations of the LTCBs are similar to those of commercial banks and are very diverse, including the securities operations concerning public bonds, securities investment, securities lending, trustee and securities agent operations. Other than the above, the LTCBs also carry out domestic exchange operations and international operations, along with the guarantee of obligation and safe keeping services.

It is obvious that interest from lending should be the most important source of income and that interest on bonds issued is the largest expense for the LTCBs. The overall yield on total funds used is slightly higher than the commercial banks' because of the larger share of funds invested in long-term lending. However, the costs for the LTCBs' funding are also higher because of the important role played by bond issues on the funding side.

Particularly in recent years, the profit margins for the LTCBs have been conspicuously smaller than those for commercial banks, not only because of the major decrease in yields on risk assets, but also because of the relatively moderate decline in the interest rates on bond issues. However, the LTCBs have a much lower cost ratio compared with commercial banks reflecting their small number of branches and employees compared with the total quantity of funds. Financial figures of the LTCBs as well as trust banks' are shown in table 7.6.

*Table 7.6* Financial figures of long-term credit banks and trust banks

| | Long-term credit banks (3) | | Trust banks' banking account (7) | |
|---|---|---|---|---|
| | ¥bn | % | ¥bn | % |
| Total assets | 78.7 | 100.0 | 70.9 | 100.0 |
| Cash and deposits | 10.6 | 13.5 | 16.5 | 23.3 |
| Call loans and bills bought | 0.9 | 1.1 | 2.4 | 3.4 |
| Securities investments | 13.5 | 17.1 | 14.8 | 20.9 |
| Loans and other lending | 45.0 | 57.2 | 28.8 | 40.6 |
| Total liabilities | 76.5 | 97.2 | 68.3 | 96.3 |
| Deposits and bonds issued | 61.2 | 77.8 | 36.1 | 50.9 |
| Call money and bills sold | 5.0 | 6.3 | 8.7 | 12.3 |
| Contingent liabilities | 5.6 | 7.1 | 4.3 | 6.1 |
| Net worth | 2.2 | 2.8 | 2.6 | 3.7 |
| Paid-in capital | 0.7 | 0.9 | 0.7 | 1.0 |
| Yield on loans and investment | | 6.30 | | 9.38 |
| Cost of deposits and funding | | 5.99 | | 10.35 |
| Profit margin | | 0.31 | | −0.97 |

*Note:* Balance sheet items are as of 31 March 1989. Operating figures are for fiscal 1988.
*Source:* Federation of Bankers Associations of Japan, *Analysis of Financial Statements of All Banks*, August 1989.

## Trust banks

At present, there are seven trust banks, other than the foreign owned trust banks: Mitsubishi Trust, Sumitomo Trust, Mitsui Trust, Yasuda Trust, Toyo Trust, Chuo Trust, and Nippon Trust. Trust business is also carried out by three commercial banks: Daiwa bank, the Bank of Ryukyu, and the Bank of Okinawa. The most important characteristic of Japanese trust banks is their role as long-term credit suppliers, reflecting a tremendous growth of loan trusts since the early 1960s. Of secondary importance is the role trust banks have played as savings institutions for the public since the end of the Second World War.

Trust banks jointly manage trust and banking business. But these two types of business have different characters and must be managed separately in accordance with the Trust Law (Law No. 62 of 1922). Thus, the trust banks have two kinds of accounts, the banking accounts and trust accounts. The banking accounts of the trust banks are identical to those of commercial banks which were described above. According to the Trust Business Law (Law No. 65 of 1922), trust banks may accept only six types of assets: money, securities, monetary claims, movable property, real estate and fixtures, and surface rights and land lease rights.

Lending forms the largest share of assets of trust banks held in their trust accounts, excluding the securities investment trusts which have been gaining a larger share in recent years. The lending within the trust accounts of banks is, of necessity, lending for plant and equipment funds due to the role of trust banks as suppliers of long-term capital. At the end of March 1989, lending for industrial equipment accounted for 43 per cent of total lending by trust accounts of banks, slightly higher than the 31 per cent for commercial banks. Also about 40 per cent of trust account lending goes to big firms with capital exceeding ¥1,000 million, while about 19 per cent of the lending of commercial banks goes to such firms.

Until about 1970, two-thirds of the securities held in the trust accounts of trust banks belonged to investment trusts while only one-third was assigned to other types of trust. Since 1975, however, the proportion of securities, and particularly of government bonds, that are applied to other trusts has risen. By the end of March 1989 this proportion stood at about 42 per cent.

Among the liabilities of trust accounts of trust banks, money trusts account for 93 per cent while the share of non-money trusts in total liabilities has remained at only 7 per cent. Until the second half of the 1960s, ordinary trusts grew very steadily, but, in recent years, specified money trusts have grown extremely rapidly and have risen to 17 per cent of total liabilities. For example, loan trusts have grown extremely rapidly because their dividend yield exceeds those on money trusts and the yields on deposits. During the period from 1965 to 1975, their share was about 50 per cent of total liabilities, but it has fallen to under 23 per cent recently because of the rapid growth of other types of trusts.

On the asset side of trust banks' trust accounts, the share of investment trust securities rose temporarily with the increase in securities investment trusts, but the share of loans recovered. After 1975, the share of loans once again declined steadily due to the weak growth of loans for plant and equipment investment. In addition, the share of securities other than those for securities investment trusts has been rising, and the assets composition of trust banks has been considerably diversified.

As described above, the trust banks have banking accounts in addition to their trust accounts. In comparing the sizes of the trust accounts and the banking accounts for trust banks, the trust accounts are of course much larger. But the sizes of the banking accounts differ widely by individual bank. For most, the banking accounts are of between 20 and 30 per cent of total assets.

All trust banks are located in large cities, and the banking accounts of these banks concentrate on lending to large corporations, just as city banks do. As a result, the deposits in the banking accounts of trust banks are primarily corporate deposits and the share of demand deposits is extremely large.

## Financial institutions for small businesses

### *Mutual banks* (Sogo Ginko)

Mutual banks were established under the Mutual Bank Law (Law No. 199 of 1951) created by post-war restructuring of the financial system. The mutual banks were developed from traditional mutual financing institutions called '*mujin*' companies. After thirty-eight years, mutual banks are now in the process of conversion into commercial banks. This is a result of the financial deregulation and the review of financial segmentation. In January 1989, there were sixty-eight mutual banks. Among them, fifty-two mutual banks were converted into commercial banks in February 1989, and ten others in April 1989. The remainders, except for two mutual banks, were converted by late 1989. Therefore, the following description focuses on the recent historic record.

There were two major differences between the mutual banks and the commercial banks: the mutual banks were restricted in granting credit to firms other than smaller businesses but were permitted to continue instalment financing operations in just the same way as the *mujin* companies (see table 7.2). However, in recent years, the instalment savings and lending portion of the mutual banks has declined. In fact, mutual banks have become similar to commercial banks. During the fast growth period, the mutual banks played an important role in developing small- and medium-sized firms, while commercial banks lent to large corporations. In addition, mutual banks grew rapidly during the process. As mutual banks expanded, they became objects of monetary policy. For example, the reserve requirement system was applied to mutual banks in April 1963 and they became eligible for the securities purchase operations of the BOJ in March 1966.

117

The business activities of mutual banks were made identical to those of the commercial banks through the legal amendment of 1981, with the exception that mutual banks might still carry out mutual instalment operations. Like commercial banks, mutual banks may take deposits or instalment savings, make loans, discount bills, and carry out foreign exchange transactions, all activities that are part of the usual banking business, but they may also engage in other business such as distribution of and dealing in government bonds and other public bonds and in securities-related operations such as securities investments, guarantee of liabilities, proxy and agent operations, and sales of gold bullion.

Mutual banks are, in principle, limited to lending to small- and medium-sized firms with capital of ¥800 million or less, or with employees of 300 or less. Under these circumstances, small businesses continue to get a significant portion of their funds from mutual banks. At the end of 1985, mutual banks provided 15 per cent of small business borrowing, while the share of financial institutions specializing in loans to small and medium-sized firms, which includes lending by credit associations and credit co-operatives, was 37 per cent.

Total deposits, CDs, and mutual instalments of mutual banks were ¥49.3 billion at the end of 1988. They had grown by less than 40 per cent over the previous five years, representing a slowdown since the shift to slower economic growth. Total outstanding loans and discounts made by mutual banks were ¥38.2 billion at the end of 1988, a growth of 36.2 per cent over the previous five years. Growth is now relatively slow due to the entry of city banks into the borrowing clientele of the mutual banks (see table 7.7).

## *Credit associations* (shinyo kinko)

The origin of credit associations dates back to the credit co-operatives of the nineteenth century, based on the Law for Small Business Co-operatives (Law No. 181 of 1949). In June 1951, the Credit Associations Law (Law No. 238 of 1951) was promulgated, and those credit co-operatives that had previously been regular co-operatives in fairly urbanized areas and that were relatively large in scale and similar to general financial institutions were classified as credit associations.

The operations of the credit associations centre on taking deposits and making loans and thus are not particularly different from those of commercial banks. However, credit associations are organized on a membership basis, so that their credit operations are limited in principle to members. In addition, their operations are limited to certain geographical areas due to their character as regional financial institutions.

The development of credit associations in the post-war period was rapid and, by 1987, they surpassed the mutual banks in total amount of

*Table 7.7* Financial figures of mutual banks, credit associations and credit co-operatives

|  | Mutual banks (68) | | Credit associations (455) | | Credit co-operatives (418) | |
|---|---|---|---|---|---|---|
|  | ¥1,000m. | % | ¥1,000m. | % | ¥1,000m. | % |
| Total assets | 58,715 | 100.0 | 77,931 | 100.0 | 21,049 | 100.0 |
| Cash and deposits | 3,731 | 6.4 | 13,780 | 17.7 | 4,122 | 19.6 |
| Call loans and bills bought | 1,902 | 3.2 | 726 | 0.9 | 20 | 0.1 |
| Securities investments | 9,465 | 16.1 | 10,324 | 13.2 | 1,522 | 7.4 |
| Loans and other lending | 39,247 | 66.8 | 46,636 | 59.8 | 12,505 | 59.4 |
| Total liabilities | 56,991 | 97.1 | 73,878 | 94.8 | 20,213 | 96.0 |
| Deposits and bonds issued | 50,969 | 86.8 | 66,540 | 85.4 | 17,031 | 80.9 |
| Call money and bills sold | 813 | 1.4 | 438 | 0.6 | 562 | 2.7 |
| Contingent liabilities | 1,607 | 2.7 | 2,429 | 3.1 | 1,128 | 5.4 |
| Net worth | 1,723 | 2.9 | 4,053 | 5.2 | 836 | 4.0 |
| Paid-in capital | 357 | 0.6 | 306 | 0.4 | 162 | 0.8 |
| Yield on loans and investment |  | 5.81 |  | 5.66 |  | 5.80 |
| Cost of deposits and funding |  | 5.32 |  | 5.25 |  | 5.30 |
| Profit margin |  | 0.49 |  | 0.41 |  | 0.50 |

*Note:* Balance sheet items are as of 31 March 1989. Operating figures are for fiscal 1988.
Mutual banks include ones converted to commercial banks in February 1989.
*Source:* BOJ, *Economic Statistics Monthly,* June 1989.

funds held. Therefore, the credit associations also held an important position in the field of financing to small- and medium-sized firms. However, like the mutual banks, the credit associations underwent a remarkable change in the content of their business in the process of development. On the deposit side, the proportion of deposits coming from non-members grew substantially, and the credit associations became more like the commercial banks.

On the basis of revisions in the financial laws, the credit associations have been encouraged to merge with each other. Thus, the number of credit associations has been reduced from 520 in May 1968 to 455 in March 1989. It is expected that the merger of credit associations will continue, as they seek a stable basis for business through economies of scale in an environment of intensified competition among financial institutions as deregulation progresses.

Deposits and CDs at the credit associations have grown by about 50 per cent over the past five years and stood at ¥66.5 billion at the end of March 1989. Time deposits are the largest portion of these total deposits, with a share of 93.4 per cent. Lending by the credit associations has grown by about 40 per cent over the past five years and stood at ¥46.6 billion at the end of March 1989. The share of credit associations in total lending to small businesses has risen steadily over the past few years. The credit associations invest their surplus funds in the call market and in deposits placed with other financial institutions including the National Federation of Credit Associations.

### The National Federation of Credit Associations (Zenshinren)

Zenshinren was established under the Credit Associations Law as the central bank for credit associations, whose members are the individual credit associations. With the emergence of the credit associations, Zenshinren was established in November 1951, by means of remodelling its predecessor, the National Federation of Credit Co-operatives which was established in 1950.

According to the law, Zenshinren may engage in (a) acceptance of deposits from, lending to, and foreign exchange operations with member associations, (b) acceptance of deposits from the government, municipalities, public corporations, and non-profit organizations, and (c) operations related to securities, and agent operations for the People's Finance Corporation.

Because the credit associations are mostly small in scale and limited in their geographical area of business, there is the possibility of major disturbances occurring from natural disasters and unforeseen emergencies. In response to this, Zenshinren established the Promotional Fund System in May 1960 and the Deposit Payments Fund Lending System in October 1971. Through these systems low-interest loans may be provided to the credit associations which are in difficulty. In addition, the Credit Associations Mutual Aid Fund System was established in October 1971 in order to improve co-operation among the credit associations.

### Credit co-operatives (shinyo kumiai)

Credit co-operatives are co-operative financial institutions based on the mutual support of owners and workers of small firms. They are organized under the Law for Small Business Co-operatives. As described earlier, credit co-operatives that were similar in nature to commercial banks were converted into credit associations. Consequently, today's credit co-operatives are more like co-operative societies than credit associations. In principle, their business is conducted only with members of the co-operatives, and thus their purpose as co-operative financial institutions is more clearly carried out.

The major expansion of credit co-operatives in the 1950s and 1960s resulted in a gap between the principles and the reality of credit co-operatives, just as in the cases of mutual banks and credit associations. In 1968, various revisions of the laws were undertaken in which the business area of credit co-operatives were expanded to include lending collateralized by deposits to municipalities and public corporations and lending to financial institutions. In addition, the capital base of credit co-operatives was improved by raising the minimum amount of capital for such institutions.

When the conversion of the credit co-operatives to the credit associations occurred in the early 1950s, only seventy-two credit co-operatives were left. However, establishment of the credit co-operatives is automatically approved unless exceptional conditions exist and a number of credit co-operatives were established in the following years. In May 1968, 544 credit co-operatives were in existence. The MOF took measures to reduce the founding of the credit co-operatives, and thereafter the merger and conversion of such institutions went on. In March 1989, there were 418 credit co-operatives.

Credit co-operatives may accept deposits and instalment savings only from: (a) members of the co-operatives; (b) the government, municipalities, public corporations, and non-profit organizations; and (c) spouses and relatives of co-operatives' members. On the lending side, the credit co-operatives may lend or discount the bills, in principle, only to members, but a certain amount may be lent to non-members. In addition to the above, the credit co-operatives may engage in domestic exchanges, payments connected with securities transactions, and agent business for designated public bodies. At the end of March 1989, total deposits and CDs, and total loans of credit co-operatives were ¥17.0 billion and ¥12.5 billion, respectively.

## National Federation of Credit Co-operatives (NFCC)

When a majority of the credit co-operatives were converted into the credit associations in 1951, the original National Federation of Credit Co-operatives was converted into Zenshinren. In 1954, however, the new National Federation of Credit Co-operatives (NFCC) was established with the remaining credit co-operatives as members on the basis of the Law for Small Business Co-operatives. The operations of the NFCC are similar to those of Zenshinren. The NFCC may accept deposits from members, the government, municipalities, and non-profit organizations. The most important lending activities of the NFCC are lending and bill discounting to participating co-operatives and their members. In addition, some loans are made to the government, municipalities, public corporations, and non-profit organizations.

### *Labour Credit Associations* (rodo kinko)

*Rodo kinko* is a financial institution in the form of a co-operative society which carries out the financial business that is necessary in order to help improve the living standards of workers and to promote the joint welfare activities of organizations such as labour unions, consumer co-operatives, and other workers' organizations. *Rodo kinko* was organized under the Labour Credit Association Law (Law No. 227 of 1953).

*Rodo kinko* accepts deposits and instalment savings from member organizations, the government, municipalities, public corporations, non-profit organizations and other qualified personnel. On the lending side, the largest share of loans goes to member organizations, and to the Japan Workers' Housing Association. There are no particular requirements on the investment of surplus funds, but the largest portion is placed with the National Federation of Labour Credit Associations as deposits or short-term lending. At the end of March 1989, total deposits, instalment savings and CDs and total lending of all *rodo kinko* stood at ¥6.1 billion and ¥2.8 billion, respectively.

### *National Federation of Labour Credit Associations (NFLCA)*

The NFLCA was established in April 1955 as the central organization for *rodo kinko* around the country. The NFLCA may accept deposits and make loans in just the same way as *rodo kinko*. However, an important function of the NFLCA is the administration of the Domestic Exchange Concentration Payment System of the Mutual Rescue Fund, and of special lending systems. In addition, the NFLCA may make special low-interest loans when a member association encounters difficulties or is subject to unusual disasters.

### *Shokochukin Bank*

Shokochukin Bank (Central Bank for Commercial and Industrial Co-operatives) is a special institution organized with government participation under the Shokochukin Bank Law (Law No. 14 of 1936), which facilitates the financing of co-operative societies of small businesses and serves small business entrepreneurs. The deposit and lending operations of the bank are limited to the organizations that contribute to its capital and to their members. At the end of March 1989, its paid-in capital was ¥233,800 million, 71 per cent of which was owned by the government. Other than the capital contribution, the government takes measures to aid the organization such as underwriting a portion of financial bonds that the organization issues. In turn, the directors of the Shokochukin Bank are appointed by the government.

The largest source of funding for the Shokochukin Bank is bond flotation, on which there is a limit of thirty times its net worth. This is permitted because the level of deposits that may be expected from member organizations and their members is not large enough. At the end of March 1989, total bonds outstanding were ¥8.5 billion, exceeding three quarters of total funding (see table 7.8). Deposits account for only 20 per cent of total funding, because there are limitations on who may place deposits: organizations qualified to contribute capital, members of such organizations, public bodies, non-profit organizations, and the authorized financial institutions.

*Table 7.8* Shokochukin Bank and Norinchukin Bank (as of 31 March 1989)

|  | Shokochukin Bank | | Norinchukin Bank | |
| --- | --- | --- | --- | --- |
|  | ¥1000m | % | ¥1000m | % |
| Total assets | 12,185 | 100.0 | 32,516 | 100.0 |
| Loans and discounts | 9,761 | 80.1 | 10,982 | 33.8 |
| Securities investments | 1,730 | 14.2 | 12,217 | 37.6 |
| Total liabilities | 11,888 | 97.6 | 32,331 | 99.4 |
| Deposits | 2,375 | 19.5 | 22,841 | 70.2 |
| Bonds issued | 8,542 | 70.1 | 5,231 | 16.1 |
| Net worth | 297 | 2.4 | 184 | 0.6 |
| Paid-in capital | 234 | 1.9 | 45 | 0.1 |

*Source: Nihon Keizai Shinbun,* 6 June 1989 and 13 June 1989.

Lending by the Shokochukin Bank was originally limited to small businesses or their co-operative societies, in line with its original intention. In response to financial deregulation, however, legal revision in 1985 permitted lending to overseas corporations established by member organizations or their members, to foreign financial institutions, to holders of Shokochukin Bank bonds or government bonds, and to depositors. The lending limit of any single borrower set by the General Council of member organizations is currently ¥2,500 million to any member organization and ¥250 million to any member of a member organization.

The revision of the Shokochukin Bank Law in 1985 expanded the limits of lending and deposit business. In addition, it permitted expansion of securities operations such as distribution and dealing in government bonds, and investment of surplus funds into monetary claims in trust. In October 1985, the Shokochukin Bank joined the government bond underwriting syndicate and initiated distribution of these bonds. Thus, the Shokochukin Bank is responding to the diversifying needs of small- and medium-sized businesses through the development of new types of financial products in an environment of financial deregulation.

## Financial institutions for agriculture, forestry, and fisheries

### Norinchukin Bank

The Norinchukin Bank (Central Co-operative Bank for Agriculture and Forestry) is the financial institution which is located on top of the pyramidal system of co-operative financial institutions for agriculture, forestry, and fisheries. The financing for these industries is carried out through organizations of co-operatives based on a spirit of mutual support and with government assistance. Such assistance is needed because it is difficult for these industries to expect the usual financing activities of financial institutions due to their character and seasonal demand for funds.

The co-operative financial institutions for agriculture, forestry, and fisheries constitute a three-tiered financial pyramid. On the top stands the Norinchukin Bank, the middle stage consists of federations of credit co-operatives in prefectures, and the bottom level consists of individual co-operatives organized in city, town, or village. The federations are formed in the middle level by each industry.

The Norinchukin Bank was established as a special corporation of limited liability based on the Norinchukin Bank Law (Law No. 42 of 1923). The bank was originally 50 per cent owned by the government but was privatized in 1959. At the end of March 1989, its paid-in capital was ¥45,000 million, all of which was subscribed by agriculture, forestry, and fisheries organizations as specified under the Norinchukin Bank Law.

The Norinchukin Bank may accept deposits from organizations which may contribute capital, non-member borrowers, the subscribers of Norinchukin Bank bonds, the public bodies and non-profit making organizations, and authorized financial institutions. Almost 90 per cent of its deposits are from organizations which may contribute capital. The Norinchukin Bank is authorized to issue financial bonds in order to raise funds. These bonds are issued in bearer form and the overall limit on their issue is thirty times the sum of their net worth.

Lending of the Norinchukin Bank is, in principle, limited to organizations which may contribute capital. However, lending to non-members is permitted unless such lending discourages the lending to member organizations. In addition, the bank invests the surplus funds in securities, call loans, and bills purchase. Recently, the securities investments increased rapidly with a growing emphasis on government bonds, while lending growth has been relatively slow since 1975. Securities holdings have risen on the same scale as lending, and the Norinchukin Bank has become the largest single institutional investor in the private sector. In addition, their call loans and bills bought have reached a very high level, and the Norinchukin Bank is a major lender of funds on the Tokyo money markets.

Other principal operations of the Norinchukin Bank include formation of an on-line communications network on a nation-wide basis for member institutions. The bank also carries out remittance transfers and payment collection services connected with domestic exchange settlement. In 1979, the bank was permitted to handle foreign exchange operations coping with internationalization of clients' activities. In March 1981, a foreign exchange on-line system began to work. In October 1982, the bank opened its representative office in New York, which was converted to branch status in October 1984.

The Norinchukin Bank Law was partly revised in 1981, following enactment of the new Banking Law in the same year. After this revision, the Norinchukin Bank was allowed, like commercial banks, to carry out securities operations such as distribution and dealing in government bonds and other public securities.

In addition to its principal operations, the Norinchukin Bank may act as agent in several types of business if an approval is granted by the government. Currently, such operations entrusted to the bank include payment of funds for government purchases of staple foods and acting as agent in lending funds of the Agriculture, Forestry, and Fisheries Finance Corporation.

Deposits placed with the Norinchukin Bank have been growing recently, due to a slower growth of lending by member organizations. At the end of March 1989, total deposits and CDs stood at ¥22.8 billion, an increase of just 50 per cent during the past five years, and bonds outstanding were ¥5.2 billion. Lending and securities held by the bank stood at ¥11.0 billion and ¥12.2 billion, respectively (see table 7.8).

*Agricultural co-operatives* (nokyo)

Agricultural co-operatives are an important basis for the agricultural field of the co-operative system, and were formed under the Agricultural Co-operative Law (of savingLaw No. 132 of 1947). The agricultural co-operatives are special co-operative organizations and their management is entrusted to the farmers who are members. Activities of these co-operatives include, not only financial operations, but also non-financial operations such as purchasing, processing, and selling of commodities, public utilities, and mutual assistance for their members. In other words, the agricultural or fisheries co-operatives are a few examples of financial institutions which may engage in non-financial business.

The agricultural co-operatives are organized throughout the country. At the end of March 1989, there were 3,936 agricultural co-operatives engaging in credit operations. These co-operatives had a total membership of eight million people, comprising almost all farmers in the nation. The credit operations in which agricultural co-operatives may engage are acceptance of savings deposits or instalment savings of members and provisions of loans necessary for farming or the livelihood of the members or for improvement of the industrial basis of conditions of agricultural areas.

The agricultural co-operatives play a very important role as savings institutions for agricultural communities, too. There are two types of savings deposits handled by co-operatives, savings deposits of a current nature and savings deposits of the nature of time deposits. Lending is also an important activity of the co-operatives. Long-term lending accounts for more than 70 per cent of the total lending outstanding from agricultural co-operatives. In March 1989, total deposits and lending of the co-operatives were ¥46.5 billion and ¥12.8 billion, respectively.

Subordinate operations of the agricultural co-operatives include handling of public funds, handling of government procurement payments for rice and barley, and proxy-lending on behalf of the Agriculture, Forestry, and Fisheries Finance Corporation.

### Credit federations of agricultural co-operatives (CFAC)

There is one credit federation of agricultural co-operatives (CFAC) in each prefecture of the nation. The CFACs are formed by the agricultural co-operatives under the Agricultural Co-operative Law. Unlike the agricultural co-operatives, the CFACs are not permitted to operate non-financial business.

The main activities of the CFACs are to accept deposits and make loans to member co-operatives, but in addition they also play a role in strengthening the credit operations of agricultural co-operatives through discounting the bills of members or guaranteeing the liabilities of members, and also in adjusting the regional surpluses or deficits of funds among the co-operatives. The CFACs are positioned in the centre of the exchange settlement system of agricultural co-operatives.

*Fisheries co-operatives, and credit federations of fisheries co-operatives*

The fisheries co-operatives formed under the Fisheries Co-operative Law (Law No. 242 of 1948) are permitted to accept deposits and to make loans, but the credit operations of these co-operatives are not as large as those of agricultural co-operatives. In March 1989, total deposits and loans outstanding were ¥1.9 billion and ¥1.0 billion, respectively.

The fisheries co-operatives that carry out credit operations have organized credit federations of fisheries co-operatives at the prefectural level. These federations are not permitted to carry out operations other than credit business.

# Chapter eight

# Private non-depository financial institutions

## Insurance companies

### *Life insurance companies* (seiho)

Insurance companies were born in Japan a little later than commercial banks. As a group they have been performing a marked role in supplying long-term funds for many years and now the insurance industry is the second largest supplier of capital after banks.

According to the Insurance Business Law (Law No. 41 of 1939), establishment of an insurance company requires a licence from the Minister of Finance. In Japan, an insurance company may engage in either life-insurance or non-life insurance business, but not in both. Currently there are twenty-five insurance companies in Japan, including five foreign affiliated companies. Life insurance companies are divided into two types of organizations: joint stock companies and mutual companies. There is virtually no difference between them. Both types of companies require ¥30 million or more of capital. Mutual companies, however, are established on condition that they have a hundred or more members.

Although the insurance companies supply financial services to those who seek protection from unforeseen accidents, at the same time they accumulate large sums of insurance premiums to provide against accidents, and use these funds to become important suppliers of funds to industries as institutional investors in the securities markets. Life insurance companies, in particular, are long-term financial institutions because mortality rates can be predicted with a great degree of accuracy and because usually the contracts are of a long-term nature, so funds received are relatively stable over a long period of time.

The assets of life insurance companies consist of small amounts of funds from many clients and must be paid out in the future to these clients. In order to protect the enrollees, safe and certain investment of the funds must be expected and therefore strict regulation of investment methods is carried out. The interest rates on lending are left to the voluntary determination of each company so far as long-term rates are concerned, but tend to be about the same as those of long-term credit banks.

Business volume for life insurance companies has shown a steady growth over the past years, with growth in the value of contracts and premium receipts reflecting an expansion of the economy and of personal incomes. As a result, the total assets of life insurance companies stood at ¥97.1 billion in March 1989, having roughly doubled in the preceding five years. In recent years, the amount of contracts outstanding in endowment insurance and other traditional types of insurance product has not risen so quickly, because of increased competition with both postal life insurance and various types of mutual insurance societies.

Lending continues to employ the largest share of assets and stood at ¥33.5 billion in March 1989. There has been, however, a marked weakening of the lending growth rate, reflecting the reduction in loan demands from the corporate sector. As a result, the share of lending in total assets declined to 34.5 per cent in March 1989 from 60.6 per cent in March 1979. The loans continue to focus on those for plant and equipment for various industries, especially the electric power, steel, and chemical industries.

The share of securities in total assets has been rising in recent years and stood at 45.1 per cent in March 1989, compared with 29.6 per cent in March 1979. In the securities market, the life insurance companies have considerable influence as institutional investors. About 40 per cent of their securities are equity investment, but the insurance companies have also been members of the government bond underwriting syndicate since it was established along with the initial issue of government bonds in 1966. They are authorized to distribute the securities that they underwrote.

Since the early 1980s, the share of life insurance companies' investments going overseas in the form of yen-denominated syndicated loans or of foreign securities has risen, reflecting the decline of corporate loan demands in Japan and the higher rate of interest abroad. In fact, the share of foreign securities in total assets rose from 2.0 per cent in March 1981 to 14.0 per cent in March 1989. Thus, the life insurance companies are diversifying their portfolios compared with the fast growth period in which their lending concentrated on loans for plant and equipment in the corporate sector.

## *Non-life insurance companies* (sonpo)

At present, there are twenty-three domestic non-life insurance companies operating in Japan. All are corporations under the regulation of the Insurance Business Law. In addition to their primary activities as providers of insurance services, the non-life insurance companies, as well as life insurance companies, play an important role as suppliers of funds for the industrial sector and as institutional investors. The maturity of their investments, however, is shorter than that of the life insurance companies, and their shares in the loan and securities markets are smaller.

A certain portion of insurance premiums of the non-life insurance industry is accumulated as reserves for contract-holders, but the largest portion is accounted for by required reserves, just as the life insurance companies. Some types of non-life insurance have premium arrangements under which a portion of the premiums are returned when the contract expires if no insurable incident has occurred. However, in most cases, the premiums are outright payments, in contrast to those of life insurance companies.

The investment of assets by non-life insurance companies is subject to the same types of regulation as that of life insurance companies, except for the fact that firms engaging in marine insurance are permitted to lend on ship mortgage. However, unlike the life insurance companies, non-life insurance companies have a character more like short-term financial institutions.

Total contracted amount for non-life insurance companies has grown steadily in recent years. Consequently, total assets of non-life insurance companies stood at ¥18.3 billion in March 1989, equivalent to about one-fifth of that of life insurance companies. Reflecting the need for maintaining liquidity, 14.0 per cent of total assets are placed in bank deposits and call loans. Lending and securities investments account for 67.6 per cent of total assets, but the share of securities investments is larger and that of loans is smaller than in the case of life insurance companies.

## Finance companies

### *Housing loan companies*

In the field of housing finance, banks and other private financial institutions play the major role, accounting for over 70 per cent of the total credit extended. In addition to the direct financing by the banks and other institutions, housing finance is also provided by housing loan companies that were jointly established by the banks after 1971. At present, there are eight such housing loan companies.

Housing loan companies rely almost exclusively on banks and other financial institutions for funding. As a result, their lending rates are higher than those of banks, but their market share has expanded very rapidly along with the growth of the number of such companies and an expansion of their network of offices. All of the housing loan companies are under the supervision of the Ministry of Finance (MOF).

The main business of housing loan companies is to extend housing loans to households on the security of real estate, and the amount of loans outstanding stood at ¥7.6 billion at the end of March 1989 (about 10 per cent of the housing loan market). The two major characteristics of loans extended by housing loan companies are that they are secured by real estate and have a long-term maturity of up to thirty-five years.

### Consumer credit companies

Consumer credit other than housing loans is divided into two types: sales credit which is provided for the purpose of payment of goods or services purchased by consumers; and consumer loans which are granted directly to consumers. It is difficult to measure precisely the volume of the consumer credit market, but the Japan Consumer Credit Industry Association estimates that consumer credit balance at the end of March 1989 was ¥35.7 billion, or about 18 per cent of private consumption expenditures. Of the total credit balance, sales credits accounted for 32.3 per cent and consumer loans for 67.7 per cent. Over the past ten years, sales credit has grown by 3.1 times and consumer loans by 4.1 times.

Various types of firms have made rapid expansion in their consumer credit. Sales credit companies (*shinpan kaisha*) have expanded rapidly in both sales credit and consumer loans, while credit card companies tied to banks and consumer credit companies have also seen fast growth in the consumer credit area. These trends indicate that the needs of consumers have shifted away from money for the purchase of durable goods, such as electric appliances and automobiles, toward education, leisure, and entertainment. It is also observed that demand has been increasing for free loans or cash loans without collaterals which may be used for any purpose.

With this growth in the consumer credit industries, some social problems have emerged concerning the unusually high rate of interest and improper collection procedures applied by cash loan companies. In coping with these problems, two laws concerning the money-lending industry were implemented in May 1983. It was thought necessary to improve and expand further consumer protection through reform in the law and the system of obtaining consumer credit information.

## Securities finance companies

Securities finance companies are specializing in the financing of securities in order to supply the funds necessary for the smooth issuance and circulation of stocks and bonds. The origin of securities finance companies dates back to post-war days. When the stock exchanges were reopened in 1949, large blocks of stock were dumped on the market because of the dissolution of the major industrial giants (*zaibatsu*). As a result, there was a serious depression in the stock market.

In order to overcome this depression and in an effort to ensure the sound development of the market, a margin trading system was introduced. Nine securities finance companies were established in 1950 for the purpose of supplying the equities and funds necessary for trading to the securities companies. In 1955, these finance companies merged into three companies in order to strengthen their services. They are located in Tokyo, Osaka and Nagoya.

The basic operation of the securities finance companies is lending to securities firms in the form of loans for margin transactions. These loans are used to supply funds necessary for margin trading in equities between the securities firms and their customers. However, loans collateralized by bonds or bond dealer financing was begun in 1960 in order to promote development of the bond market. In addition, the securities finance companies make working capital loans to the securities companies and also lend to general investors on the collateral of securities.

The securities finance companies rely, in part, on their own funds for engaging in the lending operations, but also borrow from the commercial banks and from the call market. Bank borrowing is the largest source of funds for these companies, and are generally loans on bills collateralized by bonds or stocks received in the course of dealer financing. For bond dealer financing, borrowing from the call market is collateralized by bonds and bills issued from securities firms. For loans for margin transactions, call money borrowing is collateralized by a collateral receipt for call loan transactions.

Until the mid-1970s, the securities firms constantly needed funds and hence depended highly on borrowing to raise the funds necessary for margin trading, their main line of business. In the second half of the 1970s, however, the capital base of the securities firms expanded and allowed them to rely more on their own funds. In addition, there was expansion of other means of funding, such as foreign currency loans and yen-based short-term lending from foreign banks in Japan. These developments, along with easier monetary conditions, reduced their dependence on borrowed funds.

In recent years, bond dealer financing has increased very rapidly, reflecting the expansion of the secondary bond market. In March 1989, bond dealer financing stood at ¥752,500 million, an amount less than loans for margin transactions (¥1.9 billion).

## Securities firms

### *Character of securities firms*

According to the Securities and Exchange Law (Law No. 25 of 1948), securities firms are defined to be financial institutions other than commercial banks, trust banks, and other financial institutions determined by Cabinet Order. The securities firms may engage in dealing, broking, underwriting, and selling of the stocks, government bonds, municipal bonds, government-guaranteed bonds, corporate bonds, and beneficiary certificates for securities investment trusts. Those who engage in the securities business are required to obtain a licence from the Minister of Finance for each type of business.

Financial institutions other than securities firms are prohibited from engaging in the securities business except for dealing in government bonds, municipal bonds, and government-guaranteed bonds, under Article 65 of the Securities and Exchange Law. In addition, securities investment trust management business has been handled by securities investment trust management companies since 1951. Securities firms, however, handle the largest portion of the purchases and sales of securities for investment trusts, the sales of beneficiary certificates, and the payment of dividends and redemption funds.

Therefore, most securities business is carried out by the securities firms, which play the central role in the securities markets in Japan. Moreover, the securities firms have undertaken intermediation of short-term funds with the expansion of the *gensaki* (RP) market in the 1970s. Hence the securities firms are much more important than in the pre-war period, when the major share of business was management of transactions in equities.

In March 1989, there were 220 Japanese securities firms, 130 of which were full members of all eight stock exchanges in the country, six of which were broker firms or intermediaries between the full members of the exchanges, and eighty-four of which were non-members of exchanges. In the securities markets, the four largest firms have more than 50 per cent of capital, employees, turnover, and also securities investment trust business through their affiliates. They are Nomura,

Daiwa, Nikko, and Yamaichi. In the revolutionary environment of financial services, the securities industry – and, in particular, the four largest firms – has been most active in the diversification, internationalization, and mechanization of its operations.

The diversification of operations was realized through various methods. First was the development of new types of investment trusts such as the medium-term government bond fund introduced in 1980, the interest investment fund in 1982, the free financial fund in 1985, and financial products combined with banking services. Second was the lending of money to individual customers on the collateral of public bonds in 1983. Third was to engage in selling domestic CDs, BAs, and CPs as well as foreign CDs and CPs during 1984–7. Fourth was the establishment of new markets such as the bond future market, the stock future market and the stock index market during 1985–8. These efforts were made to cope with intensified competition between the securities firms and other financial institutions.

Internationalization was advanced by several means: the largest and medium-sized securities firms established subsidiaries in overseas markets and engaged in the promotion of securities investment in Japan by foreign investors (see table 8.1). They took an active part in the underwriting of external bond issues by Japanese corporations, subscription, and sales of yen-denominated foreign issues in Japan, and other international business. Eurobond underwriting activities have grown markedly in recent years. During the first half of 1989, Japan's four largest securities firms were ranked the four largest lead-managers in the Eurobond market.

In addition, major Japanese securities firms have established banking subsidiaries in London and Zurich in recent years. These trends resulted in friction between Japanese banks and Japanese securities firms abroad,

*Table 8.1* Japanese securities firms' overseas offices by location (as of 1 July 1989)

| Location | Subsidiaries* | Representative offices |
|---|---|---|
| North America | 18 | 11 |
| Latin America | – | 2 |
| Europe | 61 | 28 |
| Near East | 5 | 4 |
| Asia | 35 | 32 |
| Oceania | 5 | 8 |
| Total | 124 | 85 |

*Note:* *Including banking subsidiaries.
*Source: Kinyu Zaisei Jijo,* 7 August 1989.

and promoted a reduction in the barriers between banking and securities business in Japan.

The securities firms are also active in mechanized operations. The largest firms created and expanded on-line systems to improve the investment information, remittance, and transfer services for customers. The securities firms created a remittance service in co-operation with mutual banks. In addition, they provided a nation-wide service for the payment of medium-term government bond funds, and for the automatic transfer and receipt of interest on public bonds through the nation-wide postal savings on-line system.

In the course of this mechanization there has been an increased tendency for small- and medium-sized securities firms to use the computer systems of the larger securities firms, so that reorganization within the securities industry focusing on the larger firms is occurring because of mechanization, development, and handling of new types of products.

## Scope of operations

The principal business of securities firms is the handling of transactions in equities. Operations concerning bond transactions have become the second line of the securities business, reflecting the development of the bond markets in recent years. Securities firms are prohibited from engaging in business other than securities operations. However, securities-related business is permitted so long as such business does not harm the public interest or investor protection. Therefore, operation of other businesses is allowed as long as approval from the Minister of Finance is granted.

With the approval of the Minister of Finance, securities firms may also engage in so-called 'accumulated investment operations'. In such operations, a client pays instalments of funds to securities firms on a regular basis, and the securities firms buy securities of equivalent value and reinvest the interest and redemption funds from the securities so purchased. Securities firms are able to handle accumulation savings accounts if they get permission.

In addition, securities firms may also engage in foreign exchange operations to the extent that the foreign exchange operations accompany transactions of Japanese residents in foreign securities investment or of foreign investors in securities investment in Japan. Foreign exchange transactions handled by the securities firms have been growing owing to the 1984 initiation of sales of foreign CDs and CPs in domestic markets, allowance of forward exchange transactions without actual demand, and the repeal of regulation on the conversion of foreign currency into yen.

*Line of business*

The securities business is divided into an issuing business in the primary markets and a trading business in the secondary markets. The issuing business includes underwriting and distributing operations. The trading business includes dealing operations on the firm's account and broking operations on behalf of its clients.

The long-term government coupon bonds, government-guaranteed bonds, and corporate bonds are usually issued through underwriting by securities firms or other financial institutions. In the case of long-term government bonds, underwriting and subscription are carried out by a syndicate composed of banks, insurance companies, and securities firms. The subscription share of the securities firms has been about 20 per cent since the late 1970s. For corporate bonds, the underwriting and subscription are usually handled by *ad hoc* syndicates composed of securities firms, including the largest four.

In the 1950s and the 1960s, trading in equities was the largest portion of the trading operations of securities firms, but, in the early 1970s, the expansion of the bond markets and RP markets raised the share of bond trading. Along with the large-scale issues of government bonds since 1975, the trading volume in bonds has exceeded trading in equities.

The earnings of securities firms come from three sources: (a) trading profits and dividends received through dealing operations; (b) management fees through broking operations; and (c) underwriting, subscriptions, and sales fees from underwriting and distributing operations. The largest portion is from fees on broking, underwriting, and distribution.

In recent years, growing earnings have strengthened the financial basis of securities firms, and, as a result, the profitability of the four largest securities firms is approaching the levels of the largest city banks. Even for small or medium-sized firms, the increase in retained profits has raised income from own-account lending concerning margin trading, and this increase in income has made a significant contribution to improving profitability.

*Regulation of securities firms*

Securities firms are subject to various regulations under the Securities and Exchange Law and other laws and regulations, in view of investor protection and sound development of the securities industry. There are two types of regulation, those concerning operations themselves and those concerning assets and accounting.

Regulations on the activities of securities firms are made on a day-to-day basis. The first is regulation of a joint operation of different types of securities business. If a company is acting as both broker and underwriter, restrictions are imposed on credit provisions by the underwriter and on the use of information relating to some issue by the employees who hold underwriting information. Second, there is regulation concerning unfair trade practices, including solicitation through provision of conclusive judgements, loss guarantees, or special profits, and prohibition of fraudulent price formation.

Securities firms are also required to observe the administrative instructions set by the Minister of Finance concerning a change or cessation of operations when problems arise concerning the soundness of the financial condition of a firm. The Securities and Exchange Law lists three cases in which a securities firm must observe the advisory orders of the Minister. The first is where the liability ratio exceeds the rate specified by the Minister. The second is the case where borrowing of cash or securities, lending or trustee assets, or securities and other assets holdings differ from the criteria determined by the Minister. The third is where a correction of asset conditions is necessary.

## Securities investment trust management companies (SITMCs)

SITMCs play a vital role in the securities investment trust transactions. The SITMCs gather funds from the general public (beneficiaries) through selling beneficiary certificates and then entrusts these funds to the trust banks (trustees). Trustees then invest these funds in securities according to the directions of the SITMC and then distribute profits or redemption funds to the beneficiaries.

Securities investment trusts are organized for investors or the general public who do not have ample funds by themselves or who are lacking in sufficient knowledge to make the securities investments on their own. The system of securities investment trusts was first established under the Securities Investment Trust Law (Law No. 198 of 1951). Originally, the management operations for investment trusts were carried out by securities firms. In order to protect the independence of management of the entrusted assets, management operations were separated from securities firms in 1960, and assigned to the SITMCs which had to be licenced by the Minister of Finance. Currently, twelve SITMCs are in operation.

There are two types in securities investment trusts: stock investment trusts, which began in 1951 when the Securities Investment Trust Law was implemented and bond investment trusts, which were newly created in 1961. The total principal of both types of investment trusts surged by 3.9 times in five years up to 1988, compared with growth in bank deposits at commercial banks of about 62 per cent. In March 1989, the principal in these investment trusts reached ¥51.7 billion, equivalent to 11.8 per cent of the total deposits of commercial banks.

Such a fast growth has occurred not only because of stable growth of the stock and bond markets, but also because of the development of new financial products such as medium-term government bond funds, new government bond funds, and international bond funds, all of which were due to the development of bond markets since 1975. Consequently, the bond investment trusts have increased their share in recent years, while the stock investment trusts which once formed the largest portion of the securities investment trust during the late 1950s and early 1960s have declined in share.

The Investment Advisory Law (Law No. 74 of 1986) was passed in May 1986 and became effective six months later. The aim of this law was to create a legal framework for the responsible management of surplus funds through a system of registration and approval of investment advisers. According to the law, an investment adviser must be registered with the Minister of Finance. By June 1989, 317 investment advisory companies made such registration.

Where an investment adviser is given discretion by a client over all or part of that client's investment decisions, together with the necessary authority to make investments on behalf of the clients, the adviser must obtain a licence from the Minister of Finance in order to carry out such discretionary investment services. In June 1987, the Minister granted licences to fifty-six qualified investment advisory companies, including seventeen foreign companies. Most of these foreign companies are affiliates of commercial banks or securities firms. The number of licensed investment advisory firms increased to 133, of which thirty-six firms are foreign, by June 1989.

### Money market brokers and foreign exchange brokers

#### *Money market brokers* (tanshi gaisha)

Money market brokers are intermediaries of transactions in the short-term money markets. They are principally regulated under the Law Concerning Control of Receiving Capital Subscription, Deposits, and Interest Rates (Law No. 195 of 1954), just as are money-lenders in general. However, money market brokers play a very important role in the money markets, and are placed directly under the supervision of the Minister of Finance.

Currently there are six money market brokers in operation. The money market brokers are engaged in dealing with or broking for financial institutions call funds, bills discount, financing bills (FBs), CDs, BAs, CPs, and interbank deposits.

In the call market, money market brokers' activities are mainly dealing, i.e. transactions on their own account with either a borrower or a lender. However, this dealing is in fact closer to a type of broking because the money market brokers are prohibited from holding a net position in call funds in order to avoid transactions risks. In the case of uncollateralized call transactions introduced in July 1985, the money market brokers act only as brokers.

In the bills discount market, money market brokers act as intermediaries by buying the bills of exchange issued by borrowing banks that are secured by the discounted bills of corporations, and selling these bills to lending banks. In this way, the individual transactions in bills are carried out on their own account by the money market brokers. However, as in the case of call transactions, actual holdings on their own account are kept within a very strict limit in order to avoid possible risks. Therefore, the largest portion of transactions is, in fact, the broker-like transaction in which a borrower and a lender are matched.

With the approval of the Minister of Finance, the money market brokers engage in trading and intermediation in transactions involving the FBs. Since May 1981, the money market brokers have sold the FBs into interbank markets that were purchased from the Bank of Japan (BOJ). This seems to reflect the BOJ's intention to develop a market in Japan like the treasury bills market in the United States.

Along with the advent of new money market instruments in recent years, money market brokers have expanded their lines of business rapidly. Since May 1979, money market brokers have functioned either as intermediaries or as parties to transactions in CDs. With the establishment of the BA market in June 1985 and the CP market in November 1987, money market brokers, together with other financial institutions, began to engage in trading and broking in transactions involving these instruments of the money markets. In addition, money market brokers carried out intermediation of interbank deposit transactions when interest rates on non-negotiable large-sum time deposits were deregulated in October 1985.

The BOJ maintains a continuous and close relationship with the money market brokers in order to implement monetary policy, and to ensure the smooth functioning of the money markets. For this purpose, the BOJ may extend loans to the money market brokers when they feel it necessary in view of financial market conditions. The BOJ's sales and purchase as a tool of open market operations are also carried out in principle through the money market brokers. In addition, the BOJ uses the money market brokers to adjust the conditions in the financial markets through sales of FBs and bills drawn for sale by the BOJ.

In line with the rapid expansion of the interbank market over the last decade, the earnings of the money market brokers have risen significantly. During fiscal 1987, for example, their operating incomes and net incomes increased 59.9 per cent and 56.2 per cent, respectively.

## Foreign exchange brokers

In the foreign exchange market, interbank transactions are assisted by the intermediaries who are called foreign exchange brokers. Currently, there are eight foreign exchange brokers operating in Japan. All brokers but one are joint ventures between Japanese money market brokers and overseas foreign exchange brokers. Foreign exchange brokers do not trade on their own account, but instead are restricted to earning fees from both buyer and seller as transactions are concluded.

The foreign exchange brokers are also engaged in broking in the Tokyo dollar-call market and Japanese offshore market, the latter having been established in November 1986. To cope with financial globalization, the foreign exchange brokers have moved to strengthen their international links. Tokyo Tanshi's affiliate, Tokyo Forex, teamed up with Tullett and Riley International. Ueda Tanshi's affiliate, Ueda Harlow is linked with Mills and Allen International.

The foreign exchange brokers in Japan have found that international broking commission rates are roughly half of those they can obtain in the Tokyo market. Nevertheless, an absolute increase in foreign exchange trading in Japan has supported a continued growth in their profitability during the 1980s.

Chapter nine

# Government financial institutions

## General view

In addition to the private-sector financial institutions, there exists a group of government financial institutions in Japan comprising the Postal Savings Service, the Trust Fund Bureau, and other financial institutions run by the government. The role of the government financial institutions is to supplement the operations of the private institutions. The government absorbs large quantities of funds through government administered postal savings, insurance, and pension schemes, and channels them into government financial institutions. These activities of the government are included in the 'Fiscal Investment and Loan Programme' (FILP).

The group of government financial institutions comprises one depository institution that receives funds and over ten institutions that lend them. The only depository institution is the Postal Savings Service and the lending institutions include two banks, one fund and nine finance corporations. The two banks are the Japan Development Bank and the Export-Import Bank of Japan. The fund is the Overseas Economic Co-operation Fund. The nine finance corporations are the People's Finance Corporation, the Housing Loan Corporation, the Agriculture, Forestry, and Fisheries Finance Corporation, the Small Business Finance Corporation, the Hokkaido and Tohoku Development Corporation, the Japan Finance Corporation for Municipal Enterprises, the Small Business Credit Insurance Corporation, the Environmental Sanitation Business Finance Corporation, and the Okinawa Development Finance Corporation

The total lending of government financial institutions was ¥83.2 billion at the end of March 1989, equivalent to 21.4 per cent of the total lending granted by all banks in the private sector (¥388.3 billion). Two government banks provided 16.4 per cent of total government lending, while nine finance corporations provided 76.8 per cent. Funds channelled through the Trust Fund Bureau were the main source of funds for government financial institutions. These borrowings from the Trust Fund Bureau were 67.8 per cent of total funding, while bond issues were 17.8 per cent, with the remaining coming from the general account and the special accounts.

### Postal Savings Service (Yubin Chokin Kyoku)

The Postal Savings Service is the division of the Ministry of Posts and Telecommunications which controls a number of post offices located throughout the country. The Postal Savings Service was established in 1874 in order to encourage thrift and savings among workers and to help stabilize the national welfare. But the system was also intended to assist in supplying capital to industry through the collection of small deposits. At present some 24,000 post offices throughout the country are in operation and carry out financial business, not only deposit taking but also handling of the Postal Life Insurance Annuity and the Postal Annuity.

There are five types of savings available: (a) ordinary savings, (b) fixed-amount savings, (c) fixed-term savings, (d) instalment savings, and (e) housing instalment savings. In line with the original intention of collecting small-sum deposits, the deposit operations of the post offices are subject to restrictions. In fact, the maximum amount for any person is ¥5 million for housing instalment savings and another ¥5 million for the remaining four types of savings, though the latter limit will be raised to ¥7 million in early 1990.

The Postal Savings Service has introduced many innovations over the past decades. Since 1973, they have initiated 'postal loans' (*yuyu* loans) that are based on postal savings as collateral. Automatic crediting of wage and salary to accounts was introduced in March 1980, and cash dispensers and ATMs were installed in 1980 and 1981. Pre-authorized payment of public utilities charges was introduced in June 1982, and automatic receiving of interest and dividends on securities began in July 1983. Particularly conspicuous has been the expansion of remittance and settlement services based on the completion of the nation-wide Postal Savings On-line System in March 1984.

The total amount of postal savings has grown rather less rapidly in recent years since the introduction of new financial products by private financial institutions. Nevertheless, during most of the post-war period, fixed-amount savings in particular constantly grew at a higher rate than total savings and stood at ¥125.9 billion in March 1989, roughly equivalent to the personal deposit balances of all banks. Among postal savings, fixed-amount savings account for about 90 per cent. Their loans outstanding are relatively small and stood at ¥616,400 million in March 1989.

Since the postal savings grew to a financial giant, it is proposed that postal savings be split into several pieces to compete with private depository institutions on an equal footing. Otherwise, the postal savings would be 'a price leader' in determining interest rates on small deposits after the entire deregulation of interest rates.

### Trust Fund Bureau (*Shikin Unyobu*)

The Trust Fund Bureau of the Ministry of Finance (MOF) is an institution that receives deposits of excess funds and accumulated funds or various special government accounts and distributes these funds to the government financial institutions, municipalities, and public corporations. Thus, the Trust Fund Bureau plays a role like a bank for the fiscal investment and loan programme of the government. The history of the Trust Fund Bureau goes back many years to the pre-war days, but it was moulded into its present form in 1951 by the Trust Fund Bureau Fund Law (Law No. 100 of 1951).

The deposits in the Trust Fund Bureau come from several sources, some of which are required by law. All postal savings, the accumulated funds of government's special accounts, and the investment portions of surpluses of such accounts are required to be deposited with the Trust Fund Bureau, although there is a minor exception. In addition, some other funds such as the treasury surpluses may be deposited with the Trust Fund Bureau. There is also the Trust Fund Bureau Special Account that was established in order to take care of the revenue on investment and expenditure of the bureau. Thus, the surplus funds and accumulations from the account also make up a portion of the funds of the Trust Fund Bureau.

At the end of March 1989, the total outstanding amount of funds available to the Trust Fund Bureau was ¥214.8 billion, 58.3 per cent of which came from postal savings and 32.4 per cent of which came from welfare pensions and national pensions (see table 9.1). The deposits in the Trust Fund Bureau must be for a minimum of one month, and interest rates must be between 2 per cent (for deposits for less than three months) and 6 per cent (for seven years or more). Since 1961, 0.8 of a percentage point extra interest is paid on the deposits of seven years or more.

The investment of these funds is required to be carried out with methods that are profitable and certain of return, and in activities that will contribute to the improvement of public welfare. There are four major areas for use of these funds. The first is the purchase of government or municipal bonds, or lending to municipalities or public corporations. The second is the purchase of bonds issued by government-supported institutions or public corporations, or lending to these bodies.

143

*Table 9.1* Assets and liabilities of the Trust Fund Bureau

|  | March 1976 | | March 1989 | |
|  | ¥bn | % | ¥bn | % |
| --- | --- | --- | --- | --- |
| Securities investments | 7.6 | 17.7 | 67.7 | 31.5 |
|   Long-term government bonds | 3.0 | 7.0 | 58.7 | 27.3 |
|   Short-term government bonds | 1.2 | 2.9 | 0.1 | 0.1 |
|   Government-guaranteed bonds | 2.4 | 5.6 | 6.0 | 2.8 |
|   Financial bonds | 1.0 | 2.2 | 2.9 | 1.3 |
| Loans | 35.2 | 82.3 | 147.0 | 68.4 |
|   General and special accounts | 2.7 | 6.3 | 26.1 | 12.1 |
|   Municipalities | 6.5 | 15.3 | 29.7 | 13.9 |
|   Government institutions | 26.0 | 60.7 | 91.2 | 42.4 |
| Cash and others | – | – | 0.1 | 0.1 |
| Total | 42.8 | 100.0 | 214.8 | 100.0 |
|  |  |  |  |  |
| Deposits of | 42.7 | 99.8 | 214.7 | 99.9 |
|   Postal savings | 24.2 | 56.5 | 125.3 | 58.3 |
|   Postal life insurance | 1.1 | 2.5 | 4.2 | 1.9 |
|   Welfare pension insurance | 12.1 | 28.3 | 65.2 | 30.4 |
|   Funds of national pension | 1.8 | 4.2 | 4.2 | 2.0 |
|   Other deposits | 3.5 | 8.3 | 15.8 | 7.3 |
| Other sources | 0.1 | 0.2 | 0.1 | 0.1 |
|  |  |  |  |  |
| Total | 42.8 | 100.0 | 214.8 | 100.0 |

*Source:* BOJ, *Economic Statistics Annual* and *Economic Statistics Monthly.*

The third is extending loans or purchasing bonds of the Energy Resources Development Corporation and the fourth is the purchase of financial bonds.

The investment must be deliberated on by the Trust Fund Advisory Council in order to ensure that they meet the policies and conditions for investment. The interest rates on lending from the Trust Fund Bureau are, in principle, identical to those on deposits at the bureau with a maturity longer than seven years. In case the Trust Fund Bureau underwrites bonds, the conditions are identical to those floated in the market place.

Most lending and bond holdings are long-term investments of over five years that are included in the FILP and require approval by the National Diet. There are also short-term investments of less than one year that are not included in the FILP, as well as some medium-term investments of between one and five years. Among the short-term investments are the purchases of government bonds that are either redeemed or repaid within one year, and lending to government's special accounts that are repaid within the same fiscal year.

As indicated in table 9.1, lending of the Trust Fund Bureau accounted for 68.4 per cent of total investments at the end of March 1989, in which loans to government-supported institutions, municipalities, and public corporations formed the largest portion (56.3 per cent). Securities holdings comprise the secondary portion, in which holdings of long-term government bonds were the most important element (27.3 per cent).

## Government banks and OECF

### Japan Development Bank (JDB)

The JDB was established in 1951 in conformity with the Japan Development Bank Law (Law No. 108 of 1951). The purpose of the JDB is to supply long-term funds to key industries, and simultaneously to supplement and promote financing by private sector financial institutions for the industrial and economic development of the nation. At the end of March 1989, the capital of the institution was ¥233,971 million, all of which was contributed by the government. Additional resources are provided by government loan and external bond issues up to a limit of ten times the net worth.

The main activities of the JDB are lending development funds, extending guarantees, providing capitalization, and related matters. Development lending is concentrated on lending of funds that would be difficult to obtain from the private financial institutions, such as the acquisition or improvement of equipment, land reclamation, and construction or improvement of existing facilities related to renewal schemes in existing cities and towns that would contribute to the economic development of the society.

Owing to a legal revision in 1985, it also became possible to lend funds necessary for the research and development of high technology that would contribute to the economic development of society and as well as industrial improvement. The purpose of this change was in response to recent conditions in which technology development has become more important. The maturity of these loans is, in principle, between one and ten years but may be as long as thirty years, if appropriate. Many of these loans take the form of joint lending with private financial institutions.

Capital contribution by the JDB was limited for many years to construction projects for large-scale industrial parks. In 1985, however, its function was expanded and allowed capital contribution in projects to promote the economic development of society and industrial improvement. The purpose of the measure is to supplement and provide incentives for the private sector through capital contribution by the JDB in new fields such as research and development of technology and urban renewal.

In March 1989, the JDB had ¥8.5 billion of loans outstanding, about the same volume as a medium-sized city bank (see table 9.2). Loans focused on basic industries such as electric power, shipping, and mining when the JDB was first established. Later, the composition of loans gradually diversified reflecting the changes in the industrial structure of the country. In March 1989, the share of electricity, gas, heat supply, and waterworks industries was 35 per cent of the total, reflecting the active stance of the JDB toward energy resource-related lending.

*Table 9.2* Government banks and OECF (as of 31 March 1989)

| | Japan Development Bank | | Export–Import Bank of Japan | | Overseas Economic Co-operation Fund | |
|---|---|---|---|---|---|---|
| | *(¥1000m.)* | *(%)* | *(¥1000m.)* | *(%)* | *(¥1000m.)* | *(%)* |
| Total assets | 8,640 | 100.0 | 5,435 | 100.0 | 5,008 | 100.0 |
| Loans | 8,454 | 97.8 | 5,225 | 96.1 | 4,774 | 95.3 |
| Investments in securities | 21 | 0.2 | 51 | 0.9 | 161 | 3.2 |
| Total liabilities | 7,791 | 90.2 | 4,222 | 77.7 | 2,872 | 57.3 |
| Borrowed money | 7,188 | 83.2 | 3,962 | 72.9 | 2,781 | 55.5 |
| Bonds issued | 471 | 5.5 | 196 | 3.6 | 74 | 1.5 |
| Contingent liabilities | 26 | 0.3 | 12 | 0.2 | – | – |
| Net worth | 849 | 9.8 | 1,213 | 22.3 | 2,136 | 42.7 |
| Paid-in capital | 234 | 2.7 | 967 | 17.8 | 2,205 | 44.0 |

*Sources: Kanpo (Government Gazette)*, 5 May 1989;
  *Nikkei Kinyu Nenpo*, Summer 1989;
  *OECF's Annual Report* 1989.

## Export-Import Bank of Japan (EIBJ)

The EIBJ was originally established in 1950 as the Export Bank of Japan, whose purpose was to provide long-term funding for export promotion based on the Export Bank of Japan Law (Law No. 268 of 1950). As its operation expanded into import finance, the name was changed to the present one in 1952, under the revised statute of the Export-Import Bank of Japan Law. The reasons behind the revision related to financing of exports, imports, and foreign investment carried out by private financial institutions, in order to promote economic relations with foreign countries, primarily through foreign trade.

Thereafter, activities of the EIBJ expanded steadily to include foreign investment finance in 1953, development project finance for foreign governments in 1957, and direct loans in 1972. In July 1975, economic assistance and some other functions of the EIBJ were transferred to the newly established Overseas Economic Co-operation Fund (OECF). The capital of the EIBJ stood at ¥967,300 million in March 1989, all of which was provided by the government. Other sources of funds come from borrowing from the government within the limit of net worth of the EIBJ. This borrowing amounted to ¥3.9 billion in March 1989 (see table 9.2).

The main activities of the EIBJ are domestic lending, direct loans, and extending guarantees. The domestic lending is offered to Japanese firms for exports, imports, and foreign investments. As a result of legal revisions in 1985, the EIBJ was empowered to lend directly to foreign corporations that were tied to Japanese firms through their capital. The direct loans take the form of loans to foreign governments, foreign banks, and foreign firms. The EIBJ also extends several types of guarantees for financial institutions that provide finance for exports and imports.

Lending by the EIBJ is, in principle, carried out as joint financing with private sector banks. Usually the share of the EIBJ is limited to 70 per cent of the total loan. Interest rates are decided on a case-by-case basis for direct loans. Maturities are, in principle, between six months and five years for export, import, and investment financing, but are determined on a case-by-case basis for direct loans.

The composition of the EIBJ loans in March 1989 indicated a 35.0 per cent share for export financing, primarily as deferred payments for plant exports. Policy considerations concerning aid to developing countries and international co-operation have been strengthening recently, so that the share of lending for import and investment finance increased to 43.8 per cent and the share of direct loans stood at 21.2 per cent. Geographically Asia has the largest lending portion at 43.7 per cent, Latin America is the second largest with 16.9 per cent, and North America follows with 12.3 per cent.

## *Overseas Economic Co-operation Fund (OECF)*

The OECF was established in March 1961 following the enactment of the Overseas Economic Co-operation Law (Law No. 173 of 1960). The purpose of OECF is to promote overseas economic co-operation and to contribute to the stabilization of the economies and the development of industries in Southeast Asia and other overseas areas currently in the midst of economic development. Until 1961, funds for economic aid had been provided to Southeast Asia and other areas indirectly through deferred credits from the EIBJ. But around 1960, a more active policy towards economic co-operation was needed and the OECF was founded.

The original capital for the OECF (¥5,400 million) came from the Southeast Asia Development Co-operation Fund within the EIBJ. Thereafter, the government added more in capital contribution, so that capital stood at ¥2.2 billion in March 1989. Additional funding of ¥2.8 billion comes from borrowing and ¥74,443 million in bonds floated by the OECF (see table 9.2). The main OECF lending is for development projects, development research, economic stabilization, and capitalization. Lending is provided to governments and government-supported institutions of the developing countries. The OECF also carries out capitalization of certain projects.

At times, there has been some overlap in the activities of the OECF and the EIBJ, because it is difficult to clearly distinguish between loans by the OECF for the purpose of economic co-operation or aid and foreign investment by the EIBJ for the purpose of trade promotion. In order to solve this problem, a reform was made in July 1975, whereby the OECF was made responsible for loans to governments for the purposes of economic co-operation, while the EIBJ was made responsible for lending to Japanese firms or citizens.

The amount of OECF lending has risen very sharply since direct loans were started in fiscal 1965. By March 1989, the accumulated financing provided by the OECF since its inception reached ¥8.3 billion, 95 per cent of which was through direct loans.

## Government finance corporations

Currently, there are nine government finance corporations in operation. All were established by legislation and their capital was fully contributed by the government. The names of these institutions, the year they were established, their paid-in capital and total assets at the end of March 1989 are shown in the table 9.3.

*Table 9.3* Government finance corporations (as of 31 March 1989)

|  | *Year of establishment* | *Paid-in capital (¥1000m.)* | *Total assets (¥1000m.)* |
|---|---|---|---|
| People's Finance Corp. | 1949 | 35.3 | 5,982.2 |
| Housing Loan Corp. | 1950 | 97.2 | 33,997.2 |
| Agriculture, Forestry, and Fisheries Finance Corp. | 1953 | 168.2 | 5,493.5 |
| Small Business Finance Corp. | 1953 | 56.7 | 6,658.6 |
| Hokkaido and Tohoku Development Corp. | 1956 | 46.7 | 877.7 |
| Japan Finance Corp. for Municipal Enterprises | 1957 | 16.6 | 12,506.4 |
| Small Business Credit Insurance Corp. | 1958 | 542.6 | 662.4 |
| Environmental Sanitation Business Finance Corp. | 1967 | 1.0 | 585.1 |
| Okinawa Development Finance Corp. | 1972 | 27.9 | 902.2 |

*Source: Nikkei Kinyu Nenpo*, Summer 1989.

Chapter ten

# Foreign financial institutions

### Expansion of foreign forces

One of the major changes in Japan's financial system in the 1980s is the rapid growth in the participation of foreign financial groups other than commercial banks. As Japan's capital outflow has increased, the foreign pressure to expand its presence in the Tokyo market has increased. The growing stock market and steady deregulation of the financial system in Japan have provided the foreign institutions with a much stronger position than ever before, although it is still tiny compared with the giants of the Japanese financial sector.

Over the past five years, there has been a dramatic change in foreign participation in the Japanese financial markets. In 1984, foreign banks and securities firms were included as regular members of the government bond underwriting syndicate. In 1985, the foreign banks were given access to the domestic trust banking sector and allowed to open securities affiliates in Japan. In the following year, foreign securities firms were granted membership to the Tokyo Stock Exchange. In addition, foreign investment advisory firms were given licences to operate discretionary investment management services in 1987 (see table 10.1).

In the banking and securities sectors, access to the financial markets has been improved for foreign companies owing to the strong pressure from foreign governments. However, foreign banks and firms still feel they have difficulty establishing a presence in money and capital markets in Japan or in competing on an equal footing with Japanese institutions. They are hampered by the long-standing and close links between Japanese financial institutions and Japan's industrial and commercial sectors. Nevertheless, it is true that many of the structural constraints limiting the participation of foreign banks and firms have been either removed or relaxed.

The fast progress in granting foreign financial institutions a greater role in Japan's financial system was mainly due to the thought of reciprocity. As Japanese big banks and securities firms have enjoyed

*Table 10.1* Function of foreign banks and securities firms in Japan (as of 30 June 1989)

|  | Foreign banks | Foreign securities firms |
| --- | --- | --- |
| Local branches | 120 ( 83) | 56 ( 50) |
| Representative offices | 127 (120) | 129 (125) |
| Foreign exchange licence | 83 | – |
| Licences for Japan offshore market | 77 | – |
| Regular member at Tokyo Clearing House | 4 | – |
| Regular member at Tokyo Stock Exchange | – | 22 |
| Regular member in the Government Bond Underwriting Syndicate | 36 | 33 |
| Permit for public bonds dealing | 18 | 48 |
| Permit for public bonds reselling | 27 | 48 |
| Trust banking subsidiaries | 9 | – |
| Securities affiliates | 22 | – |
| Discretional investment management services | 36 | |

*Note:* Numbers in parentheses stand for number of institutions.
*Source: Kinyu Zaisei Jijo, 7* August 1989.

continued access to foreign markets, then foreign groups had to be given equal access to the Japanese markets. In early 1987, the British government threatened to restrict Japanese access to the London markets, unless British securities firms were given more direct access to the floor of the Tokyo Stock Exchange. In April 1988, the US Federal Reserve Board was reluctant to approve applications by Japanese banks to acquire US primary dealers until Japanese authorities took further steps towards deregulation.

The concessions made by the Ministry of Finance (MOF) in increasing the number of issues of government bonds put up for tender, despite entrenched opposition both from the government and the banking sector, point to the MOF's sensitivities to foreign pressure. For much of 1986 and 1987, Japanese banks and securities firms have been cautious which has resulted in increased foreign criticism and pressure for greater access to Japan's domestic financial markets.

In other sectors of the financial system, foreign participation seems still severely limited. In the insurance field, for example, foreign participation is marginal, and likely to remain so. In the life insurance industry, foreign companies find it hard to achieve the critical mass to challenge the powerful force of direct sales representatives employed by the Japanese life insurance companies. However, the growth enjoyed by some of the foreign firms has been impressive in recent years. Foreign consumer finance companies, however, have had much harder experiences and most of them disappeared from the Japanese market after a few years in Japan.

## Foreign banks

### Historical background

It is notable that foreign banks had established their Japanese branches before Japan's first bank (*Dai-Ichi Kokukritsu Ginko*) was established in 1873 by the National Bank Act (Decree No. 349 of 1872), which was modelled after the National Currency Act of 1864 in the United States. In 1863, three British banks opened branches in Yokohama. These banks were the Central Bank of Western India (headquartered in Bombay), the Chartered Mercantile Bank of India, London and China (CMBILC: in London), and the Commercial Bank of India (in Bombay). These banks were called 'Anglo-Indian banks' because they were owned by the British subjects, but their operation bases were in India.

In 1864 and 1865, other Anglo-Indian banks, the Oriental Bank Corporation (OBC) and the Bank of Hindustan, China, and Japan, both of which had London headquarters, followed suit. Since the OBC was to have close contact with the newly established Meiji government, it played a significant role in forming Japan's monetary and financial system. In 1866, the Hongkong and Shanghai Banking Corporation (HSBC: headquartered in Hong Kong) opened a Yokohama branch. The HSBC was very active and extended its branch network in Asia and other parts of the world. In 1867 and 1872, two banks from the Continent, Comptoir d'Escompte de Paris (Paris) and Deutsche Bank (Berlin) opened branches in Yokohama.

As a result, eight foreign banks, all of which were European banks, opened branches in Yokohama prior to the foundation of Japan's first bank in 1873. In the early days of modern Japan, these foreign banks played a major role in five areas:

1 They handled external settlements for Japan through foreign exchange business.
2 They offered services for current and fixed deposits.
3 They provided the Japanese economy with foreign capital through their lending activities and through underwriting Japan's external bonds.
4 Some banks supplied foreign currencies by issuing their own banknotes.

5   Branch managers of major foreign banks made significant contribu-
    tions to the formation of the modern monetary and banking system
    in Japan.

Activities of the OBC and the HSBC were the most prominent. The
OBC assisted the Japanese government in the construction of the
Imperial Mint in Osaka, the railway between Shinbashi and Yokohama,
and the external bonds issued in London in 1873. But this bank went
bankrupt in 1884 due to mismanagement and the decline in silver prices.
The HSBC was very aggressive in business development and
established branches in Kobe (Hyogo) and Osaka in the early 1870s, and
in Naga- saki in the early 1890s.

Until 1873, all modern banking business had been handled by foreign
banks because no Japanese banks existed other than indigenous money
changers. The Japanese bank which engaged in the foreign exchange
business for the first time was the Yokohama Specie Bank which was
established in 1880. Therefore, foreign banks held 100 per cent of
Japan's foreign exchange business and trade finance.

In the 1860s and 1870s the foreign banks made many contributions
to Japan in the areas of trade finance and capital supply and also
pioneered modern banking operations. John Robertson and William
Cargill of the OBC and A. Allan Shand of the CMBILC offered valuable
advice to the government about the establishment of a new monetary
standard and a new banking system.

Following the enactment of the National Bank Act of 1872, *Dai-ichi
Kokuritsu Ginko* was established in Tokyo. In 1880, the Yokohama
Specie Bank was founded in order to carry out foreign exchange business. Consequently, foreign dominance of Japan's banking system
began to decline. By 1900, the Yokohama Specie Bank had more than
50 per cent of all foreign exchange business in Japan.

In 1902, a US bank, the International Banking Corp. opened banking
offices in Yokohama and Kobe. A number of other banks also entered
in the subsequent years, the Banque de l'Indochine (Paris) being the last
entrant before the outbreak of the Second World War. During the war,
American, British, and Dutch banks were forced to close down by order
of the government. The offices of foreign banks belonging to Axis
powers remained open throughout wartime.

After the Second World War, Japan was placed under the control of
the Supreme Commander of Allied Powers (SCAP), who approved the
opening or the reopening of several foreign bank branches in Japan.
Banks entering Japan included the National City Bank of New York in
1946, Banque de l'Indochine in 1947, and several other banks.
Regulatory power over foreign banks was transferred to Japan in
December 1949, and the government restricted newcomers. Since the

1970s, however, the number of new entrants began to grow rapidly, reflecting a deliberate policy.

After the Second World War, foreign banks enjoyed profitable performances for many years. From July 1946 to December 1949, foreign banks again monopolized Japan's foreign exchange business. Their position was eroded by Japanese banks after 1950. Foreign banks were exclusive suppliers of foreign currency loans (so called impact loans) for many years. However, impact loans were also eroded by Japanese banks when the foreign exchange control was lifted in December 1980. CDs, newly introduced in May 1979, provided a great help to foreign banks in expanding yen loan operations. In spite of the above, foreign bank performance deteriorated. Thus, many banks tried to deal in the securities business directly, or indirectly through their affiliates.

In order to help offset the profit squeeze from other operations, foreign banks were given greater access to trading in public bonds. In April 1984, foreign banks were allowed to join the government bond underwriting syndicate although they had only a minor share. In October 1984, three foreign banks, Citibank, Chase Manhattan, and the Bank of America were allowed to begin bond dealing, and a larger number of foreign banks were approved as well from mid-1985. It is noted that foreign banks have been allowed to establish trust banking subsidiaries and securities affiliates since late 1985.

*Current status*

Foreign banks are legally defined as branches or agents established in Japan by banks headquartered in foreign countries. As of 30 June 1989, there were 120 such branches managed by eighty-three foreign banks (see table 10.2). According to the provision of the new Banking Law a banking licence must be obtained from the Minister of Finance when a foreign bank wishes to establish a branch and to engage in banking business in Japan. Thus, foreign banks have the same legal position as Japanese commercial banks according to the new Banking Law. Because of their character, the share of foreign currency transactions in their business is large, and hence all foreign banks are authorized foreign exchange banks under the Foreign Exchange and Foreign Trade Control Law (FEFTCL).

Foreign banks also have 127 representative offices in Japan, which only require notification to the Minister of Finance under the provision of the new Banking Law. The business in which such offices may engage is as a liaison for local clients and for the collection of information. The representative offices are not permitted to carry on usual banking operations. It is also true that they represent a preparatory stage for opening a branch.

*Table 10.2* Foreign banks' branches in Japan (as of 30 June 1989)

|  | Tokyo | Yokohama | Nagoya | Osaka | Kobe | Fukuoka | Total |
|---|---|---|---|---|---|---|---|
| North America | 27 | 1 | 1 | 5 | 1 |  | 35 |
| Latin America | 2 |  |  |  |  |  | 2 |
| Europe | 31 |  | 1 | 8 | 1 |  | 41 |
| Asia | 20 |  | 1 | 15 |  | 1 | 37 |
| Oceania | 5 |  |  |  |  |  | 5 |
| Total | 85 | 1 | 3 | 28 | 2 | 1 | 120 |

*Source: Kinyu Zaisei Jijo*, 7 August 1989.

The number of foreign banks and representative offices was static during the 1950s and 1960s, but, due to increasing financial internationalization, the number of branches and representative offices has increased substantially since the 1970s. Moreover, there has been a diversification of the nationalities of foreign banks away from the concentration of banks from Europe and the United States. In the 1980s, there has been yet another increase in the number of foreign banks seeking to enter Japan, reflecting both the excellent performance of Japan's economy and expectations of further internationalization of the financial and capital markets in Japan in the near future.

Foreign bank branches have fundamentally the same power as their Japanese counterparts. The most important types of business for foreign banks are deposits, lending, and foreign exchange and trade financing, but lending operations towards Japanese firms have become the focus of business. Foreign banks are also playing an important role in the Tokyo dollar call market, the Tokyo foreign exchange market, and the Japanese offshore market.

The most important sources of funds for foreign banks are Euro-currency borrowing through their banking offices in London, because the small branch networks of the foreign banks constrain their ability to attract local deposits. Their foreign currency deposits are mainly from the government, banks, and corporate businesses in Japan. Among the yen deposits, the largest share are those of non-residents, CDs, and deposits of borrowing customers.

The lending of foreign banks in foreign currencies was formerly limited to medium- and long-term impact loans. Since deregulation in 1979, however, it has been possible to make short-term impact loans. The volume of impact loans extended by foreign banks in 1988 was $227,407 million, most of which were denominated in US dollars. At times there are surpluses of foreign currency funds; these surplus funds are lent in the Tokyo dollar call market and the Japanese offshore market. The yen-denominated lending of foreign banks, which was ¥5 billion at the end of March 1989, is almost entirely of a short-term nature and comes about through lending on bills within the credit lines. Most of the funds for such lending are raised through conversion of foreign currency into yen in the foreign exchange market or through call or bill discount markets.

The foreign exchange and foreign trade financing operations of foreign banks in Japan are almost the same as those of 'Japanese' foreign exchange banks, but some foreign banks, particularly US banks, also act as suppliers of offshore funds to Japanese banks through the rediscount of export bills which have been bought by Japanese banks or through dollar refinancing of loans made by Japanese banks. However, the importance of foreign banks in this market has declined in recent years as a result of the diversification of funding of foreign currency and the expansion of Euromarkets.

During the fast growth period (1955–70), when Japan faced a continuous shortage of capital, particularly in foreign currency, foreign banks made large profits through borrowing funds in overseas markets and lending to Japanese corporations. But the business environment for foreign banks in Japan changed dramatically due to the reduction in loan demand by corporate businesses which accompanied slower economic growth and the decline in the importance of foreign currency funding through bank borrowing reflecting the internationalization of the yen.

For foreign banks, the effect of the reduction in corporate loan demand and yen borrowing has been very important, and has been a major cause of difficulty in the local operations of foreign banks in recent years. As a result, most foreign banks are directing their efforts toward finding loan demand in the areas that remain relatively strong, such as leasing, factoring, housing loans, and consumer credit. In addition, many foreign banks have begun to engage in the securities business. In fact, thirty-six foreign banks are currently members of the government bond underwriting syndicate, and twenty-seven foreign banks have licences for the distribution of public bonds, and eighteen foreign banks have public bond dealing licences. Furthermore, twenty-two foreign banks are operating securities businesses through Japanese branches of securities affiliates where they have less than 50 per cent ownership. Nine foreign banks were allowed to establish trust banking subsidiaries in Japan in 1985 (see table 10.1).

The rapid growth of the Euroyen market since 1984, fuelled by activity in the swaps market, has provided foreign banks with special capabilities in financial engineering which have boosted their business substantially. For example, whereas most Japanese banks undertake swap transactions directly only if they have an offsetting transaction, some of the larger foreign banks are willing to take on a swap transaction and hold the risk on their own book before matching it to ancillary transactions.

Unlike the Japanese banks, the foreign banks do not have the extensive retail deposit base to provide very cheap and stable funds. Thus funding costs remain an acute issue for many foreign banks. Although given limited access to the Euroyen market, new issues by foreign banks have been sparse. Anyhow, for foreign banks to be able to make better inroads into the domestic banking sector, there needs to be a further erosion of the present concept of relationship banking. In Japan, strong personal and corporate links remain the order of the day. This serves as a natural constraint to the ability of foreign banks to penetrate the Japanese market.

Foreign banks' operations and earnings are not stable as far as Japan branches are concerned. During fiscal 1988, their loans outstanding decreased 8.5 per cent to ¥6.4 billion, which is equivalent to 1.7 per cent of total loans outstanding of all banks in Japan (see table 10.3). Among foreign banks, US banks continued to reduce their loan portfolio for five years consecutively. As a result their loans outstanding (¥800,400 million as of 31 March 1989) are currently at only one-third of the peak recorded several years ago and their share in all foreign banks declined to 12.5 per cent from about 50 per cent in the past. On the contrary, European banks have increased their loan portfolio (¥4.5 billion) very dramatically, and now they are holding 70 per cent of foreign bank loans outstanding. Particularly, French and German banks hold 21 per cent and 17 per cent shares of loans of all foreign banks in Japan.

During fiscal 1988, operating earnings of all foreign banks decreased 62 per cent to ¥10,883 million. Accordingly, after tax, profits also decreased 37 per cent to ¥17,337 million. Among eighty-three foreign banks, thirty-one banks suffered losses in fiscal 1988 against twenty in the preceding year, while those who recorded after-tax profits were fifty-two banks against sixty the preceding year. Thus, more than one-third of foreign banks are suffering losses during the term.

## Foreign trust banks

In October 1985, the MOF granted licences to nine foreign banks to engage in the domestic trust banking business. This measure responded to strong pressure from foreign banks expressed through the Japan–US Yen Dollar Committee held in May 1984. This was a momentous decision in the 120-year history of foreign banks in Japan, because this was the first chance for foreign banks to establish their banking subsidiaries.

In the early stages of discussion, all seven Japanese trust banks were hostile to any proposal that foreign trust banks be given access to the

*Table 10.3* Significant figures of foreign banks in Japan

|  | March 1988 | | March 1989 | |
|  | ¥1000m. | % | ¥1000m. | % |
| --- | --- | --- | --- | --- |
| Total assets | 19,130 | 100.0 | 21,858 | 100.0 |
| Cash and deposits | 4,616 | 24.1 | 5,759 | 26.3 |
| Call loans and bills bought | 2,353 | 12.3 | 2,962 | 13.6 |
| Securities investments | 1,010 | 5.3 | 1,305 | 6.0 |
| Loans and discounts | 7,001 | 36.6 | 6,406 | 29.3 |
| Inter-office accounts | 2,148 | 11.2 | 2,971 | 13.6 |
| Total liabilities | 19,130 | 100.0 | 21,858 | 100.0 |
| Deposits | 2,215 | 11.6 | 3,545 | 16.2 |
| Call money and bills sold | 6,960 | 36.4 | 6,308 | 28.9 |
| Borrowed money | 2,236 | 11.7 | 2,231 | 10.2 |
| Contingent liabilities | 707 | 3.7 | 659 | 3.0 |
| Inter-office accounts | 6,004 | 31.4 | 7,971 | 36.5 |

|  | (For fiscal 1987) | (For fiscal 1988) |
| --- | --- | --- |
| Operating incomes | 1,121 | 1,331 |
| Operating expenses | 1,092 | 1,320 |
| Operating profits | 29 | 11 |
| Net profit before tax | 61 | 42 |
| Net profit after tax | 27 | 17 |

*Source:* Peat Marwick Minato, *Published Financial Statements of Foreign Bank Branches in Japan.*

domestic market. The strength of foreign institutions in fund management caused grave concern to Japanese banks and they reacted harshly to the idea of foreign trust banks entering Japan and competing for the most lucrative parts of trust business. The big Japanese banks such as city banks, however, largely supported this development as a way to contribute to the eventual deregulation of the barriers between commercial and trust banking.

In October 1985, Morgan Guaranty and the Bankers Trust established banking subsidiaries for trust business in Japan. Chase Manhattan, Citibank, Manufacturers Hanover, Chemical Bank, Credit Suisse, Union Bank of Switzerland and Barclays Bank followed within a year. All of their subsidiaries are wholly owned by foreign parents with the single exception that Mitsui Trust and Banking Co. has a 5 per cent equity in Credit Suisse. However, all of these subsidiaries have relationships of various degrees with Japanese trust banks to help them establish their position in the market.

As usual, initial profitability has not been easy to achieve. However, it may take several years until foreign trust bank activities achieve a strong presence in the local economy. Most of the foreign trust banks have been successful in obtaining a portion of the trust management of special money trusts (*tokkin*). This has required them to develop their back office systems, but has given them only a minimum chance to demonstrate their fund management skills. Penetrating into the pensions sector is the ultimate goal of the foreign banks, but progress is slow.

In spite of Japanese trust banks' initial fears and criticisms of foreign banks entering the stable domestic trust banking industry, relations have improved considerably, mainly because the Japanese banks have realized the enormous difficulties that foreign trust banks have in making much headway in the domestic market. Most of the foreign trust banks have been able to expand their operations and generate revenues sufficient to cover their start-up and operating costs, owing to the boom in certain investment trusts such as special money trusts and non-money trusts (*kingai* trusts). Moving beyond that, pension fund management may take several years before any of the foreign banks has accumulated a sizeable portfolio.

During fiscal 1988, total trust assets of all foreign trust banks increased 85.8 per cent to ¥3.0 billion, consisting of ¥710,308 million in special money trusts, ¥2.2 billion in other money trust, and ¥31,289 million in pension trusts (see table 10.4).

Pension fund management in Japan is organized through a syndication system, and even though foreign banks may be permitted to bid for a portion of the funds management, it will take time to demonstrate their claim that they have much higher funds management capabilities than Japanese trust banks.

*Table 10.4* Significant figures of foreign trust banks in Japan

|  | March 1988 | | March 1989 | |
|---|---|---|---|---|
|  | ¥m. | % | ¥m. | % |
| Total trust assets | 1,616,291 | 100.0 | 3,002,881 | 100.0 |
| Special money trusts | 827,654 | 51.2 | 710,308 | 23.7 |
| Other money trusts | 736,954 | 45.6 | 2,201,716 | 73.3 |
| Pension trusts | 21,532 | 1.3 | 31,289 | 1.0 |
| Other trusts | 30,151 | 1.9 | 59,568 | 2.0 |
|  | (For fiscal 1987) | | (For fiscal 1988) | |
| Operating income | 10,485 | | 16,457 | |
| Operating expenses | 9,355 | | 13,506 | |
| Operating profits | 1,130 | | 2,951 | |
| Net profits | 29 | | 942 | |

*Sources: Kinyu Business,* September 1988; *Nihon Keizai Shinbun,* 7 July 1989.

However, operating results of foreign trust banks have improved remarkably. During fiscal 1988, their operating earnings more than doubled and net profits hiked from ¥29 million to ¥942 million, although two trust banks suffered net losses.

## Foreign insurance companies

A foreign insurer who establishes branches or agents in the insurance business in Japan is required to obtain a licence from the Minister of Finance under the Foreign Insurers' Law (Law No. 184 of 1949). Those who establish insurance companies in Japan must obtain a licence from the Minister of Finance under the Insurance Business Law (Law No. 41 of 1939). As mentioned earlier, each company may engage in either life insurance business or non-life insurance business, but not in both.

In the field of life insurance, foreign companies have established sixteen branches in Japan, eleven of which are engaging in contracts with resident foreigners only. In other words, only five branches are engaging in insurance business with Japanese. In addition, there are three subsidiaries of foreign insurers, and two joint-ventures of foreign and Japanese companies. These subsidiaries and joint-ventures are incorporated in Japan. In the field of non-life insurance, thirty-seven foreign insurers have established thirty-seven branches and engage in non-life insurance business in Japan.

### *Foreign life insurance companies*

In general, foreign insurance companies hold only a tiny market share in the life insurance sector in Japan. There are far fewer foreign companies in life insurance than in non-life insurance, with only five branches – Combined Insurance Company of America, American Life, United Omaha, Nationale Nederlanden, and American Family. In addition, the Life Insurance Company of North America, Equitable, and Prudential have wholly owned subsidiaries, and Allstate and Pruco have joint-ventures with Japanese partners. These were established after 1975.

Although the foreign insurers' market share is very small, their income has risen much faster than the industry average in recent years, rising 31.3 per cent in fiscal 1984, 28.6 per cent in fiscal 1985 and 33.6 per cent in fiscal 1986. They are poised for even faster growth in the future following the MOF's approval of the introduction of variable policies. The rising affluence of society and concern for adequate provision for retirement are creating among depositors and investors a much greater sensitivity to return and a greater willingness to take risks, which gives the foreign companies the potential to write a larger amount of business.

While the foreign life insurance companies were much slower to move into Japan than the non-life insurance companies, the environment is much freer and is likely to become more so over the coming decade. The introduction of variable life policies, and the possibility of policies being introduced which are much closer to investment trusts, demonstrate a willingness of the MOF to permit policies carrying higher risks. This may also generate a higher return for policy holders than traditional, strictly regulated policies.

The MOF has allowed banks to begin marketing products in association with foreign life insurance companies. For example, the Mitsubishi Bank and the United Omaha Life Insurance began offering time deposits, with the interest used to pay for insurance premiums. It is obvious that the marketing of insurance-related products by banks will give the foreign life insurance companies a broader distribution network in Japan, which will help them boost their share of the market.

At the end of March 1989, total life insurance contracts held by five branches of foreign insurers were ¥32.3 billion or 2.6 per cent of total figures of foreign and Japanese insurers in Japan. Total assets held by foreign life insurers were ¥896,700 million or 0.9 per cent of the market. Total premiums, received by foreign insurers during fiscal 1988 were ¥400,400 million or 1.6 per cent of the market.

### Foreign non-life insurance companies

The foreign non-life insurers (with thirty-seven branches) are reasonably active in Japan, although eight of them are members of the British Insurance Group (BIG). A number of them have little more than a representative function in Japan, largely for re-insurance purposes, although they are confident that there will be sufficient liberalization in the market which will give them a proper role. There are also a small number of international insurance brokers increasingly active in Japan. They have carved out a useful niche working with those of Japan's big manufacturers who are moving production facilities overseas. This may, in turn, give them access to some further business in the domestic market when there is any liberalization.

Among foreign non-life insurers in Japan, the largest is AIU Insurance, followed by Cigna group and BIG. AIU initially succeeded in Japan with auto-policies and has gradually expanded from this base. It is estimated that the foreign insurers hold 70 per cent of the entire share, with Cigna holding an estimated 20 per cent and BIG around 5 per cent.

The disadvantage of not having long-standing links with the large industrial group makes it hard to penetrate into the corporate sector, because most of Japanese conglomerates tend to place their insurance contracts with an insurer in their group.

At the end of March 1989 foreign non-life insurers' total assets were ¥278,580 million representing a 1.3 per cent share of the market in Japan. During fiscal 1988, their net premium revenues increased 8.2 per cent to ¥78,402 million, compared with a 14.9 per cent increase recorded by Japanese insurers.

### Foreign securities firms

The rapid expansion of the Tokyo stock market and Japan's abundant current surplus in recent years have been a beacon to the large international securities firms. In fact, the number of foreign securities firms moving into Japan has substantially increased in recent years. In 1972, Merrill Lynch opened a Tokyo branch for the first time as a foreign securities firm. In August 1978, another firm opened a Tokyo Branch. As of 1 July 1989, fifty foreign securities firms, including twenty-two affiliates of foreign banks, operate fifty-six branches in Japan. In addition, 129 representative offices were established by foreign firms.

Those who open branches of securities businesses in Japan are required to obtain licences from the Minister of Finance under the Law Concerning Foreign Securities Firms (Law No. 5 of 1971). Those who open representative offices are only required to give notice to the Minister, although they may not engage in securities business in such offices. Since December 1985, affiliates of foreign banks, if the banks' ownership is less than 50 per cent, have been allowed to open branches to handle securities business in Japan.

The attraction for foreign firms is not only the rapid growth in trading levels of equity and bond markets, but also the fact that the capitalization of Tokyo's stock market has exceeded New York's since April 1987. Foreign firms have been successful in obtaining a larger presence in the primary government bond market. After a long patient struggle, foreign securities firms were successful in joining the government bond underwriting syndicate in April 1984 and in gaining a larger share within the syndicate. Currently, thirty-three foreign securities firms are members of the syndicate and are given a share of 7.9 per cent. In addition, some of the bigger foreign firms' aggressive bids in a limited number of bond tenders, on occasion outbidding the larger Japanese firms, have been a signal of their determination to carve out a sizeable portion in their market for government debt in Japan.

The level of activity of the foreign firms has also been fuelled by the rising volume of trading of US treasury bonds in Japan. Following the sharp increases in the exposure of Japan's institutional investors to these securities in recent years. Trading is minuscule compared with volumes dealt in New York, but it has expanded.

The growth in volume traded by the foreign firms has been impressive, although in terms of stock transactions they rank well below Japanese firms. Morgan Stanley, which has the largest operations among the foreign securities firms, is ranked about thirtieth in stock trading according to its estimates and seems to boost its position further in the medium term. However, since the four largest Japanese securities firms directly control about 50 per cent of the trading in stocks, building up a significant presence in Japan will be very difficult for the foreign firms.

In November 1985, six foreign and four Japanese securities firms were permitted to be members at the Tokyo Stock Exchange. Such foreign firms include Morgan Stanley, Jardine Fleming, Merrill Lynch, S.G. Warburg, Goldman Sachs, and Vickers da Costa. This permission was in response to the strong requests of foreign firms to join and to reciprocate the treatment given to Japan's Nomura Securities who had filed an application to be a member of the London Stock Exchange. In addition, sixteen foreign and six Japanese firms became members of the Tokyo Stock Exchange in May 1988.

Reflecting their best efforts, the operating performance of foreign securities firms has been improving steadily. During the six-month period ending 31 March 1989, foreign securities firms in total recorded operating earnings of ¥8,760 million, compared with an operating loss of ¥19,210 million during the previous term (1 October 1987 to 30 September 1988), and net loss decreased to ¥3,790 million from ¥25,480 million. Between these periods, the number of firms registering operating earnings increased from nine to twenty and those registering net profits increased from five to sixteen firms. It is obvious that the initial investment for office and equipment and membership of the exchange is a very heavy burden for most foreign securities firms.

Given the tough competition in Japan, few doubt that foreign firms will find it difficult to expand their operations rapidly, although the force of their latest push is a clear indication of their intentions. The rapid expansion of the number of employees of the foreign securities firms in Japan has given rise to speculation over just how long it will be before one of the foreign firms emerges as large enough to rival one of the four largest Japanese firms.

In May 1986, the Investment Advisory Law (Law No. 74 of 1986) was enacted to create a legal framework for the responsible management of surplus funds through a system of registration and approval of investment advisers. Where an investment adviser is given discretion by a client over all or part of that client's investment decisions the adviser must obtain a licence from the Minister of Finance. By June 1989, thirty-six foreign firms were granted licences for discretionary investment services by the Minister.

### Overseas foreign exchange brokers

Reflecting the expansion and internationalization of the Tokyo market, foreign brokers have a presence in the Tokyo market, but their strategy has changed from branch operation to joint venture in recent years.

The first arrival was Astley & Pearce, a major foreign exchange broker in London. In December 1978, Astley & Pearce established a Tokyo branch to engage in the foreign exchange broking business. In June 1981, another London broker, N.W. Marshall & Co. established its Tokyo branch by acquiring Minami & Co., a small Japanese broker.

Since the performance of Astley & Pearce was not satisfactory, this company was sold in 1983 to the Nittan A.P. Co., a newly established joint venture, 67 per cent of which was owned by Nippon Discount & Co. and 33 per cent by Exco International. In the same year, London brokers, Tullett & Riley Co., and R.P. Martin & Co. bought equity interests in Japanese brokers, Tokyo Forex Co. and Kobayashi Co., respectively.

Two years later, the Tokyo office of Marshall and Co. was sold to Hatori Marshall Co., a joint venture of Hatori and Co., a Japanese broker, and Marshall. In addition, two joint ventures were established between Japanese brokers and European brokers in 1985. They are Meitan Tradition Co. formed by Nagoya Tanshi Co. and Tradition Service Holding SA in Switzerland, and Ueda Harlow & Co. owned by Ueda Tansi Co. and Mills and Allen International in London. Further, in November 1988, Yagi Tanshi Co. sold its foreign exchange division to Yagi Euro Corp., the newly established joint-venture between Yagi Tanshi Co. and Euro Broker Capital Markets Inc. in New York.

As a result, currently seven foreign brokers have a presence in Tokyo in the form of joint ventures. Some European brokers have also established joint ventures with Japanese brokers in Singapore and Hong Kong. These developments mean that foreign brokers' access to the Tokyo market was very difficult, but that they are willing to help Japanese brokers who have been forced to quickly learn international market practice.

Chapter eleven

# Interbank clearing systems

## Changing structure of payment mechanism

With the rapid development of computer and telecommunications technology, a great change has occurred in methods of payment in Japan. First, there has been a decline in the use of cash money, which is the primary means of payment, since alternative means such as account transfers, credit cards, and prepaid cards have been developed in recent decades. Second, the use of transaction accounts has been reduced due to new financial products that combine features of transaction and investment accounts, such as the composite account (*sogo koza*). Third, there has been a rapid advance in the mechanization and automation of payments operations and systems, as seen by the spread of cash dispensers and automated teller machines (ATMs) or in the spread of on-line computer systems in depository institutions.

In addition, the settlements network has rapidly broadened its scope and become more integrated, due to jointly operated on-line cash dispensers at depository institutions, the expansion of the Data Telecommunications Systems of All Banks in Japan (Zengin System), and completion of an on-line, nation-wide computer network for the Postal Savings Service. In fact, since 1980, various depository institutions have linked their generalized computer systems with those of other banks and have created systems to convert deposits to cash by means of cash dispensers and ATMs. Thus, the banks have created a system under which cash may be withdrawn from machines belonging to other banks so long as the machines are within the same system.

Recently, the Bank of Japan (BOJ) has computerized transactions between the BOJ and its client depository institutions. In addition, there will be a gradual development of computerized networks between banks and their customers, called 'firm banking' and 'home banking'. As a result of the further use of data telecommunications for financial transactions, it is expected that the settlements function provided by depository institutions will expand in the future, and that there will be a further increase in the efficiency of the payment mechanism as a whole. Consequently, the convenience of making settlements will increase substantially.

On the other hand, however, the risks of accidents with computer systems and also the system risk among depository institutions that accompanies the huge increase of fund flows are also expected to rise. Therefore, the continued maintenance of a safe financial system raises several problems concerning the payments mechanism. Among these problems are not only those mentioned above, but also that of ensuring the safety of the system as a whole through the sound management of the individual depository institutions that comprise the system. Even so, it is true that clearing systems among the depository institutions are much more important.

### Clearing houses

The clearing house is an organization under which depository institutions in a certain area assemble at a specified time every business day in order to exchange cheques payable at other institutions as well as drafts, promissory notes, bills of exchange, bond coupons, postal money order receipts, stock dividend receipts, and other such instruments. The clearing house is a traditional form of interbank settlement and dates back to the nineteenth century. Japan's first clearing house was set up in Osaka in 1879. Eight years later, the Tokyo Clearing House was established.

Currently, there are 183 clearing houses designated by the Minister of Justice in Japan. Most of these houses are operated by the bankers' associations in respective regions. The participants in the clearing houses include not only commercial banks, but also trust banks, long-term credit banks, mutual banks, credit associations, credit co-operatives, and other institutions either as direct participants or indirect participants. Foreign banks operating in Japan are also participating in either capacity. In addition, the main and branch offices of the BOJ and prime offices of the Postal Savings Service participate in the clearing houses in the appropriate regions and exchange tax receipts, bills rediscounted, government cheques, and postal money orders.

The clearing balances of individual participants are normally settled by means of transfers among their current accounts with the BOJ. In the areas where the BOJ does not have branches, settlements are carried out through interbank deposits at a specified bank. The form of bills and cheques is standardized by the Federation of Bankers Association of Japan (*Zenginkyo*). The depository institutions which receive bills or cheques are required to observe the magnetic ink character recognition

(MICR) system for amounts and code numbers of individual institutions. Introduction of the MICR system has mechanized the clearing operations so that the burden of such operations has been tremendously reduced compared with earlier years.

In order to maintain the safety of credit transactions, the clearing houses have implemented the suspension of transaction system since 1887. Because the cheques and bills brought to the clearing houses are viewed as legally binding payment obligations, the issuer of a cheque or bill that is dishonoured due to insufficient funds or for other reasons is subject to the posting of a notice of failure to pay. Those who issue dishonoured bills again within six months are subject to a two-year prohibition from current account and lending transactions with participating depository institutions of the clearing house.

The Tokyo Clearing House is the largest one in Japan, with 597 depository institutions participating as of 30 June 1989, eighty three of which are foreign banks, including four direct participants. In 1988, the Tokyo Clearing House accounted for 36.8 per cent of the total volume of transactions and 83.0 per cent of the total clearing amount of the 183 designated clearing houses. Tokyo's share has been rising and this trend represents the recent rapid concentration of financial business in the Tokyo area.

The Tokyo Clearing House has been engaged in mechanical processing since 1971, utilizing large sorter-readers and computers. All processing of MICR-printed bills and cheques brought in by participating institutions is processed automatically, including their classification by participants, calculation of the value of receipts and payments, and balance of each institution. Transaction amounts at the clearing houses are given in table 11.1.

*Table 11.1* Transaction amount of main payment systems (billions of yen)

|  | Clearing house | | Foreign exchange yen settlement | | Zengin system | |
|---|---|---|---|---|---|---|
|  | Total | Per day | Total | Per day | Total | Per day |
| 1982 | 1,795 | 5.8 | 773 | 3.1 | 405 | 1.4 |
| 1983 | 1,913 | 6.4 | 998 | 4.0 | 478 | 1.6 |
| 1984 | 2,244 | 7.8 | 1,291 | 5.1 | 577 | 2.0 |
| 1985 | 2,693 | 9.1 | 1,596 | 6.4 | 707 | 2.5 |
| 1986 | 2,882 | 10.2 | 2,227 | 9.0 | 845 | 3.0 |
| 1987 | 4,173 | 15.1 | 3,183 | 12.7 | 1,023 | 3.7 |
| 1988 | 3,992 | 14.5 | 3,959 | 16.0 | 1,347 | 5.0 |

*Source:* Federation of Bankers Associations of Japan, *Payment Systems in Japan*, 1988.

## Domestic fund transfer settlement system

There are two methods for those who send money to other parties through depository institutions. One is to transfer funds to the bank account of the recipient, in which case the Zengin System plays an important function. Another method is to send money by remittance via mail or telegraph to the designated bank. Net balances resulting from such fund transfers are also cleared among their current accounts with the BOJ.

The Zengin System, established in 1973, is a huge on-line network system linking all private depository institutions in Japan. Since the Zengin System was completed, domestic fund transfers have increased efficiency and the complicated operating procedures are no longer required. Every depository institution may now handle fund transfers through the Zengin System very easily and quickly. Debit or credit balances as a result of funds transfer between participating institutions are settled at the BOJ. Transactions through the Zengin System are subject to a centralized calculation of the value of receipts and payments for each institution at the centre of the system, and the results are reported to the BOJ on the following business day.

On the basis of notification from the centre of the Zengin System, the BOJ effects transfers between respective banks' current accounts for domestic fund transfer settlements held for interbank settlement. The interbank settlement of funds transfer under the Zengin System thus takes place on the business day following the day of notification. The transferee bank credits the customer's account on the day of notification or on a designated day, so that the fund is available for the customer. In order for a bank to be protected from the risk of failing to settle the net balance, participating banks are required to provide deposits, government bonds or other collateral with the BOJ, while banks that belong to a particular group bear joint responsibility for settlement within the group.

Depository institutions participating in the Domestic Fund Transfer System include member banks and associate member banks of the bankers association, and other institutions participating through agents. Member banks and associate member banks comprise 163 banks which maintain the funds transfer settlement accounts with the BOJ. These banks settle their receipt and payment balances arising from the daily fund transfers at the BOJ. Institutions participating in the system through agents consign settlements of fund transfers to their agents banks who are members or associate members of the system. The number of institutions participating through agents stands at 5,135 at the end of 1988.

## Automated clearing house (ACH)

The Tokyo Bankers Association introduced a magnetic tape exchange system or so-called 'Automated Clearing House' (ACH) in 1973, in order to deal rapidly and efficiently with clerical work relating to the large number of transactions among member banks. The ACH has been established for such items as wages and salaries, pensions, and stock dividends, requiring large volume transfers covering more than one bank on a fixed date. The system is conducted currently at the Tokyo Clearing House and the Osaka Clearing House. The Tokyo system is managed by more than 100 depository institutions.

All of these transfers used to be made on a transfer slip basis. With the progress in computerization at banks and corporate businesses, transmission and receipt of data now occur through magnetic tapes. *Zenginkyo* introduced the ACH in 1973 for the direct credit of stock dividends. Application of ACH was extended further to: (a) direct payroll credits in 1975, (b) direct pension payment credits in 1977, and (c) direct dividend credits on loan trusts in 1983.

Direct payroll credits can be used to explain the ACH system. First, the remittee bank supplies data for each employee to the Tokyo Clearing House no later than three days before pay-day. Then, the Tokyo Clearing House processes the information supplied, and encodes this on a magnetic tape. Finally, the remittee bank, two days before pay-day, uses this tape to credit bank accounts designated by payee employees. Funds settlement between banks and through ACH operations is conducted through the clearing house.

While the ACH in the United States and the Bankers' Automated Clearing Service (BACS) in the United Kingdom process both credit and debit operations, the Japanese ACH system handles only credit operations. The ACH system is to be up-graded by data transmission through the new Zengin System.

## Shared ATM networks

Since the early 1970s, Japanese banks have been stepping up the installation of cash dispensers to reduce office work, save labour, and shorten customers' waiting time. More recently, automatic depositors and ATMs have also been adopted. The uses of ATMs are confined to deposits, withdrawals, transfers, and balance reporting. ATMs also make small loans through credit cards. The number of these machines installed stood at approximately 62,000 sets in September 1988 (see table 11.2).

Most of these machines are connected on-line with the host computers of depository institutions. At the beginning, cash withdrawal or deposits through machines could be applied only to the machines of the

*Table 11.2* Shared ATM networks (as of 30 September 1988)

| Institutions | Name | Start time | Member banks | Number of ATMs | Number of cards issued (million) |
| --- | --- | --- | --- | --- | --- |
| City banks | BANCS | Jan. 1984 | 13 | 16,554 | 53.47 |
| Regional banks | ACS | Oct. 1980 | 64 | 17,522 | 48.32 |
| Trust banks | SOCS | April 1983 | 7 | 782 | 2.15 |
| Mutual banks | SCS | Oct. 1980 | 68 | 7,056 | 16.06 |
| Credit associations | SNCS | Nov. 1980 | 455 | 10,313 | 20.37 |
| Agricultural co-operatives | Zenkoku Nokyo Chokin Net Service | March 1984 | 3,956 | 9,100 | 9.13 |
| City banks, regional banks, and mutual banks | NCS (Nippon Cash Service) City banks 13 Reg. banks 23 Mutual banks 17 | Nov. 1975 | 53 | 382 | – |

*Source:* Federation of Bankers Associations of Japan, *The Japanese Banks,* 1989.

bank in which one had an account. However, in 1975, Nippon Cash Service (NCS), a joint venture among banks, was established as a shared ATM network whose ATMs were installed at public places. Furthermore, shared ATM networks have been set up, i.e. BANCS by the city banks and ACS by the regional banks, and SCS by the mutual banks. The ATMs of any depository institution are available within the respective group of banks. For interbank settlement, the clearing house or Zengin System is employed.

Although large-scale use of shared ATMs has been largely confined to co-operation within each group of banks, there has been increased use of shared ATMs across group lines by individual institutions in certain regions. Plans for co-operation among depository institutions are currently under preparation to surpass the ATM network of the Postal Savings Service, which has built a nation-wide network, as well as to respond to the widespread need among customers for shared ATM networks.

The city banks and regional banks, including newly converted ones from mutual banks, are prepared to integrate shared ATM networks of BANCS, ACS, and SCS by February 1990. In addition, trust banks, (SOCS), credit associations (SNCS), foreign banks, and agricultural co-operatives are considering joining the proposed integration of ATM networks. As a result, perhaps almost all ATM networks of private depository institutions will be united into a single but huge ATM network by the end of 1990 and a depositor may withdraw deposits at any ATM in Japan.

### Foreign Exchange Yen Settlement System

Settlement of international transactions normally takes place in the financial centres of the countries whose currencies are employed as settlement currencies, i.e. by the clearing house interbank payments system (CHIPS) in New York or a similar interbank system in London. The Foreign Exchange Yen Settlement System has been in operation since 1984; used by the Tokyo Bankers Association for the purpose of rapid and efficient settlement in yen on transactions connected with foreign exchange dealings among banks. This system is described as the Japanese version of the CHIPS.

Settlement of yen transactions related to foreign exchange used to be done in the following way: the bank which has received funds transfer instructions from an overseas bank draws a BOJ cheque on the receiver bank and sends a messenger with it to the receiver bank together with funds transfer instructions. The receiver bank then presents the cheques at the BOJ on the same day.

Internationalization of the Japanese economy has increased the use of the yen as a settlement currency for international transactions. To facilitate the efficiency and safety of these settlements a new system was introduced in October 1980. In the same way as in the clearing system, funds transfer instructions of participating banks are exchanged at the Tokyo Clearing House for calculation on the value of payments and receipts, and their balances according to banks. Under instructions from the Tokyo Clearing House, settlement of the balances is made through credit-debit transactions between the current accounts held with the BOJ at 3.00 p.m. on the same day.

As of 31 May 1989, a total of 146 banks, including fifty-nine foreign banks, are participants in the Foreign Exchange Yen Settlement System. The volume handled during fiscal 1988 amounted to ¥3,959 billion, averaging ¥16.0 billion a day. The amount is equivalent to the total clearing amount throughout Japan.

### BOJ financial network system (Nichigin Net)

Settlement of funds for the interbank transactions are completed by the transfer of funds between current accounts held with the BOJ. In order to raise the efficiency of these functions and to ensure the security of the settlement mechanism, the BOJ recently completed a huge nation-wide on-line network system, which is called 'Nichigin Net'. This system has linked the nation's entire depository institutions to a single, on-line

171

network, replacing paper-based transactions such as the use of the BOJ cheques with electronic transactions.

Participants in the Nichigin Net include depository institutions having current accounts with the BOJ, securities firms participating in government bond book entry system, money market brokers, and life and non-life insurance companies participating in the call and bill discount markets. Participants and the BOJ are connected under this system by extensive terminals installed at the participants' offices and the BOJ's operation centre.

The initial operation started in mid-August 1988, with plans to gradually expand its scope of operations thereafter. The areas to be covered in the initial stage of operation include on-line fund transfers between individuals banks maintaining current accounts with the BOJ, on-line transmission of data to confirm unsecured money market transactions, and on-line processing of interbank fund transfer instructions concerning foreign exchange yen settlements.

The Nichigin Net recognizes the importance of the security and confidentiality of transactions. Spare equipment is provided and circuits between the BOJ head office and branches as well as its telephone centre are duplicated. Encryption of data on circuits and the application of password and ID number to input data are being applied.

Part IV

# Monetary authorities and monetary policy

# Chapter twelve

# Monetary authorities

## Ministry of Finance (MOF)

*Powerful ministry*

The MOF is one of the most powerful departments of the Japanese
government and is central to the functioning of Japan's financial system
and the establishment of financial policy. The MOF also monitors and
controls activities of all financial institutions in the private and public
sectors. Actually, regular audits on all banks, securities firms, and
insurance companies, both domestic and foreign, are carried out in
conformity with statutory laws. The MOF also exerts considerable
unofficial 'guidance' in directing the activities of all participants in the
financial system in Japan.

In legal terms, the MOF is responsible for setting fiscal and monetary
policy, collecting taxes and customs duties, organizing and allocating
the government budget, floating government bonds, and overseeing
foreign exchange transactions and foreign investment. It also manages
the Trust Fund Bureau (Shikin Unyobu), which forms a *de facto* bank
within the government. Its power extends far beyond the statutes with
extensive private-level contact and consultation with all participants in
the industry. Nothing may happen without approval, either implicit or
explicit, from the MOF.

The MOF has played a key role in deregulating the financial system
and its continued support is vital if this process is to be sustained. Senior
officers of the MOF play the lead role in international negotiations in
defining and pursuing the process of deregulation in Japan. Power
rivalries among the MOF bureaux play an important role in determining
the outcome of negotiations for deregulation or for changes to the
financial system. There are, equally, factions across party political lines,
which may also have a bearing on the MOF's attitude to issues at hand.

Deregulation has moved fastest where it has not overtly threatened
domestic interests. For example, the MOF's International Finance

Bureau could support the opening up of the *samurai* and *shogun* bond markets during the 1970s since they posed no threat to the existing financial structure. On the other hand, deregulation in areas threatening the vested interests of Japanese financial institutions has been slow. For example, due to the conflict between the long-term credit banks and the securities firms over the expansion of the domestic corporate bond markets, the opening of the market came only after extensive discussion, and only small amounts of ground were conceded each time.

The MOF has shifted progressively over the past five years as it has become increasingly appreciative of the need to change the financial system to ensure that Japanese institutions continue to be allowed to expand overseas. The decision to speed up the approval process for foreign borrowers wishing to tap yen-markets is tangible evidence of the change of attitude, as are the decisions to adopt a shelf registration system, which started in October 1988.

Any new product can be introduced only after approval is granted by the MOF. Any new entrant to the market also needs to obtain approval. If the change involves something new that has not been done before, the approval process can be excruciatingly slow, since the MOF officials will painstakingly assess every aspect of the proposal before approval. When foreign banks were proposing to introduce yen-yen swaps products, the MOF and the Bank of Japan (BOJ) held exhaustive discussions to clarify exactly the full implications of the proposal before allowing these deals to be marketed to domestic financial institutions in 1986.

Often criticized for deregulating too slowly, the MOF can move quickly to head off potential structural difficulties emerging in the finance and banking system. For example, as they followed market demand for longer-term borrowing, the city banks began lending longer-term, resulting in severe mismatching of their portfolios. Even though they were restricted to borrowing funds for a maximum of two years, the MOF allowed the city banks to access long-term funds through swaps involving Euroyen funding. This move highlights the flexibility of the authorities in sidestepping existing lines of demarcation within the financial system, if necessary.

Besides controlling development of the financial system, the primary roles of the MOF are setting economic policy and drawing up government budgets. The degree of moral persuasion the MOF holds over the financial sector can work with stunning effect. In early January 1988, for instance, when the yen was peaking against the US dollar, the MOF put strong pressure on Japan's financial institutions to stop the heavy selling of US dollars. This move had a fundamental influence in effecting the turn-round of the exchange rates at that time.

## Supervisory power over financial institutions

The MOF headed by the Minister of Finance holds enormous power over Japanese and foreign financial institutions operating in Japan. One power is to grant licences and approvals to the financial industry. The new banking law and other statutes stipulate that commercial banks and other depository institutions, insurance companies, securities firms, and securities investment trust companies obtain proper licences in order to engage in business. In addition, the financial institutions engaging in foreign exchange business and trust business require extra approval for such business.

The MOF is responsible for ensuring that financial institutions observe requirements imposed by laws and related regulations. Thus, commercial banks and other financial institutions are required to submit reports on business and financial conditions semi-annually to the MOF, whose bank examiners may make field examinations at any institution. The institution's legal lending limit is, in principle, 20 per cent of net worth of each institution, with some exceptions (see table 7.2).

In addition to legal requirements, the MOF sets 'administrative guidance' within its jurisdiction. In case of commercial banks, the following guide-lines are imposed by the MOF.

(a) Net worth to risk assets ratio must be higher than 7.25 per cent by March 1991 and 8.0 per cent by March 1993, for banks with overseas branches, in compliance with the standard set by the Bank for International Settlements (BIS).

(b) Current assets to total deposit ratio must be higher than 30 per cent, in order to consolidate the assets structure of banks and to raise their liquidity.

(c) Fixed business assets to net worth ratio must be less than 50 per cent (but desirable at 40 per cent).

(d) Dividend to net income ratio must be less than 40 per cent.

Needless to say, the MOF has control over government financial institutions other than the Postal Savings Service. Presidents of the Export–Import Bank of Japan, the Japan Development Bank, and the Overseas Economic Co-operation Fund are appointed by the Prime Minister, but most of these presidents are chosen among ex-senior officers of the MOF. Presidents of nine government finance corporations are appointed by the Minister of Finance, in many cases from among ex-officers of the MOF.

The power of the MOF is extended even to the BOJ. The Governor and Vice-Governor of the BOJ are appointed by the Cabinet, but managing directors, advisers and auditors are appointed by the Minister of Finance. The MOF has the statutory power to supervise the BOJ, to set limits for banknote issues and to issue orders if necessary. In addition, a number of activities of the BOJ are subject to approval of the Minister. Such activities include establishment of branch offices, amendments of by-laws, budget planning, and other extraordinary matters.

## Bank of Japan (BOJ)

### Historical background

The BOJ, the central bank in Japan, was originally founded in 1882 under the Bank of Japan Act (Decree No. 32 of 1882). The original form was modelled on the Banque Nationale de Belgique as described earlier. Its equity was owned by the government (55 per cent) and the private sector. The BOJ was reorganized during the Second World War under the Bank of Japan Law (Law No. 67 of 1942).

Because the Bank of Japan Law was enacted during the wartime, there have been several discussions concerning revisions in the post-war period. However, no major reforms have been made so far, the only exception being the establishment, in June 1949, of the Policy Board as the highest decision-making body within the BOJ. The Policy Board is modelled after the Board of Governors of the Federal Reserve System, which was suggested by the Supreme Commander of Allied Powers (SCAP).

Article 1 of the Bank of Japan Law stipulates that the purpose of the BOJ includes control of the currency, adjustment of finance, and maintenance and fostering of the credit system, pursuant to the government policy, in order that the nation's economic powers might adequately be enhanced.

The expression is out of date, but it is generally understood that the objective of the BOJ is to foster currency stability and to maintain orderly credit conditions, in order to promote steady development in the Japanese economy. The BOJ is in continuous contact with financial markets through its day-to-day operations. This contact helps to foster currency stability and the maintenance of orderly credit conditions, and thus contributes to stable economic development.

### Functions

The functions of the BOJ are not different from those of the central banks in other countries. There are four major functions: (a) banknote issuing, (b) acting as a bank for financial institutions, (c) acting as bank for the government, and (d) conducting monetary policy through the first three functions.

Over the past decades, the BOJ has gradually mechanized its operating system in order to perform these functions. In recent years, advanced techniques in data processing, telecommunications, and computer systems have been introduced not only to inter-office telecommunications, but also financial transactions between the BOJ and its client institutions.

### Function of banknote issuing

The Bank of Japan Law grants the BOJ the power to issue banknotes, which circulate as legal tender for any transactions both public and private. The system of banknote issuance is the so-called 'elastic maximum issuing limit system'. This was instituted as a temporary measure in March 1941, but the system became permanent according to the enactment of the Bank of Japan Law in 1942.

Article 29 of the Bank of Japan Law prescribes that the BOJ is authorized to issue banknotes, but does not mention responsibility concerning convertibility. The maximum issuing limit for banknotes is determined by the Minister of Finance after consultation with the Cabinet Council. Since 21 December 1988, the limit has been ¥32.6 billion. When the BOJ feels it necessary, it may issue banknotes exceeding the limit, but continuance of such excess issuing for more than fifteen days requires approval of the Minister.

Moreover, for excess issuance exceeding fifteen days, the BOJ must pay an issuing tax determined by the Minister, which is currently 3 per cent per year. Banknotes issuance by the BOJ must be secured by assets of equivalent value. The assets eligible for the purpose include trade bills and other bills, loans, government bonds or other bonds, foreign exchange, and gold and silver bullion. However, there exists no special specie reserve under the current system.

### Function as a bank for financial institutions

The BOJ currently has transactions relationships with virtually all of the important financial institutions, including the city banks, the regional banks, the long-term credit banks, the trust banks, the foreign banks, the mutual banks, the credit associations, the National Federation of Credit Associations, the National Federation of Credit Co-operatives, the Shokochukin Bank, the Norinchukin Bank, the securities firms, the securities finance companies, and the money market brokers.

The BOJ may open current accounts for client financial institutions. These accounts earn no interest. These are used for settlement of clearing transactions, remittance or transfer of funds, call and other transactions among financial institutions. In addition, all transactions of financial institutions with the BOJ – for example, payments related to securities trading or to BOJ lending – are passed through these current accounts. The balances of these deposits are counted as reserve deposits required by law.

The BOJ may discount bills of and extend loans to financial institutions. Bill-discounting by the BOJ is re-discount of bills that have already been discounted by a financial institution for its client. The BOJ's bill-discount operations are carried out only for bills that have been designated as acceptable for re-discount and not for all trade bills. The BOJ's loans are made directly to financial institutions and are collateralized by bills or securities that have been approved as a qualified collateral by the BOJ. Currently qualified collaterals include government securities, government-guaranteed bonds, financial bonds, certain municipal bonds or corporate bonds that the BOJ has considered as appropriate.

The rates of interest on the BOJ's discount and loans are publicly announced and are known as official discount rates. When the term 'official discount rate' is used, however, it generally refers to the discount rate applied to trade bill re-discount, which is 4.25 per cent since 25 December 1989. In addition, an extra lending system was introduced in March 1981. Under this system, the BOJ may make loans at a rate different from the official discount rate where it is necessary for appropriate management of financial markets.

The BOJ may sell and buy bills and securities with financial institutions in order to supplement open market operations. Trading in both long- and short-term government securities has been carried out, but currently such transactions concentrate on the purchase of long-term bonds. The trading of bills is of two types, trading of bills held by financial institutions and the sale of bills issued by the BOJ.

The BOJ acts as the clearing institution for the settlement of domestic fund transfers as described earlier. Balances of domestic fund transfer are settled through exchange settlement accounts with the BOJ. The BOJ also acts as the central institution for the government bond book-entry system started in 1980 in order to facilitate secondary transactions in government bonds. The purpose of this system is to contribute to the development of a secondary market in government bonds by rationalizing delivery and custody.

Functions as a bank for the government

The BOJ handles both deposits and lending transactions with the government and also acts as agent for the government in government bonds and foreign exchange transactions. The BOJ carries out the receipt and the payment functions of the government. All receipts of the government, including tax and other revenues, are entered into the government's current account with the BOJ, and all expenditures of the government are made by government cheques drawn on the BOJ. No interest is earned on this account.

The Bank of Japan Law stipulates that the BOJ is to carry out the operations of the government treasury. The scope of this business is not limited to the payment and receipt of funds into government deposits with the BOJ. It includes handling the securities either held by the government or in the custody of the government. In addition, a portion of the treasury operations is entrusted to the commercial banks and other financial institutions in the private sector. The BOJ acts as an agent for the government in all clerical matters concerning government bonds such as the issuing, redemption, interest payments, and registration of the securities. An agency system has been established to deal with government bonds.

By law there are no limitations on the lending of the BOJ. However, the Public Finance Law (Law No. of 1947) prohibits, in principle, the underwriting by the BOJ of government bonds with maturity of longer than one year or extension by the BOJ of term loans with maturity of longer than one year. These provisions were made on the principle of ensuring sound finance for the government. Indeed, since 1948, there has been no underwriting of long-term government bonds by the BOJ and no long-term lending to the government.

For short-term cash management of the government, however, the BOJ has provided credit by means of underwriting of the financing bills (FBs). In principle, such bills are to be subscribed in the market place. In fact, however, the interest rates on them are rather low, and the portion sold in the market is extremely small. As a result, the BOJ is the underwriter for the largest portion. In 1985, the treasury bills (TBs) with maturity of less than six months were issued for the first time in order to facilitate the roll-over of the government bonds then coming due. Because TBs differ in character from FBs, however, the BOJ is prohibited from underwriting them.

Foreign exchanges belonging to the government are currently held by the Foreign Exchange Fund Special Account. On the basis of the Foreign Exchange Fund Special Account Law (Law No. 56 of 1951), the BOJ currently carries out the clerical work concerning payments in yen and foreign exchange through this special account, as agent for the Minister of Finance. Since the foreign exchange trading involves exchange rates smoothing operations, the BOJ intervenes in the foreign exchange market in its capacity as agent of the Minister.

*Organization*

The BOJ is a special corporation organized under the Bank of Japan Law. Its paid-up capital is ¥100 million, of which ¥55 million is contributed by the government and the remaining by the private sector. Contributors have no privileges other than a 5 per cent dividend per annum. Net income from operations during any business period is delivered to the treasury, after the deduction of dividend and reserve accumulation.

### Policy Board

The BOJ's Policy Board established in 1949 is the highest policy-making body of the institution. Its duties are administration of the business of the BOJ, control of currency and credits, and operation of other means of monetary policies so as to meet the needs of the national economy. The specific areas in which the Policy Board has jurisdiction are rather broad and extend to all the major policy instruments such as official discount rates, open-market operations, and reserve requirements, and also include regulation of major market interest rates. However, the introduction, change or abolition of reserve ratios are subject to approval of the Minister of Finance.

The Policy Board consists of seven members: the Governor of the BOJ, two representatives of the government (one each from the MOF and the Economic Planning Agency), and four others representing the city banks, regional banks, commerce and industry, and agriculture, who are appointed by the Cabinet. Of these seven, the government representatives do not have voting powers, so that decisions are made by majority vote of the Governor and the appointed members. The chairman of the Policy Board is elected by vote of the members with voting rights, but as a matter of custom the Governor is elected.

### Officers and offices

The executive officers of the BOJ include the Governor, Vice-Governor, seven managing directors, five auditors and a number of advisers. The Governor represents the BOJ and conducts the operations of the BOJ in accordance with the policies determined by the Policy Board. The Vice-Governor and the managing directors assist the Governor in the conduct of the BOJ's operations while auditors inspect the operations of the BOJ. The advisers may express to the Governor their opinions on matters of importance concerning the operations of the BOJ. The Governor and the Vice-Governor serve five-year terms, the managing directors four- year terms, the auditors three-year terms and the advisers two-year terms, with reappointment permissible.

The head office of the BOJ is domiciled in Tokyo, and there are thirty-four branches and twelve liaison offices in major cities throughout the country. In addition, the BOJ has representative offices in New York, London, Paris, Frankfurt am Main, and Hong Kong. These offices liaise with foreign central banks and do research on foreign economies.

## *Relationship with the government*

Under the existing laws, the BOJ is under the control of the Minister of Finance. In addition to the detailed provisions concerning individual activity, the Minister has general powers of order over operations and supervision, along with the right to appoint and dismiss managing directors. These provisions reflect the wartime nature of the laws. Nevertheless, the Minister and the BOJ maintain close contact and co-operation on a regular basis, and the powers of order have never, in fact, been used.

However, one cannot deny that the Minister of Finance has a strong influence over every aspect of the BOJ. From 1957 to 1960, the Research Committee on Financial System, discussed a revision of the Bank of Japan Law. In the course of discussion the biggest issue was how to specify the independence of the BOJ. On this matter the committee could not reach a unified conclusion. The result was a report with a set of plans: plan A and plan B, in cases of disagreement.

In cases in which the Minister believes that there are fears that the BOJ's policies would create barriers to the achievement of government policy and in which agreement could not be reached on these matters by the Minister of Finance and the Governor of the BOJ, plan A calls for the Minister to give direct instructions to the BOJ. Plan B calls for a request by the Minister for the Policy Board to put off decision-making for a certain period, after which the Policy Board would resume its decision-making as usual. No conclusion about how to deal with such cases has been arrived at, and the issue remains unsolved yet.

Chapter thirteen

# Monetary policy

## Objectives of monetary policy

Among the final objectives of monetary policy, it is common to list such objectives as higher employment or the support of economic growth, and equilibrium in the balance of payments. However, the most important is price stability or currency value stability. The central bank pursues all three objectives at the same time, but problems arise when there are trade-offs between these objectives.

The historical experiences of both Japan and other countries have indicated a couple of critical problems in the dilemma of 'stability vs growth' and the 'domestic vs external'. In the former case, the problem is whether to view price stability or employment (i.e. economic growth) as more important. In the latter case, the problem is whether to view the domestic objective of price stability or the external objective of balance of payments equilibrium as more important.

In Japan, there were no serious trade-offs between the three objectives until the late 1960s. In 1969, however, monetary policy confronted the two types of trade-offs for the first time, when inflation began while the balance of payments was in surplus. At that time, the Bank of Japan (BOJ) preferred price stability and tightened monetary policy. As a result, economic growth slowed down, and the balance of payments surplus expanded further, which helped increase pressure to revalue the yen. Thereafter, there occurred several instances which required a solution to this dilemma.

Between 1969 and 1973, monetary policy failed to choose a first priority. In the earlier period, price stability was seen as being important, whereas the later period saw instead an emphasis on economic growth and the balance of payments equilibrium. These measures resulted in the hyper-inflation and the balance of payments deficits that accompanied the first oil crisis of 1973, and the serious recession after the crisis. Based on this experience, the BOJ strengthened its belief that price stability was indeed a pre-condition for sustaining employment and economic growth, at least in the foreseeable future.

A more important factor was that the fixed exchange rate system was shifted to a floating exchange rate system in February 1973. This change meant that equilibrium in the balance of payments was, in principle, left to the self-equilibrating power of the foreign exchange market. Thus, the central bank of each country was in the position to take responsibility for the stabilization of prices in its own country. Since 1975, the BOJ has recognized this situation and has carried out a monetary policy with the primary objective of a stable value of the currency. However, it is true that the floating rate system has not been successful in adjusting the balance of payments imbalance even among the major countries.

## Instruments of monetary policy

The central banks' major instruments of monetary policy are lending policies, open-market operations, and changes in legal reserve requirements. During the fast growth period in Japan, the most important role in the monetary policy was played by the lending policy, including changes in the BOJ discount rate. In addition, so-called 'window guidance', that is, the central banks' control on loan growth at the commercial bank level, was used as a supplementary measure. These instruments of monetary policy were most effective because of the over-borrowing by corporate businesses and the over-lending of the financial institutions.

On the other hand, one result of policy operations focusing on lending was that the commercial banks, and particularly city banks, came to depend excessively on borrowing from the BOJ. Coping with this situation, the BOJ introduced the so-called 'new scheme for monetary control' in 1962. Under this scheme, money required to accommodate economic growth would be supplied through the purchase of government bonds rather than through lending. Other instruments were developed, such as bills discounted by the BOJ after 1972, and after 1981, financing bills (FBs), though on a limited scale.

However, there still remain barriers to the proper utilization of open-market operations, that is, flexible operations in open markets in which non-financial institutions may participate. In order to ensure the effectiveness of monetary policy in the process of financial deregulation, it will be necessary to utilize open-market operations on a day-to-day basis. Therefore, it has become even more important to create thoroughly open-market operations, similar to the treasury bills market in the United States.

*Lending policy*

The lending policy includes adjustment of the official discount rate and other lending rates, and adjustment of the credit ceiling of the financial institutions. The adjustment of the official discount rate influences the funding costs of financial institutions, directly through the higher costs of borrowing from the BOJ, and indirectly through a higher level of interest rates in the short-term money markets. The commercial banks and other financial institutions may change their attitudes towards lending and securities investments in response to such changes in funding costs. Such movements on the part of financial institutions may result in changes in the money supply. In turn, the effects spread to the economic activities of corporate businesses and households. This is called the 'cost effect' of discount rate adjustments.

In addition, discount rate adjustments have 'announcement effects' which have a psychological effect on the behaviour of financial institutions, corporate businesses, and households, based on their expectations of how the economy will be affected by changes in the discount rate. For example, when the discount rate is raised, such a change will indicate a restrictive attitude towards business activities. Thus, one might expect market movements to reflect the psychological effect of cautious attitudes towards production and investment prior to the cost effect of the discount rate.

In November 1962, in order to reduce the dependence on BOJ lending by financial institutions, the BOJ established credit ceilings for the city banks. The credit ceiling system was part of the normalization of financial conditions under the new scheme for monetary control and is currently applied to the ten largest city banks. Under this system, the BOJ establishes credit ceilings on a quarterly basis for each of these banks and, in principle, does not lend more than these limits. In cases where lending exceeds ceilings, that lending is not allowed for more than two weeks, and at interest rates 4 percentage points above the discount rate.

In March 1981, the BOJ introduced a special lending formula with an interest rate determined regardless of the official discount rate. This facility is to be used as a means for financial adjustment in cases where it is needed for the appropriate management of money markets. An example might be the flexible response to disruptive influences felt in the foreign exchange markets by the active inflow of short-term capital generated from changes in overseas interest rates. So far, no use has been made of the special lending facilities, and no interest rates for them have been set. If it were necessary to use this facility, the lending would be carried out along with changes in interest rates in response to changes in overseas interest rates and domestic market development.

## *Open-market operations*

In the real sense of the term, 'open-market operations' are central bank activities in the open markets when it trades in short-term bills. Through these operations, the central bank can directly change the reserve position of commercial banks and indirectly change interest rates, thus resulting in changes in credit activities in terms of both quantity and cost, and in an adjustment in the money supply. Such operations are called open-market operations because the central bank trades with open-market participants through money market brokers.

In Japan, such operations were originally limited to exceptional cases of supplementary augmentation of lending since the open markets were not developed. In November 1962, the BOJ sought to make bond operations more flexible along with an introduction of the credit ceiling system described earlier. Through bond operations the BOJ tried to supply the money necessary for economic growth instead of supplying such funds through lending by the BOJ. Originally, the bond-trading operations were bilateral transactions with financial institutions at fixed rates and with repurchase agreements. In February 1966, however, the system was changed to the outright sale at the market price, as the bond market was reopened.

In January 1966, the BOJ decided to sell FBs which were in its portfolio to the money market brokers for the purpose of offsetting as much as possible the seasonal fluctuations of demand and supply of funds, thus contributing to the adjustment of market conditions. In addition, there were to be agreements for repurchase on the day of redemption according to the instructions from the BOJ. Such operations, however, were replaced with bill operations after 1972.

Active operations in the bill discount market commenced in June 1972. However, the open-market operations in Japan were not opened to non-financial institutions for a long time. Under such condi- tions, open-market operations did not have a direct effect on the money supply. Even the market sales of FBs continue to be rather exceptional. At present, the BOJ is engaged in trade operations as follows: government bonds, bills discount, the BOJ's own bills, and FBs. Only recently, however, the BOJ initiated an operation of CPs which formed an open market.

After June 1978, a system of bidding for bonds was introduced to replace the system of using the prices for bonds listed on the stock exchange. This change was made in order to improve the functioning of interest rates and to facilitate the use of securities operations. In May 1979, with the mechanization of book-keeping tasks concerning the bid calculations for government bond operations, the BOJ decided to make its securities operations more flexible in conjunction with the move towards deregulation of interest rates. So-called 'quick' operations were introduced in June 1979. Thus, the amounts sold are determined on the day of the bid and the purchaser is notified.

In May 1981 the BOJ reopened its sales of FBs as a means of absorbing funds during periods of excess liquidity. It was the first time since the end of the Second World War that the BOJ had engaged in the open-market operations in the real sense of the term. Until 1981, the bills were sold only to money market brokers who did not resell these bills. Since 1981, however, resale by money market brokers to the financial institutions has been allowed, and the financial institutions have then resold the bills to corporate businesses.

In the beginning, such sales of FBs were limited to periods of excess liquidity, but in 1985 they were also used in a period of tight liquidity so that the duration for which FBs were held in the financial institutions became longer. However, a large-scale market in FBs that could act as the centre of the open money market does not exist because FB business is still limited.

In May 1989, the BOJ initiated the sale and purchase of CPs as a means of open-market operation, but it is only at an experimental stage. It is true that the BOJ desires to strengthen policy instruments for open-market operations.

## Reserve requirement

The Law concerning the Reserve Deposit System (Law No. 135 of 1957) requires depository institutions to deposit, in non-interest bearing accounts with the BOJ, a certain ratio of their deposits and other liabilities. The reserve requirement was initially applied to the commercial banks, the long-term credit banks, and the trust banks only, but was later expanded to other depository institutions such as the foreign banks, the mutual banks, and the credit associations.

A reform to reserve requirements was made in May 1972, as suggested by the Research Committee on Financial System in 1971. The purpose of the reform was to respond to changes in the financial environment accompanying the progress towards internationalization and to help increase the efficiency of monetary policy. Under the reform, the range of institutions to which the requirement applied and the type of liabilities to which it applied expanded. In addition, the maximum reserve ratio was raised from 10 per cent to 20 per cent, and the limit for reserve requirements on foreign currency and non-resident liabilities was set at 100 per cent. Also, reserve requirements on increases in liabilities was introduced.

Since November 1976, reserve requirements have been applied to non-resident free yen deposits and foreign currency liabilities. Until

1980, non-resident free yen deposits were the only deposits convertible to foreign currency without permission. During the second half of the 1970s, reserve requirements were extended to increase the balances in the non-resident free yen deposits. In April 1979, newly created CDs were also subject to reserve requirements.

Another legal amendment was carried out in May 1986, for the purpose of introducing a progressive schedule of reserve ratios. This revision was made in order to respond to the progress in financial deregulation and to ensure the efficiency of monetary policy. Under the progressive reserve ratios, tranches are established according to the outstanding amounts that are subject to reserve requirements, and higher reserve ratios are applied to the higher tranches. This reform will make it possible to use the reserve requirement system more flexibly.

During the periods of tight money and subsequent relaxation until around 1980, reserve requirements were changed relatively frequently. Together with lending policy and open-market operations, they were a powerful policy instrument for the adjustment of the liquidity position of depository institutions. Current requirements are shown in table 13.1.

### Window guidance

In view of market conditions, the BOJ has customarily provided guidance to the financial institutions to keep the increase in their lending to clients within a limit that the BOJ feels is appropriate. Such guidance was particularly important when the BOJ tried to curtail lending by major financial institutions such as the city banks. This type of guidance is, in general, called 'window guidance', and the form of guidance is changed from time to time according to financial conditions. Reflecting these conditions, the guidance sometimes takes the form of regulation of loan growth and sometimes the form of guidance of overall positions.

This guidance was primarily targeted at the city banks that had high levels of borrowings from the BOJ. In the tight money period of 1964, there were directives to control increases in lending on a quarterly basis, and the objects of such guidance were expanded from the city banks and the long-term credit banks to include the trust banks and the regional banks. In the tight money period of 1967, the financial institutions subject to guidance were again expanded to include the larger mutual banks. In the tight money period after January 1973, the scope of guidance was expanded further to include the larger credit associations and the larger foreign banks; that is, almost all of the financial institutions. In addition, the guidance suggests not only the restraint of overall lending, but also the restraint of lending to trading companies and the securities firms.

*Table 13.1* Required reserve ratio*

| | Time deposit or CDs (%) | Other deposit (%) |
|---|---|---|
| For balance of deposits | | |
| Commercial banks, trust banks, long-term credit banks, mutual banks and credit associations** | | |
| on amounts exceeding ¥2.5 bn. | 1.75 | 2.5 |
| on amounts from ¥1.2 bn. to ¥2.5 bn. | 1.375 | 2.5 |
| on amounts from ¥500,000m. to ¥1.2 bn. | 0.125 | 1.875 |
| on amounts from ¥50,000m. to ¥500,000m. | 0.125 | 0.25 |
| Norinchukin Bank | 0.125 | 0.25 |
| For securities issued and outstanding | | |
| Specialized foreign exchange banks and long-term credit banks | 1.25 | |
| For money trusts including loan trusts | 1.25 | |
| For foreign currency deposits | | |
| from residents | 0.375 | 0.5 |
| from non-residents | 0.25 | |
| For non-resident yen accounts | 0.25 | |
| For non-resident yen transferred from JOM (Japan offshore market) | 0.25 | |

*Notes:* *Effective since 1 December 1986.
   **Excluding mutual banks and credit associations with deposit balances less than ¥160,000 million at the end of fiscal year.
*Source:* BOJ, *Economic Statistics Annual*, 1988.

After 1975, the tight money policy was gradually relaxed, and, from July 1977, a new formula was introduced under which every financial institution was requested to submit voluntary lending plans. However, a sort of consultation with the financial institutions was maintained in order to continue appropriate management of the money supply. In 1979, a strict guidance was implemented that was similar to ones in previous periods of tightening, but in the second half of 1980, this guidance was gradually eased along with the change in policies. Since early 1982, the lending programmes of the individual financial institutions surfaced again to replace window guidance.

Although window guidance is a moral persuasion, it has been so far a powerful instrument supporting the effectiveness of monetary policy. If a restrictive guidance is continued for long periods, there emerges discrimination among financial institutions between those which are subject to controls and those which are not. In addition, the lending shares within one type of financial institution tend to be fixed. Thus window guidance should be a supplementary measure of monetary policy supporting other orthodox instruments, such as lending policy, and be used primarily during the tight money period.

However, the role of window guidance may decline gradually, as financial deregulation and internationalization go on, as the effectiveness of monetary policy working through interest rates grows, and as the diversification of funding sources for corporate businesses progresses.

## Operations of monetary policy

### Operating targets of monetary policy

The distance between the policy instruments of the central bank and the final objectives are very remote and certain time is needed before effects become visible. Thus the central bank must pay attention to a change in operating variables in the course of the transmission process, and has to carry out monetary policy by making judgements from time to time about the effects of policy on these intermediate variables. Such variables are known as the operating targets of monetary policy (see figure 13.1).

There are two stages in the operating targets, i.e. the operating variables which are close to the central bank, and the intermediate objectives which are closer to the final objectives. Because the operating variables are close to the central bank, they are affected directly by policy instruments. But their relationship with the final objectives is somewhat obscure. Indeed, the intermediate objectives are rather remote from the control of the central bank and are only indirectly affected by the policy instruments. On the other hand, their relationship with the final objectives, such as the price level, is relatively stable.

Therefore, the transmission mechanism for monetary policy goes from policy instruments to operating variables, to intermediate objectives, and finally to final objectives. The BOJ conducts its final adjustments watching the movement of interest rates in the interbank markets as its operating variables. Careful and continued attention needs to be given to the intermediate objectives of increases in lending, particularly the growth in lending by the city banks. There are two reasons for such action.

First, since Japan's interest rates were set at a relatively low level for many years, there were few interest rates that reflected demand and supply of funds in the financial markets and hence few that could be useful as intermediate objectives. Interest rates on deposits and yields of newly issuing bonds were particularly inflexible and even the extremely important lending rates such as short-term and long-term prime rates were subject to regulation and also were determined regardless of funding costs. As a consequence, these interest rates lacked flexibility.

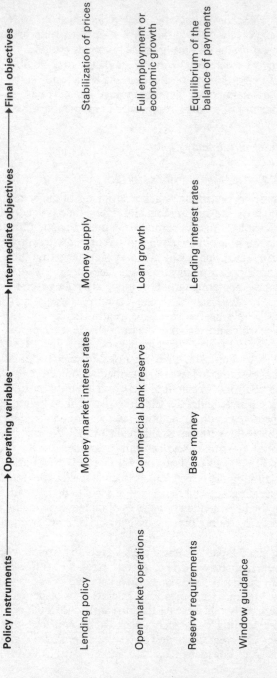

*Figure 13.1* Transmission mechanism of monetary policy
*Source*: BOJ, *Wagakuni no Kinyuseido*, 1986.

The *gensaki* market and the secondary market have developed steadily in recent decades, but even these markets remained small until the late 1960s and did not fully reflect forces of demand and supply in the financial markets. It was learned that the *gensaki* rates became extremely high in tight money periods. In these circumstances, the interbank market rates were the only rates which could fluctuate freely, but they were not intermediate objectives but operating variables.

Second, private sector investment activities were dependent upon bank borrowing entirely because of the situations of so-called 'over-borrowing' by the corporate sector during the fast growth period with its investment and export oriented growth. Thus, an increase in bank lending was a leading indicator of corporate investment activity, so that the increase in bank loans could work as an appropriate intermediate objective during the fast growth period as corporate investment was the major force supporting growth.

## Intermediate objectives

In July 1975, the BOJ announced that it recognized the money supply as an intermediate objective. Accordingly, a change in monetary control took place in Japan. Since then, the BOJ has made it a rule to announce, at the beginning of every quarter, an estimated growth rate of the average outstanding balance of the money supply in relation to the corresponding period in the preceding year. This estimated value is called a forecast for the current quarter. Initially, the money supply meant M2, but the meaning was changed to M2 + CDs, when CDs were introduced.

The reasons for the shift to money-focused policy were due to several changes in the financial structure of Japan's economy. One of these changes was the increased difficulty in recognizing exactly what information on interest rate movements gave about the effectiveness of monetary policy. This difficulty was generated by the gradual acceleration of inflation in the second half of the 1960s followed by the intensified inflation throughout the world after the first oil crisis.

For example, when interest rates rise, it is impossible to judge conclusively whether this rise has taken place because of high inflationary expectations, because of an increase in money demand generated by overheating of the business activities, or because of a decrease in money supply as the effects of tightened monetary policy permeate through the economy. If the real reason is either of the former two factors, then there is a need to tighten monetary policy further, but if the latter is real reason, such action is no use. An indicator that does not allow such judgements is inappropriate as an intermediate objective.

Another change of the financial structure leading to the shift to money-focused monetary policy was Japan's experience in the early 1970s. As a result of the excess growth of money supply in 1971 and 1972, the growth ratio of M1 and M2 peaked at around 30 per cent over that of the corresponding period in the preceding year. Then the consumer price index rose to two-digit levels from 1973 to 1975. In order to combat this inflation, a long and painful adjustment process continued until 1977.

The third point of change was the reduction in the fund deficit in the corporate sector, reflecting the downward kink in economic growth, and the expansion of deficits in the public sector leading to large-scale flotations of government bonds. As a result, creation of the money supply was no longer limited to increases in lending to the private sector, but now included the substantial government bond underwriting by the banks.

The money supply that accompanies banks' underwriting of government bonds was accumulated as cash balances in internal funds of the corporate sector, and effected an increase in corporate liquidity, and thus became the financial support for corporate activities. The money stock became a buffer between increases in lending to the private sector and aggregate spending activities. Thus watching loan growth meant watching the increase in the money supply; after 1975, however, it became necessary to use the money supply itself as the intermediate objective.

Normally, the monetary indicators used as intermediate objectives for monetary policy are base money (cash and bank reserves), money in the narrow sense (M1), and money in the broad sense which might include M2 and M3 (see table 13.2). In view of its experiences, the BOJ emphasizes an indicator that falls in the category of broad money, that is, M2 + CDs. There are three reasons for this. First, M2 + CDs have the closest relationship to income and expenditure, in the sense that they are leading indicators that affect the latter two variables in the future. The second reason for using M2 + CDs is its superior controllability. In addition, the statistics on M2 + CDs have a high degree of reliability, and they are not inferior to base money or M1 with respect to reporting time.

The BOJ announces the 'forecasts' on M2 + CDs, which do not mean 'target' in the strict sense of the word. However, the policy actions of the BOJ are included in the determination of these forecasts, and in this sense the forecasts represent increases in the money supply that the BOJ is willing to allow. The BOJ pays close attention to the effect the growth of money will have on future income, expenditure, and prices. If undesirable effects seem possible, they take policy actions immediately.

*Table 13.2* Definition of money supply

| | |
|---|---|
| M1 | Cash in circulation plus demand deposits with the BOJ and depository institutions of group A less cash held by these institutions |
| M1′ | M1 plus non-demand deposits held by corporate businesses |
| M1′ + CDs | M1′ plus CDs issued by depository institutions of group A |
| M2 | M1 plus non-demand deposits with BOJ and depository institutions of group A |
| M2 + CDs | M2 plus CDs issued by depository institutions of group A |
| M3 | M2 plus total deposits with depository institutions of group B less cash held by these institutions |
| M3 + CDs | M3 plus CDs issued by depository institutions of group B |

*Notes:* Cash includes bank notes issued by the BOJ and subsidiary coins issued by the government.
Group A includes commercial banks, trust banks, long-term credit banks, mutual banks, credit associations, the Norinchukin Bank, and the Shokochukin Bank.
Group B includes labour credit associations, credit co-operatives, agricultural co-operatives, fisheries co-operatives, and Postal Savings Service.
*Source:* BOJ, *Economic Statistics Annual*, 1988.

At such times, the forecasts include changes in policy action and move gradually in the desirable direction.

## Monetary control and operating variables

The BOJ's ability to control interbank interest rates is based on its power to influence demand and supply conditions of funds in the interbank market through its lending policy and open-market operations. In other words, the BOJ's ability to control interest rates is based on its power to affect the path along which reserves are accumulated. Under the current system, required reserve levels are determined on the average deposits over the period of one month, but the reserves must be accumulated from the 16th of the current month to the 15th of the following month.

If repayment of BOJ loans or other factors causes financial adjustments in the market such that the quantity of reserve deposits continues to be less than required reserves for a time, then reserve accumulation gradually falls behind the schedule. Consequently, the financial institutions begin to look for borrowing in the interbank market in order to increase their reserve accumulation, and the demand–supply will gradually become tight and raise interbank interest rates.

Even without forcing reserves to a low level, a delay in the reserve accumulation path can cause interest rates in the market to rise gradually. It is also possible, in contrast, for the BOJ to accelerate the reserve accumulation path through the supply of lump sums for purchase of bills. In such cases, the demand–supply situation in the interbank markets gradually becomes easier and interest rates decline.

Changes in the interbank market rates affect the money supply primarily through three channels, i.e. effects on the banks' portfolio selection, financial disintermediation, and effects of the interest rate fluctuation on spending in the private sector. The first was the traditional transmission channel during the fast growth period, while the second and third are channels provided since the development of open markets and the more flexible movements of interest rates in these markets.

The relative importance of these transmission channels of policy effects differ according to the character of interest rates in the financial system. For example, as bank lending rates and bond yield become more flexible, then the first channel becomes weaker and the third one becomes stronger. If deposit interest rates become more flexible, then the second channel becomes weaker and the third channel becomes stronger. In all cases, however, influence over interbank interest rates ensures the controllability of the money supply.

## Monetary policy and financial deregulation

### Financial deregulation and money supply

It is generally understood that the deregulation and internationalization of the Japanese financial system will continue to advance along with the development of various financial innovations, such as new financial products, new methods of trading, and new types of markets. In order to cope with changes in the financial structures, new efforts are needed in the management of monetary policy.

One of the major motives underlying the development of financial deregulation in Japan has been the large-scale flotation of government bonds since 1975, the simultaneous development of open financial markets with free interest rates, and new financial products. Since 1975, the problems that accompany such large-scale flotations of government bonds, and in particular worries about inflation, have been very much in the public eye. Thus, the shift to an easy monetary policy during 1975 to 1978 was accompanied by frequent debates concerning the danger of excess liquidity that might accompany large-scale issues of government bonds.

Such debates flared up when growth of the money supply rose even slightly and when the MOF began to stress their programme of fiscal equilibrium. The MOF always worried about inflation as one of the dangers of large-scale bond flotations. But such worries would not necessarily be borne out in all cases, because the link between accumulated government debts and increases in the money supply, and thus inflation, would be determined by the form of government bond issues and the lending stance of the BOJ.

In Japan, the largest portion of government bond issues have been underwritten by commercial banks and other financial institutions. These transactions may result in an increase in the money supply, but the increasing ratio of the money supply since 1975 had been on a gradual downward trend. Because the BOJ did not passively supply base money to encounter the occurrence of inadequate reserves, the commercial banks were forced to reduce their position of credit through such measures as calling loans or selling bonds, and thus had no choice but to return the money supply to its original level. Thus, the control of the money supply may depend upon the BOJ's attitude.

In view of the control of the money supply, deregulation of resales of government bonds by commercial banks in April 1977 was an epoch-making event. This is because the deregulation allowed the banks to sell bonds to overcome the deterioration that accompanied the BOJ's refusal to supply more base money. As a result, there was a decreasing danger that the BOJ would passively supply base money and thus permit the increases in the money supply that accompany underwriting of government bonds.

After such deregulation, the commercial banks became more active in their resales of government bonds, and these bonds, which had now become more liquid, were in large part purchased by corporate businesses and others in the private non-banking sector. This was possible because corporate businesses faced a new financial situation in which the degree of their net demand for funds had fallen with the shift towards slower economic growth, and in which they could diversify the investments of their own funds without much consideration of their long-standing relationships with banks. The large-scale flotation of government bonds that took place after 1975 was to a large extent purchased by individuals and corporate businesses in the private non-banking sector.

*Financial innovation and money supply*

Financial innovation in Japan may be divided into two types. The first was innovation that helped to reduce the balance of transaction accounts, where interest rates are zero or regulated at low levels. Examples include reduction on the use of cash through automatic crediting of salaries to bank accounts, cash dispensers, and ATMs and reduction of saving deposits through the invention of composite accounts. The second type of innovation created new financial products on which are paid market interest rates. Such examples are CDs, MMCs, and medium-term government bond funds.

At first, the development of financial innovations that transmitted funds into the open markets led to financial disintermediation and reduced the money supply. The development of new types of financial products that involved government bonds also made it easier not only for corporate businesses but also for individuals to hold government bonds. The outflow of funds into the open markets from the depository institutions led to a reduction of the lending ability of these institutions. In addition, the development of new products such as the medium-term government bond funds took place in a form that increased the holding of government bonds by individuals.

When considering financial innovation, other effects must also be recognized. First is the change in the character of the money supply indicators that are the intermediate objectives of monetary policy. With the development of financial innovations which help reduce cash and transaction accounts, the growth rate of M1 will decline, and its fluctuations will gradually become smaller. As a result, it will not be representative as an indicator of transaction volume. Moreover, if the new financial products resulting from financial innovation function either as cash or quasi-money, the definition of the money supply must be revised.

Second is the change in the demand function for broad money. As a result of financial innovations, there will be an increase in the share of assets within M2 or M3 that reflects market interest rates. As a consequence, M2 and M3 will become gradually less sensitive to fluctuations in the market interest rates. Moreover, an increase in the growth rates of M2 and M3 may be expected because asset selection for investment motives will increase its concentration on high-yield and low-risk assets included in M2 and M3.

As a result of these changes in money demand, several problems will arise in the use of the definition of M2 and M3 as intermediate objectives for monetary policy. There is a possibility that it will become more difficult to control M2 and M3 from the supply side through fluctuations in market interest rates as in the past. Also, there is the possibility that M2 and M3 will begin to move simultaneously with transactions in the economy and that they will lose their function as leading indicators of policy objectives, such as nominal GNP and price levels.

*Deregulation and the effectiveness of monetary policy*

As indicated earlier, there are three channels through which effects of monetary controls are transmitted: effects on the banks' portfolio selection, financial disintermediation, and of effects interest rate fluctuations on private expenditures. The relative importance of these transmission channels will change as interest rate regulations are gradually repealed. As a larger portion of the money supply falls into categories that fluctuate with market interest rates, there will be a weakening of policy effects through the first and second channels.

In the course of financial deregulation, the effectiveness of monetary policy will be maintained mainly through the effects of interest rate fluctuation on private expenditures, because the interest rates in open markets and the interest rates on bank loans and deposits will be more flexible. This means that the influence of monetary policy on the money supply will act through demand-side factors rather than supply- side factors such as disintermediation. Needless to say, effectiveness of transmission of monetary policy through this channel depends on a sufficiently high interest elasticity of expenditure in the private sector.

In other words, ensuring the effectiveness of monetary policy in a deregulated financial world means that it is important to strengthen the transmission of policy effects through the third channel. As open markets expand, both at home and abroad, and as increases continue in the quantities of free interest rate assets, maintaining the money supply at an appropriate level will require further adjustment of interest rates in the short-term money market. Therefore, the BOJ must nurture not only the interbank market but also open markets, particularly the FBs market.

## Internationalization and monetary policy

### Flow of capital and money supply control

International financial transactions were entirely deregulated for Japanese residents in accordance with the enforcement of the revised Foreign Exchange and Foreign Trade Control Law in December 1980, and the repeal of conversion quotas from foreign currency to yen in June 1984. In addition, Euroyen transactions have been free from regulation since June 1984, too. Flows of foreign capital into Japan seem to have no effect on the domestic money supply unless this capital was absorbed by the monetary authorities.

When foreign capital flows into Japan, such capital must be converted into yen if it is paid for a domestic transaction. Thus, when transactions are made with those who are in the non-bank sector, the foreign capital inflow means only that the holders of the money supply may change, and the total quantity of money does not change. If the counterpart to the foreign exchange transaction is in the banking sector, then the money supply rises along with the purchase of the foreign currency. But if reserves are insufficient and the BOJ do not supply extra base money,

199

the banking sector must either collect loans or sell securities in an amount equivalent to the foreign capital inflow, and the money supply will return to its original level.

In the short run, the exchange rate and interest rates will probably change, but the effects on the domestic economy are likely to be only transitional and small in scale. In the absence of excessive intervention in the foreign exchange markets, the effectiveness of monetary policy will be maintained even in the case of more vigorous capital flows.

The effects of Euroyen transactions are fundamentally the same as that of the inflow of foreign capital. Whether yen deposits are domestic deposits or Eurodeposits, the payment reserves behind these deposits will remain in Japan through yen-denominated claims on domestic banks. As long as the Eurobank does not bring payment reserves against yen into Japan, the bank cannot simultaneously increase its lending and deposits in Euroyen. Moreover, the total money supply in yen determines the total quantity of payment reserves against yen-denominated deposits as a whole, including Euroyen.

Therefore, the interest rates in the Euromarket are determined within the same framework as are the interest rates in the markets for domestic reserves that are controlled by the supplier of such reserves or the BOJ. Hence, Euroyen rates are affected by domestic short-term yen interest rates through interest arbitrage. From the viewpoint of monetary control, the Euromarkets are the same as domestic open markets such as the *gensaki* market. The only distinction is that the Euromarkets are located abroad.

Euroyen interest rates and *gensaki* interest rates have been most closely related since the deregulation of capital inflow and the approval for non-resident participation in the *gensaki* market in 1979. Indeed, the interest arbitrage has been most effective since repeal of conversion quotas from foreign currency to yen in June 1984. Nevertheless, certain problems concerning control of the money supply (i.e. reserve requirement ratios and the definition of monetary indicators) remain unsolved.

If the Eurobank does not keep 100 per cent reserves against its Euroyen deposits and lends these reserves directly to the domestic non-bank sector which creates Euroyen deposits, there will be an increase in the total yen deposits in the domestic and Euromarkets, resulting in an increase in the total money supply. In order to prevent such a development, it is necessary to impose direct reserve requirements on the yen deposits or yen lending of Eurobanks. In fact, however, it is most difficult to impose such requirements against deposits with foreign banks.

Another issue is whether to include Euroyen in the money supply statistics, and this problem is a somewhat technical matter. If large shifts were to occur between Euroyen deposits and domestic yen deposits, then it would be only natural for there to be differences between the calculation of a domestic money supply that includes only domestic yen deposits and the total yen money supply that also includes Euroyen deposits. The determination of which types of Euroyen to include in money statistics is extremely difficult and is determined only after examining every factor.

### Foreign exchange rates and the monetary policy

Fluctuations of foreign exchange rates have major impacts on the operations of monetary policy. Since the shift to the floating rate system in 1973, the foreign exchange market has moved very flexibly. When the floating rate system started, it was believed that monetary policy would be more independent under the floating rate system than it had been under the fixed-rate system. But looking at more than sixteen years of experience, it is hard to say that the floating rate system has functioned as adequately as was expected.

The first problem has been that the short-term price elasticity of export and import volumes has been rather low, so that 'J-curve effects' (recovery of equilibrium in current account balances) have required very long periods of time. As a consequence, the foreign exchange market has had a repeated tendency to overshoot the levels of exchange rates that correspond to equilibrium. The second problem has been that the foreign exchange markets have diverged from the levels corresponding to purchasing power parity not only in the short-term, but in the medium-term as well. As a result, disequilibria in the current account have continued in the medium-term and have stimulated protectionism.

Due to these problems generated from the floating rate system, it is not practicable for the BOJ to focus solely on the performance of domestic equilibrium even though the final objective in the conduct of monetary policy is the stability of price levels in Japan. A major consideration must also be paid to the level of foreign exchange rates which reflect external equilibrium and interest rate differences between Japan and major foreign countries.

# Future outlook

It is generally understood that the financial markets of the world are becoming a united global market as a result of financial deregulation, internationalization of financial institutions, and the securitization of financing throughout the world. Under these circumstances, Tokyo is becoming one of the three largest financial centres, in addition to New York and London. Tokyo has some important strengths that may enable it to move into a leading position. These include a fundamentally strong economy, a high rate of domestic savings, and a fortunate geographical location.

One of Tokyo's principal strengths is a powerful economy which is the second largest in the free world after that of the United States. The Japanese economy had a hard time coping with a series of drastic changes that occurred in the 1970s. It was inevitable that business activities would be seriously depressed, but the depression bottomed out in November 1986. Since then, the Japanese economy has expanded steadily, though its growth is not quite as fast as in the fast growth period, but the current boom seems to be the longest in the post-war period. For fiscal 1987 and 1988, Japan's real economic growth rate was 5.2 per cent and 5.1 per cent, respectively.

Another strength of the Japanese economy is the large volume of monetary assets supported by a higher rate of savings. A recent survey disclosed that Japan's total financial assets were ¥1,325 billion at the end of 1988, or 3.6 times the GNP. One of the prime factors leading to such a large volume of liquidity has been the high rate of savings in Japan. The savings rate from household incomes remains well above 15 per cent. There are no changes which appear likely to reduce the savings rate in Japan or to lower significantly the volume of monetary resources available in Japan. If the yen remains strong, the external purchasing power of Japan's monetary assets will rise, contributing to Japan's potential as a capital exporter.

The third point to contribute to the growth of the Tokyo market as a major financial centre is Japan's location in the Pacific basin. Tokyo is geographically well-positioned to be the leading financial centre to fill a gap left by New York and London. Tokyo is the only major market open when the New York and London markets are closed. In addition, up to the year 2000, the countries in Asia and the Pacific region are expected to achieve higher rates of growth as a group than any other area of the world. Tokyo has strong traditional ties to the regions, and its financial institutions have considerable experience in evaluating projects, in pro- viding financial resources, and in dealing in these regional markets.

Although there are some problems in Tokyo, such as a higher cost of living and office space, Tokyo appears to be the fastest-growing and most attractive of the three major centres from the viewpoint of international financial business. Thus, the Tokyo market will present numerous opportunities for financial institutions, particularly as the restructuring of the economy and the upgrading of the physical infra- structure stretch into the 1990s. It is to be hoped that Japan can also direct its capabilities for adaptation to assume its growing role in the world economy.

# Appendix 1: Chronology of financial deregulation

| Year | Month | Steps for deregulation |
|------|-------|------------------------|
| 1970 | Dec | First 'samurai' bond issued by Asian Development Bank. |
| 1979 | Mar | Sears Roebuck issued unsecured straight bonds in Tokyo. |
|      | May | Negotiable CDs are introduced. |
| 1980 | Dec | Revised Foreign Exchange and Foreign Trade Control Law enforced. |
| 1982 | Apr | New Banking Law enforced. |
| 1983 | Apr | Banks begin to distribute public bonds. |
|      | June | Short-term Euroyen loans to non-residents permitted. |
|      | Aug | Banks begin to close business on second Saturday every month. |
| 1984 | Apr | Purchase of foreign CDs and CPs permitted for residents. |
|      |     | Foreign exchange forward contracts without actual demand are allowed. |
|      |     | Medium-term yen loans to non-residents are deregulated. |
|      |     | Foreign banks are allowed to join the Government Bond Underwriting Syndicate. |
|      | May | Report of Japan–US Yen–Dollar Committee released. |
|      | June | Regulation of conversion of foreign currency into yen is liberalized. |
|      |     | Short-term Euroyen loans to residents are deregulated. |
|      |     | Banks start dealing in public bonds. |
|      | Dec | Overseas branches of Japanese banks and foreign banks are allowed to issue six-month Euroyen CDs. |
|      |     | Non-residents are allowed to float Euroyen bonds. |
| 1985 | Feb | Foreign exchange brokers are allowed to engage in international broking. |
|      | Mar | MMCs are introduced. |
|      |     | Medium-term and long-term Euroyen loans to non-residents are deregulated. |
|      | Apr | Residents are allowed to float Euroyen convertible bonds. |
|      | June | Yen-denominated BA market is established. |
|      | July | Banks are allowed to issue foreign currency denominated bonds in overseas markets. |

|  |  | Uncollateralized call transactions are introduced. |
|---|---|---|
| 1988 | Aug | First '*shogun*' bond is issued by World Bank. |
|  | Oct | Bond future market established. |
|  |  | Interest rates on non-negotiable large-sum time deposits are deregulated. |
|  |  | Foreign banks are allowed to establish trust subsidiaries in Japan. |
|  | Nov | Residents are allowed to float Euroyen straight bonds. |
|  | Dec | Less than 50 per cent affiliates of foreign banks establish Tokyo branches for securities business. |
| 1986 | Feb | Government issues TBs in discount form. |
|  |  | Six foreign securities firms obtain regular membership at Tokyo Stock Exchange. |
|  | June | Foreign banks are allowed to issue Euroyen bonds. |
|  | Aug | Banks close business on third Saturday every month. |
|  | Oct | Government begins to offer super long-term (twenty years) government bonds. |
|  | Nov | Investment Advisory Law is enforced. |
|  | Dec | Japan Offshore Market is established. |
| 1987 | Feb | Overseas branches of Japanese banks are allowed to underwrite foreign CPs. |
|  | Apr | Banks are allowed to issue convertible bonds in the domestic market. |
|  | May | Banks, securities firms, and insurance companies are allowed to trade in overseas financial futures markets. |
|  | June | Osaka Stock Exchange begins to trade 'Osaka Stock Futures 50'. |
|  | Sept | Auction for super long-term government bonds is implemented. |
|  | Nov | Auction for long-term government bonds is partially implemented. |
|  |  | Domestic CP market is established. |
|  |  | Foreign firms are allowed to issue Euroyen CPs. |
| 1988 | Jan | Foreign firms are allowed to issue domestic CPs (*samurai* CPs). |
|  | Apr | Maximum term of Euroyen CDs is extended to two years. |
|  | Sept | Stock index futures is started (TOPIX and NIKKEI-225). |
|  | Dec | MOF sets new capital to assets ratio in response to BIS accord. |
| 1989 | Jan | City banks introduce new formula for prime lending rate. |
|  | Feb | Fifty-two mutual banks are converted into commercial banks. |
|  |  | Banks close business every Saturday. |
|  | Apr | Bonds option trading is started. |
|  | May | Medium- and long-term Euroyen loans to residents are allowed. |
|  | June | Super MMCs are introduced. |
|  |  | Tokyo Financial Future Exchange is established. |
|  | July | Overseas deposits by residents are deregulated. |
|  | Dec | US T bond market is established. |

# Appendix 2: List of laws and decrees related to banking and finance

| | |
|---|---|
| Agricultural Co-operatives Law | Law No. 132 of 1947 |
| Agriculture, Forestry and Fisheries Finance Corporation Law | Law No. 355 of 1952 |
| Anti-Monopoly and Fair Trade Law | Law No. 54 of 1947 |
| *Bank of Japan Act | Dec. No. 32 of 1882 |
| Bank of Japan Law | Law No. 67 of 1942 |
| *Banking Act | Law No. 72 of 1890 |
| *Banking Law | Law No. 21 of 1927 |
| Banking Law, new | Law No. 59 of 1981 |
| Commercial Code | Law No. 48 of 1899 |
| Credit Associations Law | Law No. 238 of 1951 |
| Deposit Insurance Law | Law No. 34 of 1971 |
| Environmental Sanitation Business Finance Corporation Law | Law No. 138 of 1967 |
| Export-Import Bank of Japan Law | Law No. 268 of 1950 |
| Fishery Co-operatives Law | Law No. 242 of 1948 |
| Foreign Exchange Bank Law | Law No. 67 of 1954 |
| *Foreign Exchange Control Law | Law No. 83 of 1941 |
| Foreign Exchange and Foreign Trade Control Law | Law No. 228 of 1949 |
| Foreign Exchange and Foreign Trade Control Law, revised | Law No. 65 of 1979 |
| Foreign Exchange Fund Special Account Law | Law No. 56 of 1951 |
| Government Bond Law | Law No. 34 of 1906 |
| Hokkaido Tohoku Development Corporation Law | Law No. 97 of 1956 |
| Housing Loan Corporation Law | Law No. 156 of 1950 |
| Industrial Co-operatives Law | Law No. 34 of 1900 |
| Insurance Business Law | Law No. 41 of 1939 |
| Investment Advisory Law | Law No. 74 of 1986 |
| Japan Development Bank Law | Law No. 108 of 1951 |
| Japan Finance Corporation for Municipal Enterprises Law | Law No. 83 of 1957 |
| Labour Credit Associations Law | Law No. 227 of 1953 |
| Law Concerning Foreign Securities Firms | Law No. 5 of 1971 |
| Law Concerning Foreign Insurance Companies | Law No. 184 of 1949 |

| | |
|---|---|
| Law Concerning Joint Operation of Trust Business by Banks | Law No. 43 of 1943 |
| Law Concerning Reserve Deposit System | Law No. 135 of 1957 |
| Law Concerning Control of Receiving Capital Subscription, Deposits and Interest Rates | Law No. 195 of 1954 |
| Law for Small Business Co-operatives | Law No. 181 of 1949 |
| Loan Trust Law | Law No. 195 of 1952 |
| Long-Term Credit Bank Law | Law No. 187 of 1952 |
| Mutual Bank Law | Law No. 199 of 1951 |
| *National Bank Act | Dec. No. 349 of 1872 |
| Norinchukin Bank Law | Law No. 42 of 1923 |
| Okinawa Development Finance Corporation Law | Law No. 33 of 1972 |
| Overseas Economic Co-operation Fund Law | Law No. 173 of 1960 |
| People's Finance Corporation Law | Law No. 49 of 1949 |
| Postal Savings Law | Law No. 144 of 1947 |
| Public Finance Law | Law No. 34 of 1947 |
| *Savings Bank Act | Law No. 73 of 1890 |
| *Securities and Exchange Law | Law No. 22 of 1947 |
| Securities and Exchange Law, revised | Law No. 25 of 1948 |
| Securities Investment Trust Law | Law No. 198 of 1951 |
| Shokochukin Bank Law | Law No. 14 of 1936 |
| Small Business Credit Insurance Corporation Law | Law No. 93 of 1958 |
| Small Business Finance Corporation Law | Law No. 138 of 1953 |
| Temporary Interest Rate Adjustment Law | Law No. 181 of 1947 |
| Trust Law | Law No. 62 of 1922 |
| Trust Business Law | Law No. 65 of 1922 |
| Trust Fund Bureau Fund Law | Law No. 100 of 1951 |

*Laws which are no longer effective.

# Bibliography

## Books and mimeographs

Allen, G.C. and Donnithorne A.G. (1954) *Western Enterprise in Far Eastern Economic Development – China and Japan*, London: George Allen & Unwin.

Bank of Japan (1986) *Wagakuni no Kinyuseido (Financial System in Japan)*, Tokyo: 1986.

Black, John R. (1883) *Young Japan – Yokohama and Yedo*, New York: Baker, Pratt & Co.

Bortoluzzi, A. (1984) *Foreign Banks in Japan*, Research Paper, Tokyo: Institute for International Trade.

Collis, Maurice (1965) *WAYFOONG – the Hong Kong and Shanghai Banking Corporation*, London: Faber & Faber.

Federation of Bankers Associations of Japan (1984) *Banking System in Japan*, Tokyo.

—— (1987) *Financial Liberalization and Internationalization in Japan*, Tokyo.

—— (1988) *Payment Systems in Japan*, Tokyo.

—— (1989) *Japanese Banks 1989*, Tokyo.

Fox, Grace (1969) *Britain and Japan, 1858–1883*, Oxford: Oxford University Press.

Nippon Tanshi Co., Ltd. (1988) *Short-term Money Markets in Japan*, Tokyo.

Peat Marwick Minato (1987) *Banking in Japan*, Tokyo.

Research Committee on Financial System (1987) *Report on Specialized Financial System in Japan*, Tokyo: Federation of Bankers Associations of Japan.

Robin, Brian (1987) *TOKYO – A World Financial Centre*, London: Euromoney Publication PLC.

Suzuki, Yoshio (ed.), (1987) *The Japanese Financial System*, Oxford: Oxford University Press.

Tatewaki, Kazuo (1982) *Kinyu Daikakumei (Great Financial Revolution)*, Tokyo: Toyokeizai Shinposha.

—— (ed.) (1986) *Kinyukakumei to Ginkokeiei (Financial Revolution and Bank Administration)*, Kyoto: Horitsu Bunkasha.

—— (1987) *Zainichi Gaikoku Ginkoshi (History of Foreign Banks in Japan)*, Tokyo: Nihon Keizai Hyoronsha.

Tschoegl, Adrian E. (1987) *Foreign Banks in Japan*, Research Paper, Tokyo: Bank of Japan, Institute of Monetary and Economic Studies.

Viner, Aron (1987) *Inside Japan's Financial Markets*, Tokyo: *The Japan Times*.


## Periodicals

*A Collection of Foreign Banks' Financial Reports* (annual), Tokyo, Nihon Keizaisha Ltd.

*Analysis of Financial Statements of All Banks* (semi-annual), Tokyo, Federation of Bankers Associations of Japan.

*Chosa Geppo* (monthly review), Tokyo, Bank of Japan, Department of Research and Statistics.

*Diamond Industria* (monthly), Tokyo, Diamond Lead Co. Ltd.

*Economic Statistics Annual*, Tokyo, Bank of Japan.

*Economic Statistics Monthly*, Tokyo, Bank of Japan.

*Ginkokyoku Kinyu Nenpo (Banking Bureau Yearbook)*, Tokyo, Ministry of Finance.

*Japan Economic Journal* (weekly), Tokyo, Nihon Keizai Shinbunsha.

*Kanpo (Government Gazette*, daily), Tokyo, Ministry of Finance, Printing Bureau.

*Kinyu Business (Financial Business*, monthly), Tokyo, Toyokeizai Shinposha.

*Kinyu Zaisei Jijo (Money and Finance*, weekly), Tokyo, Kinyuzaisei Jijo Kenkyukai.

*Monetary and Economic Studies* (semi-annual), Tokyo, Bank of Japan, Institute for Monetary and Economic Studies.

*Nihon Keizai Shinbun (Japan Economic Journal*, daily), Tokyo, Nihonkeizai Shinbunsha.

*Nikkei Kinyu Nenpo* (semi-annual), Tokyo, Nihonkeizai Shinbunsha.

*Okurasho Kokusai Kinyukyoku Nenpo (International Finance Bureau Year-book)*, Tokyo, Ministry of Finance.

*Okurasho Shokenkyoku Nenpo (Securities Bureau Yearbook)*, Tokyo, Ministry of Finance.

*Published Financial Statements of Foreign Bank Branches in Japan* (annual), Tokyo, Peat Marwick Minato.

*Tokyo Business Today* (monthly), Tokyo, Toyokeizai Shinposha.

# Index